Naming and Reference

The Problems of Philosophy
Their Past and Present

General editor: Ted Honderich
Grote Professor of the Philosophy of Mind and Logic
University College London

Other books in the series:

Now available in paperback

Naming and Reference
The link of word to object

R. J. Nelson

London and New York

First published 1992
by Routledge
11 New Fetter Lane, London EC4P 4EE

Simultaneously published in the USA and Canada
by Routledge
a division of Routledge, Chapman and Hall, Inc.
29 West 35th Street, New York, NY 10001

Typeset in 10/12pt Times by Witwell
Printed in Great Britain by TJ Press (Padstow) Ltd, Padstow, Cornwall

British Library Cataloguing in Publication Data
A catalogue record for this book is available from the British Library.

Library of Congress Cataloging-in-Publication Data
Nelson, R. J. (Raymond John),
Naming and Reference/R. J. Nelson.
p.   cm. – (The problems of philosophy)
Includes bibliographical references and index.
1. Reference (Philosophy)   2. Semantics (Philosophy)
I. Title.   II. Series: Problems of Philosophy (Routledge [Firm])
B105.R25X45   1992   91–45969
12′.68–dc20

ISBN 0-415-00939-1

To the memory of my mother and father
Florence and Emil Nelson

Contents

Contents

Preface

Of all things distinctively human the first is language, and the second is how and why this is so. Man studying himself is not new. Systematic thought about language and man goes back to Plato's *Cratylus* or before and is a central theme in philosophy and cognitive science today.

Strangely, the connections of language with the world are not much better understood now than they were in Plato's time. Significant advances have been made in linguistics, even in structural semantics, but they have not included much of importance about the relation of names to things named. Much is known about the syntactical structure of phrases and sentences, but not about the word-to-world hook-up of the component words.

This book is about that semantical connection, about reference of language to the world. In it I adopt what has come to be called a 'causal' or 'direct' theory of reference, which goes back to John Stuart Mill and has been recently advanced by Saul Kripke. Using various computer models, I explore meaning and reference of words to objects and the relation of these semantical phenomena to perception, belief and truth. In this work I use parallel, connectionist brain/mind models, and not the programming, sequential models of mid-century artificial intelligence research.

My theory suggests an alternative to Chomsky's psychology of language. Gerald Edelman's work on modern brain biology has produced convincing evidence that certain mental capabilities, notably visual perception, are best explained as evolutionary phenomena. On my view, reference is closely related to perception. It then follows that language, if the causal theory is right, is acquired in an evolving individual brain, 'bottom up', without any constraints imposed by a learner's putative innate knowledge of principles of universal grammar. Thus if we get down to an understanding of word–world linkage, we seem to be forced to a position that denies the native, species-specific character of language as resting on an a priori cognitive structure, except for genetically determined constraints that have little to do with tacit knowledge in Chomsky's sense of the word.

At the present time I do not think there is any hope of grasping the subtleties of reference without some familiarity with the lore. Therefore, in the first few chapters I review notions of reference beginning with Locke's *An Essay Concerning Human Understanding*. This review takes us fairly far back in time, as one of Locke's two views is essentially Augustinian and resembles what passes today for 'semiotic'. Next comes Peirce, whose profound views on logic and language influence my own adoption of Kripke; and then sketches of Frege, Russell, Tarski, Carnap and Quine – enough, I believe, to give the flavor of the problem of reference and meaning as it has come to us in this century. This material presupposes some familiarity with basic logic.

The remaining chapters introduce the causal theory and Jerry Fodor's cognitivism and culminate in Chapters 8–11 with a fairly detailed presentation of my own views. The present account extends the mechanist philosophy of my book *The Logic of Mind* (1989a).

This book is a product of a good deal of thought, writing and lecturing over the past thirty years or so. I have a debt to Rudolf Carnap that goes back a good many years before that. I have been deeply influenced by Quine who, whether I agree with him or not on all points, has been a standard of clarity and excellence in all things.

I have benefited from many discussions and communications with John Corcoran, Donald Davidson, Christopher Hill, Mortimer Kadish, Jack Kaminsky, Robert Lover, Colin McLarty, Peter Nelson, Vernon Rowland, William Thomas, John Wallace and very specially with my dear wife Hendrieka Nelson. My sincere thanks to all.

CHAPTER 1

Introduction

1. From words to things

Anyone given to reflection is likely to have strong feelings about what counts as an important philosophical question. 'Does God exist?' ranks high, as does 'Is man a machine?' and 'Are there rational grounds for moral judgment?' However, 'Ought poetry reflect the politics of its age?' ranks pretty low, except for literary critics and otherwise unoccupied philosophers.

The nature of reference of words is one of the high questions. It does not seem to be very exciting, even for a philosopher, until you notice that the question, 'Does the word "God" refer to anything?' asks the same thing as 'Does God exist?' An answer to one is surely an answer to the other.

Yet there is certainly a difference. The verbal question is slightly irritating. 'Does God exist?' calls for a plain yes or no. And if you are an agnostic you can drop it. But 'Does "God" refer?' hints at trouble: some one is kidding you or wasting your time. It is hard to deny that 'God' unlike 'Spfch' refers to or means something, but that doesn't mean God exists. Or does it?

On the other hand it seems nothing needs less explanation: we all speak and listen more or less successfully every day. The pronoun 'I' refers to me, 'you' to you; the noun phrase 'this desk' refers to the proverbial desk before me, and 'this book' to this very book. Nothing could be less open to wonder or worry than the objects of words. As to 'God': if you believe, the word refers and if you do not it is fiction, and that's the end of it.

However, things are not as simple as that. Does 'I' refer to you? Does '1010' refer to ten or to one thousand and ten? Does '1010' refer to anything for one-year-old Johnny? To what? To anything

1

for a computer? What do you mean by 'refer?' Do computers refer when a programmer makes symbol declarations? Does the name 'Hamlet' refer? What about 'zero'? What about 'the least rapidly divergent series'? Does 'tachyon' refer? If so, to what? If not so, why do some people have theories about them?

One might easily make a case that the question 'what is reference?' is the hardest, if not the most important, in all of philosophy – not to say in linguistics and cognitive science. One contemporary writer insists that in spite of the spectacular gains in linguistic theory of the past thirty years, especially Chomsky's transformational grammar, and the 'heroic efforts to understand the dimension of language associated with meaning and reference, we are as much in the dark as ever' (Putnam 1975: 215).

If learned agreement among investigators – all using the same publicly available data and all born from the same cultural background – is taken as a measure of the success of a science, the study of reference is the biggest failure around. No issue has been faced in more diverse and incompatible ways. Reference is being pursued right now as a part of semantics, semiotic, linguistics, ontology, epistemology, analytical philosophy, psychology, anthropology, cognitive science, computer science, neuroscience, metaphysics and, most recently, physics; and the action has generated zero output. Contemporary research attracts no prizes.

One reason for the mess is difference in aim. Logicians want to know the role of reference in reasoning in science and in philosophy itself. Cognitive scientists want to know how it figures in concept formation or in the dynamics of communication. Neurobiologists want to know whether it is locally distributed or scattered over the cortex. None has broken ground, although most inquirers now agree (it took 2500 years from Plato to get to this point) that the relation of word to thing is governed by causal law much as other phenomena in natural science are. Indeed, this is the line we shall pursue.

In order to get on with the complexities of the subject, I want to identify the basics and set up a strawman for a bout of needling.

When people speak with one another they talk of things which they observe, avoid, seek, think about, or describe in some way. Pronouns like 'you' and 'I' *refer* to individual objects, you and me, present in discourse. Proper names like 'Russell' 'Lady Ottoline' 'Gibraltar' and 'Arcturus' refer to particulars which might not be within sight or hearing but do or did exist somewhere at one time.

Common names and adjectives *apply* universally to many objects, not only to one thing. For instance 'philosopher' applies to any philosopher you choose; not only to Russell, but to Plato, Kant and Wittgenstein. 'Tree' applies to all trees, 'tangos' to tangos, and so on.

Suppose Jones informs us that Bertrand Russell was a philosopher and also a mathematician, uttering the sentence

Bertrand Russell was a philosopher and also a mathematician.

In this sentence, 'Bertrand Russell' is a name of or refers to the person Bertrand Russell. 'Philosopher' is a predicate and is true of or applies to any philosopher. In general, *predicates* describe or attribute properties or qualities to objects named by *names.*[1] Both sorts of word carry semantical weight and make sense to one who knows English, even when they are isolated from the whole sentence.

What Jones says about Russell is true. However, terms refer and apply in false sentences as well. 'Russell was a Swedenborgian' is false, so far as I know, and therefore 'Russell was not a Swedenborgian' is true. In this sentence 'Russell' refers the same as before, and 'Swedenborgian' applies to Swedenborgians. 'Not' has the force of denying that 'Swedenborgian' applies to Russell.

The words 'not', 'and' and 'also' occurring in these sentences are not names and do not refer (in any clear way) to anything; moreover, they are not predicates and thus convey no news about things. Their office is connective. Of course names and true predicates can be fashioned out of almost any words. An example is 'he is an also-ran' where we have given 'also' a bit of independent sense by joining it with 'ran' to make a predicate. But playing it straight, I'll assume that all speakers of English, including ourselves, know in a rough way which parts of the language have independent meaning and which do not. For a logician's abstract approach the separation of glueing material from the main items is easy – names and predicates carry the semantical burden and the 'ands', 'ifs' and 'neithers' come along to connect words into full sentences. We shall follow this approach.

The theory of reference is about referring terms of languages, i.e. about names, predicates, the objects they refer to or apply to, and for whom. It is a part of semantics, which also studies meaning as well as reference. The difference between the reference or application of a word and its meaning or sense is subject to great dispute. But we can see at once that the two do not coincide.

For instance 'mermaid' *means* half fish, half girl, but does not *apply* to anything, i.e. there are no mermaids. Again, 'liver' does not mean the same in English as 'heart?' yet 'has a liver' and 'has a heart' *apply to exactly the same* animals.

Conversely, a term could mean one thing and refer to many. For instance, in 'I am reading this sentence', 'I' has a fixed meaning but a different referent for each reader – one for you (you) and another for me (me).

Just what the difference is for proper names is not clear. Some thinkers deny that proper names like 'Russell' have meaning on a par with that of predicates. For example, they might argue that you cannot give a definition of 'Feynman' while you can of 'physicist'. Anyone who understands English knows what 'physicist' means, approximately; on the other hand he or she might know English, yet not know what 'Feynman' designates: does it refer to an Austrian mountain, an Italian sports car, an American physicist, or a rabbi? Others say a name plays a meaningful role of some sort whether it refers or not. 'Cerberus' does not name anything, although it means a three-headed dog, and 'Pegasus', which is also empty, means a winged horse.

Again, contrary to the view that proper names do not mean anything, 'Russell' and 'Bertie' refer to the same individual, for friends, but do not mean the same; for 'Russell = Russell' tells you nothing, while 'Russell = Bertie' conveys some knowledge you might not have had before you were told.

The distinction between meaning and reference is far less clear than a few obvious examples suggest, especially when you consider that many other expressions (such as 'comprehension', 'ground' 'sense', 'intension' and 'connotation') have been used by logicians with not quite the same meaning as 'meaning' but for the same thing – some dimension other than reference. Some philosophers, notably Bertrand Russell at one stage in his thought, used 'meaning' in about the same way as we are using 'reference' so that for him the meaning of a proper name was its object. Since there is no such thing as God, according to the Russellian atheist (I am not saying Russell was an atheist), 'God' is a meaningless word. For the non-Russellian atheist, however, it is meaningful but has no referent.

The more common view is that meanings are not ordinary objects, whatever they are, but possibly goings-on in the head, or platonic entities, or properties of things. For the time being we will stick with substantial objects 'out there', and allow meaning to dwell in a methodological limbo.

For this reason I will focus on reference, not meaning, in this introduction. This policy neither requires that we abolish the use of 'meaning' nor bans concepts of meaning or intension from our ruminations. It just requires that we do not pretend to have a theory of meaning or to allow meaning a place in the theory of reference until we are in a stronger position than we are now to say what it is. Thus you can say 'perhaps the meaning of the term "horse" is one thing and the reference another' or 'a word might be meaningful, but not apply to anything' and be understood, without being able to offer an explication of the word 'meaning' or even to justify the implied distinction of meaning from reference. You can walk without knowing leg anatomy and you can talk grammatically without knowing a thing about grammar; moreover, you can use semantical terms, including 'meaning' without having a theory of semantics. But do not confuse habit and theory.

The distinction between the familiar use of concepts and the explanation of them calls for a distinction between *pretheory* and *theory*. This distinction is extremely important throughout all of science, but here in particular. 'Mass' does not mean the same to a piano mover as it does to a physicist, although we fancy it applies to the same objects for both. And pretheoretical use of 'meaning' by ourselves does not convey what it might mean, one day, in theoretical semantics. Meanwhile, we have no business using the concept as a building block for a theory. One of our aims right now is to see why.

The theory of reference overlaps grammar, although the questions it raises here are largely independent of it. Sentences are built of referring terms and other lexical items; so syntax presupposes a fund of names and predicates. On the other hand we face a reverse tendency when we note that terms are frequently identified as such according to grammatical context. For instance in 'red is her favorite color', 'red' is the name of the object red, while in 'The spot is red', 'red' is a predicate. A somewhat more subtle example: 'she is a pretty little girl' has an occurrence of 'pretty' that is adverbial if the sentence is read in one way and adjectival if read in another.

What counts as a name and what counts as a predicate sometimes depends on the *use* of terms. You can use them variously, as in 'Russell' to speak of Russell or to talk about the name itself; for example 'Russell' contains seven letters. One might also use a name, jocosely, as a predicate: 'Schmid is no Russell' or even 'that is Russell'.

Familiar uses of sentences are to assert facts, make declarations, admonish, entertain or to illustrate points of grammar. There is no language without speakers, listeners, writers and readers; they are responsible for reference through utterance. But for the time being let these users dwell in the background while we abstract out just the reference relation itself.

To put the matter as plainly as possible, then, we shall focus on the relation between names or predicates and things: the relation between 'Russell' and Russell, 'philosopher' and philosophers, '0' and zero, 'quark' and quarks, 'she' and she, 'the author of *Hamlet*' and Shakespeare, and 'the chief designer of the first stored program computer' and the foremost investigator of the mathematical theory of games.

Now anyone seeking a robust intellectual diet might be inclined to quit this business right here: if ' "Russell" refers to Russell' is a harbinger of things to come, linguistic reference must be pretty thin stuff. The relation between the name 'Russell' and the man could not be nearly as intriguing as the relation between Russell and Whitehead or between Russell and Lady Ottoline Morrell. What's in it?

To answer the dare, let us set down some tentative definitions which might warm us to the fact that ' "x" refers to x' is very interesting stuff indeed.

Let us write a list of some of the name–thing pairs that most who understand English would accept; it is in effect a very long (infinite) report of English speakers' pretheoretical knowledge of what refers to what. Eventually it is this knowledge which has to be explained. The first entry pairs 'Abel' with Abel etc., and may (temporarily) be thought of as expressing that 'Abel' refers to Abel.

'Abel' – Abel
'Abel' – Eve's second son
'Bach' – Bach
'Christ' – Christ

'God' – God
'the author of *Romola*' – George Eliot
'Russell' – Russell
'Lady Ottoline' – Lady Ottoline
'the president of the United States in 1991' – George Bush
'1' – 1
'4/4' – 1
'π' – 3.141592 . . .
'the principal inventor of the digital computer' – the coauthor
of *The Theory of Games and Economic Behavior*
'Pegasus' – Pegasus
'Titania' – Titania
'Titania' – the fairy queen in *A Midsummer Night's Dream*
'Peaseblossom' – Peaseblossom
etc.

Notice that this list includes grammatically proper names like 'Abel' and the numeral '1' and also definite descriptions. The latter are complex names whose constituents are usually the definite article 'the' strung together with an expression forming a descriptive phrase. Examples above are 'the president . . .' and 'the principal inventor . . .', which describe certain people.

We do not presuppose any more than a speaker of ordinary English would; namely, we do not take it (although we might) that Abel, Bach and God actually exist(ed), while Titania does not. I will return to this after introducing the more technical ideas we need. For the moment let us assume that each name or description on the list names at most one thing, but perhaps not any.

Proper names and descriptions are not the only referential terms in ordinary English. Indefinite pronouns such as 'some' and personal pronouns and demonstratives are others. But they are not names.

First, let us look at 'some'. Suppose you hear a noise in the next room and infer that someone entered it. 'Someone' refers to an individual, and 'entered the room' applies to him or her. At nearly the same time you infer from hearing a sigh of comfort and a squeak of a spring that someone sat down in a chair. You express your belief by 'someone entered the room' and 'someone sat down in a chair'. From these sentences you certainly cannot infer 'someone entered the room and sat in a chair', as the affair could include two persons.

On the other hand, on the occasion of Jones entering the room, consider 'Jones entered the room' and 'Jones sat in a chair'. It clearly follows *ceteris paribus* that 'Jones entered the room and sat in the chair' is true. In the second case there is a simple, direct, valid inference, and in the first not. Failure in the first case can be traced to the indefiniteness of the pronoun 'someone'. Someone entering the room need not be the same as someone sitting in a chair. 'Someone' indefinitely refers to at least one thing, not at most one thing as proper names and descriptions do. 'Some', 'most' and 'all' do not definitely refer and are not to be counted as singular terms.

As to definite pronouns 'I', 'he', 'they', etc., demonstratives 'this', 'that', etc. and space–time words 'here', 'now', 'then' etc., all fix their references by pointing or nodding in immediate experience involving speakers and listeners. Hence these words are denominated collectively as *indexicals*. Within context, indexicals point to exactly one referent, not counting halucination or bad perceptual mistakes. In this respect they are something like proper names. However, out of context they refer to nothing. For example 'that girl' uttered in the absence of girls does not refer to anyone unless speaker and listener have a context – probably established in an ongoing conversation – in mind.

Again, while we await a waiter, 'I am hungry' is about me, if I am the speaker, but is about you if you are. The speaker in this example is itself the context. Indexical terms have fixed reference in use, unlike 'someone', and they can play the same sort of role in inferential context as 'Jones' does in the foregoing example.

So far we have a classification of logical names into proper names, definite descriptions, definite pronouns and indexicals. These are collectively *singular terms*. The other major class consists of predicates, which we call *general terms*. Singular terms are distinguished from general terms by their linguistic role, which is either logical, grammatical, psychological or a bit of each. To explain what I mean by 'linguistic role' in a way not presupposing the very ideas to be later explained – reference and application – is not an easy task. But let us suppose we can define both 'singular term' and 'general term' in order to get on with our venture. It is enough to say here that in very simple sentences like 'Russell is a philosopher' singular and general terms are coupled by predication to form true or false declarative sentences about individual objects (Quine 1960: 96). One plays the role of selecting an object and the other of attributing something to it.

Some, but not all, singular terms have another property beyond role. They are subject to *disquotation*. We say that the move from 'Abel' to Abel is an act of disquotation because quotes are removed to go from one term of the relation to the other. I will call the move from 'Abel' to Eve's second son (second entry on the list on page 6) *indirect disquotation*. We get indirect disquotation in two steps. First, note that Eve's second son is the same person as Abel; second, owing to this identity, substitute 'Eve's second son' for 'Abel' in the right-hand side of the first entry of the list. This yields the second entry, and justifies it.

We assume throughout this book that our list includes all disquotable singular terms of English. But it is not required to include all indirect disquotations as these depend upon items of knowledge that not all people have. Not everyone knows Abel is Eve's second son or that the principal inventor of the digital computer wrote a book on economic theory.

Now 'I', 'you', 'that', 'now' and 'here' etc. are also singular terms. But they cannot be added to the list. For example.

'I' – I (or me),
'you' – you
'that' – that
'now' – now
'here' – here

are either senseless or totally indefinite. Clearly these terms do not refer to any eternally fixed objects ('that' refers to which that?) outside of context. This is the same as noting that there are no fixed descriptions free of context that could be put in for 'I' etc. in the ill-fated disquotations.

So let us separate singular terms according to the following scheme. Included in one totality are proper names and descriptions, which are disquotable or indirectly disquotable, and in the other those that never go on the list; these include indexicals, which depend on context, and words like 'some' and 'all' which do not uniquely refer.

The list makes no distinction between names that refer to an object and names that do not. In order to include both I will use the expression 'p-reference', which is short for 'purported reference.' This notion affords a way of postponing an extremely hard problem and at the same time highlighting it for eventual solution. Everyone knows that 'Titania', 'the 100th President . . .' and 'the fourth moon of the innermost planet of Arcturus' do not definitely refer: the first is fictional; the second is futuristic and hence might not be considered to be about an actual object; and the third is speculative. All three are names, but none clearly names anything. So we skirt around the question of their objects for the time being by having them *purportedly* refer.

We are now (finally!) ready for a tentative definition of 'p-refer'. One way to do this is just to summarize our list. A name N p-refers, we say, if and only if it and its mate are on the list of English names, entry subject to the informal and intuitive considerations just noted.

> N p-refers to o if and only if either N = 'Abel' and o = Abel, N = 'Abel' and o = Eve's second son, or N = 'Bach' and o = Bach, and so on.

This is almost the same as Tarski's (1931) summary of disquotation relative to 'refers'. We shall return to it in Chapter 5. It can be nicely packaged in the following definition:

> (0) N p-refers to o if and only if N is the same as some term 't' on the list, and $o = t$.

> (Hill 1987: 2)

Note that we have a right to apply this definition to listed names only and not, broadly, to singular terms like 'I' or 'you' for the reasons discussed.

> To illustrate (0), suppose N = 'Abel' and o = Abel. Then we have 'Abel' p-refers to Abel if and only if 'Abel' is the same as some 't' on the list and Abel = t.

In fact 'Abel' is the same as some 't' on the list, namely 'Abel', and t = Abel.

The definition (0) does characterize 'p-refer' in a noncircular way, as a good definition should; it can also be seen at a glance that the definiens and definiendum are equivalent. However, the information (0) conveys is nearly zero. It does not tell a thing about the nature or the anatomy of reference. All it really does, minor surface complexities aside, is summarize the idea using the logical particles 'same as' (identity) and 'there exists', plus the list of names everyone knows. Applied to Russell, this theory says that 'Russell' p-refers to Russell since 'Russell' is the same as some name 't' on the list, and t = Russell. Now substitute 'Russell' (which is permitted as it is on the list) for 't' and you get that 'Russell' p-refers to Russell just when 'Russell' is the same as 'Russell' and Russell = Russell.

But why the razzle-dazzle? If that is all there is to it, and we cannot have Lady Ottoline, why not take up beekeeping or industrial management?

2. Referential metaphysics

On the contrary, if philosophy is your game you will find puzzles galore of quite a subtle sort lurking in this trial definition. Let us begin with theology and descend from there.

Does God exist? Well, notice that the right-hand side of (0) is just a moderately clever way of saying 'there is a t such that 't' = N and t = o.' So if 'God' p-refers to God, there is a t such that God = t, i.e. God exists. If we suppose 'God' does not p-refer to God, 'God' does not belong on the list of names, contrary to our assumption that it includes all disquotable names. People and preachers use 'God' with purported reference every day. So it is absurd to suppose the word does not p-refer. So God exists.

Using this argument you can prove anything exists that has a name. For instance, Peaseblossom and Titania exist in some strange world with God and the irrational number 0, to the distress of Pythagoreans.

These fragile arguments are meant to encourage a deeper look into reference and not to introduce serious theology or ontology – although the proof of God's existence might nicely supplement Anselm's *Proslogium* or Thomas's *Five Ways*.

But they are too easy. Something must be wrong with either (0) or the the reasoning or both. As informal arguments go, both seem valid. However, the argument plays on an ambiguity in the concept of existence which is hardly tolerable. (0) does mention some name 't' for N to be identical to; but the existential status of the object referred to, t, is quite worrisome, as we have just observed.

A simple remedy is to add explicitly to (0) the condition that the objects of reference actually exist, but not just in some worrisome sense. Then if 'God' refers to God, God exists. Here's the new tentative theory, this time for reference itself, not for p-reference.

(1) *N* refers to *o* if and only if *N* is the same as some '*t*' on the list, *o* = *t* and *t* exists.

Now if 'God' refers to God, then since 'God' is on the list, 'God' = 'God', God = God and God exists. Therefore He exists. On the other hand if 'God' does not refer, we do not derive a contradiction as before, but only that God does not exist. The trouble with (1), of course, is that a thing like Pegasus can exist in one sense (because his name is on the list), but not in another (because he does not actually exist in space-time). We will return to this point in §4.

If we want to avoid the corrupt theology and ontology it appears we have to abandon (0) and with it the present effort to get a theory of purported reference started. Assuming we really had a characterization of the role of singular versus general terms that was noncommital on reference – and so captured the notion of p-reference only – we could be on our way. But we do not have one, and adoption of (1) means we tie reference to existence. As things stand, a name is not a name unless it refers. This is intolerable for science and everyday talk as well as for theology and fiction.

Meanwhile let us introduce a first definition of 'application' for general terms. The explication of 'applies to' stems from a very long (infinite) list of general terms *P* of English: 'animal', 'barbershop', 'citizen of York', 'philosopher', 'overwhelmingly fond of Margaret' and so on. Then we write, where *P* is any predicate

(2) *P* applies to *o* if and only if either *P* = 'animal' and *o* is an animal, or *P* = 'citizen of York' and *o* is a citizen of York, and so on.

This just imitates the list of names preceding (0). We shall forgo the problems entailed in imitating (0) itself. Again the definition is formally all right as no circularity is involved, and it appears to be adequate for the intended technical use, as we shall show. (2) just says that a predicate applies to an object *o* provided that *o* has the attribute the predicate expresses. Quite obviously, this is redundant, and the light it sheds for our quest seems pretty feeble. However, we might flatter ourselves that this view of predication is essentially Aristotle's and is central to modern logic.

For completeness we might also introduce application more

generally for relational predicates such as '*x* is larger than *y*', '*x* is the spouse of *y*', '*x* is between and *y* and *z*', '*x* gave *y* to *z* for *w*' etc. But this would needlessly complicate a very complex subject and so we shall drop it.

Sometimes I shall use 'reference' generically, having in mind either reference proper (1) or application (2). Both relations are vaguely 'referential' in ordinary English and both have to do with the relation of words to things.

Now let us temporarily drop application proper and return to theology and reference. At this point it is tempting to invoke meanings – names mean, even though they might not refer. 'God' is just as meaningful to the atheist as to the theist, and 'Titania' is meaningful even though fictional.

But assuming 'being meaningful' is not just vague talk for 'being a singular term with purported reference', this does not buy us anything. As things stand, we do not have a respectable notion of meaning at all, much less a distinction between singular and general meanings. 'Nonreferential names are significant because they have meaning', if not simply idle, just expresses our naive feeling for language. Words, words, words.

Perhaps we can evade the problem by adopting the suggestion that 'God' and '0' really refer to concepts of individuals, or more explicitly, to individual concepts in our minds. If so, use of the words would not commit us to beliefs in God and 0, but only to ideas in the mind. Such a convention would also allow sensible talk of the fictitious Pegasus and Titania as well as of God and numbers.

But saving the principle that names must name things in order to be names by invoking an individual concept in the mind for 'God' to bear, we have steered ourselves straight back into the philosophical wilderness we sought to avoid by rejecting meanings. We now have a concept for 'God' to refer to, ordinary full-blooded things for most other names to refer to, and nothing for 'Pegasus' or 'the 100th President' unless it be a concept of Pegasus for one and a possible President for the other. In exchange for all this we have a less than satisfactory notion of God for either the believer or the skeptic to work on and an equivocal definition of 'refers'.

The main fault here, however, is that having names name concepts in selected cases licenses the practice of *ad hoc* solutions for individual problems. It endorses populating our ontology at will, showing no regard for evidence, argument or proper science.

13

That is certainly not the way we want our theory to go – any more than the theoretical physicist wants four special concepts of force. Of course the complexities the physicist copes with are brought on him in the course of inquiry in mid-stream. But he would be mad if he set out to study physical phenomena by imposing on himself different theories for different cases before his science got off the ground. So would we. *Ad hoc* tinkering with ontology is not a rational approach to reference or any other scientific question.

However, we might invoke a blanket limitation, a requirement that *all* names refer to, and *all* predicates apply to, concepts of individuals. This approach would commit us to referential belief in everything, including God and Titania, that could be pinned down by rummaging through our heads. But it would condemn all of science to conceptualism willy-nilly or, for the more robust of us, to Cartesian quandries about the relation of actual things to ideas in the mind. Locke has the problem, and we shall find instruction in considering his views on words in the next chapter.

A nineteenth-century view which is still held says that all names refer to objects, to be sure, but some objects are *possible*, not actual. These possibles are neither concepts nor actual things, although they are modes of being. One of this ilk claims that 'Pegasus' refers to a possible object that does not exist, and that 'God' refers to a possible object that perhaps does actually exist. We might adopt possibles forthwith simply by construing the worrisome version of existence in (0) as 'possible existence?' This would seem to help clarify 'purportedness' as well.

Purveyors of this stuff are not above pushing impossible possibles, e.g. the objects referred to by 'the round square cupola on Berkeley's Tower' or 'the real root of $x^2 + 4 = 0$'. The notion is plainly a purely gratuitous device for upholding a conviction that names, to be names, must refer to something. By our standards, unactual impossible possibles are no solution to reference, and we reject them – although they will turn up again.

Still another strategy might be to limit reference to physical objects. Then if 'God' is to refer, it must be to an existing physical being. The pleasing consequence of this convention, for the atheist, would be that God as usually conceived of does not exist. Of course this means the atheist must be willing to practise philosophy by edict, not by argument. I shall return to this point in a moment.

However, as with the original (1), we would still not know what to do with fiction and speculation, as physicalism does not help reclaim a decent concept of purportedness. 'Purports to refer to a physical thing' is less transparent, I think, than 'purports to refer'. Some philosophers, notably Gareth Evans (1982), deliberately eschew questions of ontology such as I have raised and settle for inquiry into reference of names under the assumption that all names including variables refer, if they refer, to spatiotemporal particulars. Of course he tries, 'like a cautious builder, to have a thought for the constructions which must at some later time be added' (ibid.: 3).

But a troubling question hounds the theory even if we keep clear of theology, fictions and speculational entities. To see it let us also add to our theory of application (2) the clause that the object *o* be physical. Then, for example, 'red' applies to *o* if and only if 'red' is the same as some predicate 'F', *o* is a physical object and *o* is F. But this restriction stymies all talk of pains, sensations, thoughts and of course numbers. If they are to apply, the terms 'thought', 'pain', 'deity' and 'number' must be of physical things by edict or else of nothing at all. The move would be of a piece with the earlier blanket restriction of reference and application to concepts. The only advantage of physicalism here is that more thinkers in today's intellectual climate tolerate hard bodies than soft images and other mental things.

Further, this alternative would hardly appeal to one who takes philosophy of mind seriously; it begs the question of mind and body. For instance, it blocks debate on the pros and cons of the identity theory: either one is saddled with materialism a priori and not by reasoned argument; or else mental terms do not apply to anything, and if they do not apply, the identity theory is empty. For note, the sentence 'every mental event is identical to the event of excitement of a nerve fiber', which, I take it, is a reasonably adequate expression of the theory, would have to be reckoned trivially true under physicalism (unless the mind is in the heart or glands) and not debatable; or otherwise vacuous because 'mental' does not apply to anything in our ontology.

Blanket materialism would put a large group of assorted scientists, who are often Intersabbatical Materialists, at a great disadvantage. If 'this spiritual thrill' might refer to something nonphysical – if the identity theory is debatable – on Sunday, then they are intellectually safe, as their faith can take over. If it is not debatable, as under the blanket assumption, then they are no better off on Sunday than on Monday.

We have tentatively questioned a theory, (0), that allows purported reference, so names can be names without objects; the only alternative seems to be to play around with ontology – if you cannot solve a problem, add or subtract an entity or two. Nevertheless, let us keep a hold on physicalism without fully embracing it, aware that the decision to hold is tentative and allows serious questions to stand.

At this point it is fair to ask whether there is an alternative to ontological juggling in order to satisfy the demand that names be names. Many philosophers think there is a way – down a divided path. I have in mind certain dual theories of reference that distinguish between two kinds of reference (and application): *absolute* reference and reference *relativized* to use.

The basic idea is this. Objects are involved in reference only when names are *used* to refer. Consider our first version of a definition in (0): a name p-refers just when it is on a list paired with its disquote or indirect disquote. But a person actually using a name to refer is doing something more than idle listing. A speaker of English often uses 'Russell' to refer, while he uses 'Pegasus' in story writing or criticism without intending to refer at all.

Let us write 'reference*' for the notion of using to refer, i.e. for the idea of reference involving a user who has in mind to name an object. There is to be no question of an object of reference – which is just an abstract semantical relationship – but only of an object of reference*.

Now reference* is one among a number of uses of terms which include description, admonition, instruction etc. For instance, a term might be used to refer*, or alternatively be used as part of a non-naming expression to describe a situation, admonish someone, declare fealty etc. without intending a referent, i.e. an existent object. Khomeini might use 'Allah' in 'Allah is watching' to refer* to Allah; or in a less frightening mood comment that 'good Muslims declare their faith in Allah five times a day'. In the first case he uses 'Allah' to refer*; in the second he does not, but only uses it to describe a Muslim practice (one might say).

The old, familiar relation (0) is said to be a *semantical* relation, and the relation that incorporates a user is said to be a *pragmatical* one.[2] According to one possible version of this dual theory semantics is to be devoted to the study of the relation between words and things, including reference and application. Semantical relations are in principle no different than other relations which can be studied abstractly as in mathematics. Given this view, it is a mistake to add clauses '*t* exists' or '*t* is physical' to definitions of 'refer'; reference has nothing to do with existence or other material questions. Reference* does.

One possible interpretaton of this position is that the reference studied in pure semantics of this kind is p-reference. Expressing a term referentially*, however, or asserting or denying a sentence is a matter for pragmatics, a theory which proceeds differently than the relations (0)–(2).

It seems clear that reference construed as abstract relation has few of the amusing (or irritating!) metaphysical consequences we coaxed out of (0) and (1). It seems to escape the puzzles and eschews the scheme, disquotation lists and all, that sets them up. Unfortunately I shall have to argue later that theories relating true reference and application to use in this way are incomplete; indeed they presuppose objects and other semantical entities much as (1) does. However, I am willing to let the dual theory stand as a therapeutic offering for the moment. It seemingly resolves the ontological enigmas at one stroke. Meanwhile we shall carry on with (1) and (2) as devices for use in stirring up problems and return to a more systematic discussion of use* in Chapters 4 and 6.

3. Plato, Aristotle and numbers

Let us return to reference and ontology. Except when writing about physicalism I have said little about (2). Are there ontological problems that plague application?

In relation (2) of §2 there is no condition of existence, while of course there is in relation (1). As we have seen, we require existence in (1) to guarantee a stock of objects; no object, no reference. But attribution of a property by application of a predicate is not reference to an object. (2) does seem to presuppose the referentiality of '*o*' but it does not specify existence of properties or attributes. For instance, if there are no mermaids, our theory entails that 'mermaid' applies to nothing. It neither affirms nor denies that there is such a thing as the attribute mermaid. Here the proper

17

existential question is whether 'there' refers, not whether 'mermaid' does, for 'mermaid' is a predicate, not a name.

But we have agreed to give the issues about reference of names a temporary rest. What about reference of predicates? Whether they refer or not, and to what, brings us to a semantical version of the classical problem of universals.

Imitating the analysis of reference of names in §2, let us write:

(1) P refers to o if and only if P is the same as some 'F', $o = F$ and F exists.

where it is to be understood that P is a general term, not a proper name. Assuming there are referring predicates, (1) entails classical realism. For instance, ' "mermaid" refers to mermaid' entails by (1) that mermaid exists. This conclusion is by no means the same as 'there are mermaids' or 'mermaids exist', which follows from ordinary application as in ' "mermaid" applies to mermaids'.

The business is somewhat confusing as in one sentence 'mermaid' is a name and in the other a predicate. To eliminate the ambiguity let us replace 'mermaid' in 'mermaid exists' by 'mermaidness' while retaining 'mermaid' for the predicate. To be very explicit, let us write

(i) 'mermaidness' refers to mermaidness

and

(ii) 'mermaid' applies to mermaids.

Sentence (i) implies there is such a thing as mermaidness. Sentence (ii) imples only that there are mermaids. Note we could have (i) true and (ii) false, (i) false and (ii) true, both true, or both false; so the two are completely independent.

The Platonist could accept (i) true and (ii) false – there is an Idea of mermaidness but it is not instantiated – or both (i) and (ii) true, if there be mermaids. The Aristotelian could accept (i) false and (ii) true, if there be mermaids, or both (i) and (ii) false. But he would in no case accept uninstantiated mermaidness – (i) true.

In effect, in semantical terms (this is the main point) the Platonist believes that general terms *refer*, while the Aristotelian believes they only *apply* to individual things.

Using the concept of reference to spell out the difference between semantical Platonism and nominalism is not a new idea; it is a center-piece in Quine's (1960) ontology, and we shall meet it again.

A more interesting feature of this way of expressing classical realism is that it fails to divide off nominalism from Aristotelian realism. Both of these schools deny that predicates refer; both deny the existence of a substantial form or idea mermaidness. Nominalists and Aristotelians are in accord when the issue is put in our semantical way; predicates apply to things but do not refer to anything.

The Aristotelian medieval tradition, relying on metaphor, had it that universals are in particular things; they exist in things, but have no separate existence. Today most philosophers would, I believe, express essentially the same by saying a particular realizes or instantiates a universal. On the other hand the medieval nominalist holds that universals are names only and are neither in or out of individual things; nor are they universal concepts, as they were for Abelard and, in even modern times, for many empiricists.

Is there something about application that explains the difference?

One possible way to make sense of the difference is to bring human beings back into the story. How the relation of application is understood by a language user might be the key. To see what I mean, think of application as a triadic relation, 'F' applies to o for an individual i. Then determination of whether F applies to a particular o is affected by i's cognitive role. Let us tentatively redefine 'F applies to o' in this triadic spirit as follows:

(2) 'F' applies to o if and only if there is a cognitive agent i such that i determines that o is F.

Note that (2) is totally unrelated to reference*. Here we are thinking of the speaker or listener as determining the very *nature* of application, not as using a pre-formed (so to speak) semantical linkage for this or that particular purpose.

I am suggesting that the key to the dispute between nominalism and Aristotelian realism lies in 'determines'. For the latter, determination rests with Creative Reason (or the Active Intellect, in the thought of St Thomas) which abstracts the universal form F from o. This act is a determination of what the thing is and consequently of the true application of 'F' to o. For the nominalist, on the other hand, the determination is effected directly by application of the term '*F*' either arbitrarily ('extreme nominalism'), by virtue of a similarity of the object of which '*F*' is predicated to other things it is predicated of, or by virtue of a kind of matching procedure that presuppposes recurrent properties.

In following this semantical strategy, I want to suggest that Platonism versus anti-Platonism is a question of reference, while the finer distinction between Aristotelian realism and nominalism is one of how application of a predicate is determined by an agent. This requires analysis of reference and application as three-termed relations.

There is some significance in this old-fashioned business. We shall show that there is no adequate theory of reference as a simple two-way word to thing relation even in the instance of proper names. And by inserting the language speaker we shall establish a way of settling old philosophical scores and at the same time take steps toward a timely theory of reference and human cognition.

Let us not discard relation (1) without saying something about the putative indispensability of abstract reference for science. I have in mind mathematical objects.

Although in everyday and scientific life we do not boggle at reference of mathematical terms like 'five', '5 + 7' or 'the set of numbers less than 100^{100}', their objects are not concrete. One reason we worry little about ontology of whole (positive) numbers is that they make the management of money a joy. Nevertheless, from the point of view of semantics, numbers (unlike physical objects) are nowhere to be seen. Here reference is more obscure than ever.

My dictionary records 'five' as an adjective, i.e. a logical predicate; for example there are five men on a basketball team and five points in the Calvinist controversy with the Arminians. From a grammatical viewpoint 'five' modifies 'men' in the first example and 'point' in the second. However, unlike 'tall', which also modifies 'men' in 'there are tall men on a basketball team', 'five' does not apply to individual men, but to a set of men, a team. This the proverbial schoolboy learns today in elementary logic or modern mathematics courses.

'Five' is also the name of a number. By (1) above, ' "five" refers to five' implies that 'five' is the same as some '*Q*' and five (or fiveness) = *Q*. So the abstract object five is a property or set of sets. If we insist that the set 'five' applies to must exist on pain of 'five' not applying to an object, then we see that the objects of reference must include both sets and properties (or sets) of sets as well as individual physical things.

Despite its shortcomings, we might now take reference and application of terms to individuals as in §1 and §2 and supplement them with concepts of reference and application to sets and sets of sets as required for mathematics and science. This defines our tentative ontology: '*N*' in (1) of §1 is to range over names of numbers, functions and sets as well as names of physical objects; and 'refers' is to pair names with these objects.

I earlier complained of the practice of making ontic decisions by edict, i.e. of introducing concepts for 'God' and 'Pegasus' to refer to, just so the names are not empty. But now what about numbers and sets? We have admitted them along with physical objects – while being unsure of what to do with God and Pegasus, the speculative and the fictional. Is this not as arbitrary as importing concepts for 'God' to refer to, as we did when on our subjectivist tack?

The answer is clearly no. In the mathematical case we are accepting the conclusions of more than a century of work in the foundations of mathematics. We could reject them only from the standpoint of an apriorist philosophy of mathematics that fancies itself above ordinary logic. Numbers have been around a long time, and no other precise (class of) interpretations other than the set interpretation seems to be adequate for mathematics and science. We do not introduce sets and sets of sets by edict; we do so because we cannot pursue pure mathematics without them. But God as a concept in the mind is a proposition whose sole merit is to abet a suspect theory of reference. It draws on a philosophical tradition that was abandoned with perukes; and it has low appeal anyway to serious devotees of the religious life. It is not only not intellectually indispensable; no one opts for it.

4. *Three commandments*

Having shown how the explanation of reference in (1) of §2 is related to some problems in philosophy, I now want to look into some of the issues in semantics proper.

There are many things wrong with relations (0) of §1 and (1) of §2 although the basic idea of disquotation they are designed to capture probably must be a part of any adequate theory of reference. After reviewing the shortcomings I will return to a summary discussion of disquotation.

Disquotation slights reference of indexicals and demonstratives, and I shall try to make up for this in later chapters.

We pay a lot for what we get out of (0) and (1). The problem is that the disguised quantifier hidden in '*N* is the same as some "*t*" on the list' in (0) is a substitutional quantifier (explained in Chapters 3 and 5) and is responsible for the crazy theology in §2. If we make its use explicit, (0) reads: 'there is a *t* such that "*t*" = *N* and *t* = *o*' etc. When we put 'God?' in for *N* and 'God' for *o*, we got 'there is a *t* such that "*t*" = "God" and *t* = God; ergo God exists'. Opinion differs as to whether the notion of existence expressed in this cheerful deduction has anything to do with actual existence, like Johnsonian rocks or the solution of $x + 1 = 4x + 9$. In writing (1) I assumed it did not, and so added '*t* exists' explicitly. You do not have to be Bertrand Russell to see that this yields two notions of existence buried in (1). In plain English, (0) is conceptually untidy and (1) messes things up even more. But at the moment it is all we have got that is close to being a theory.

A name is a name owing to its linguistic role. Yet can one explain role without tacit appeal to a referent? The fact is, there are names having no referent. This is one of the chief puzzles about reference and is a reason for introducing the notion of p-reference.

We tested four proposals for guaranteeing objects of some sort for all names.

(i) We rejected-out-of-hand the proposal that fictional and speculative names might be meaningful though non-referring, and that meaningfulness confers the right to call a purported name a name. Notice that a sturdy notion of meaning would not help to find an explication of 'name' anyway, for conferring a meaning or sense on 'Titania' would not make a name out of it or help decide whether it has a bearer. It was a name early on. Besides, we do not at this point allow meaning as a technical notion, but only as a pretheoretical one we either have to clear up or clear out.

(ii) Another alternative is to generate entities needed to fill gaps as the gaps turn up. Let 'God', 'the fourth moon . . .' and 'Titania' refer to concepts or ideas in the mind. Or let their bearers be denizens of a world of fiction or of nonactual possible worlds. Thus they are names with reference, but without reference to actual things. Both of these options might be left open, although they violate a basic commandment we should be reluctant to breach: do not introduce entities *ad hoc*.

(iii) A complementary alternative is to restrict the philosophical domain of discourse to safe objects, like the physical and mathematical: practice safe reference. If fictional and spiritualistic terms are excluded from the game we do not have to worry about spawning unwanted impossible possibles. But this does not solve the reference problem of 'the fourth moon of Arcturus?' or 'Bach's 203rd Church Cantata?' or 'tachyon?' all of which would be physical but for their existential impoverishment. We still have nonbearing names with us. If our aim is to understand language, the mind and the relations among minds and between minds and the world, whole domains must not be eliminated by edict.

(iv) Another approach (end of §2) divides off the word–thing relation from use and the user, and studies it as an abstract relation. I suggested the notation 'reference' for the abstracted relation and 'reference*' for actual referring. Then living reference, assertion etc. become matters of reference* and can be relegated to psychology and cognitive science. Nonbearing names simply would not be used in making statements, but only for fictions or for noncommittal descriptions. Moreover, puzzles about empty names could be evaded in the abstract theory since it could use the supposition that all names refer: 'supposing that all names refer, we get a theory of reference, as follows . . .'.

The trouble is that relegating questions of reference, truth, and so forth to use* obscures the role of the agent-user as constitutive of primary reference. To retain the agent is of course precisely to block the move to abstraction. The proposal to abstract from use and consign questions of assertibility to psychology of language use* obscures the nature of the anatomy of reference. I will return to this topic in Chapter 6.

At this stage of inquiry, application does not present the same puzzles as reference beyond identifying the stock of general terms to be listed and of finding an explanation of their linguistic role. Frege (Chapter 3) will have a good deal to say about the role of predicates in semantics. There are no objects to worry about since we decided not to use predicates as names of individuals (except that number-words like 'five' are to be taken as names of sets, which we allow in our ontology along with physical objects). If a predicate like 'mermaid' does not apply to anything, then we just use negation in the appropriate places. Unlike a name, which is not a name without a purported object, a predicate does not have to have anything to be of.

What we are to pursue, then, is a theory of reference of naming expressions that relate to physical objects and numbers (but not to the exclusion by edict of mental or heavenly things) including fictional and speculative names. A good theory must, at the least,

> Explain disquotation; each disquote on the complete list of
>   English should be entailed by the theory.
> Explain what is meant by 'purportedness'.

I will refer to these requirements jointly as 'condition (*R*)' in what follows.

These requirements assume that the list contains singular, disquotable terms only. We have no theory, so far, explicating 'singular term' except vaguely in terms of logical role.

Note that the first condition can be satisfied using (0) of §1 – just plug in for '*N* ' and '*o*' using the original list – but this explanation is trivially circular. What we intend by (*R*) is a genuine explanation, and we shall see what the nature of it must be at the end of Chapter 5. We shall see there that the theory must explain how names link to objects.

Note also that (0) in §1 gratuitously introduces purportedness. (*R*) says we want an honest-to-goodness explanation of how empty names like 'Titania' can be names at all.

We also insist that the theory we are in pursuit of meet three regulations:

Commandments

>   I Do not use circular definitions; do not pass off a pretheor-
>   etical idea as a new technical idea
> II Do not add entities *ad hoc*
> III Do not appeal to entities you cannot explain (individuate)

These are probably not independent; but I am particularly concerned to stress I. Explication of pretheoretical ideas in terms of themselves is endemic in studies of reference and meaning. I would list violations of I in the notion of natural sign (Chapter 2) as an explanation of disquotation; and of Fregean sense (Chapter 3) as an explanation of meaning (and possibly of purportedness).

II is violated by the doctrine of possible objects introduced for words like 'Titania' and 'Pegasus' to name.

III is violated by the confused use of 'exists' in item (1), §2. The doctrine of possible objects also violates (III).

CHAPTER 2

Natural Signs

1. Reference themes

Talking about things is so distinctively human that special effort is needed to see that there is anything puzzling in it. It takes work to discover that naming, a natural ingredient of speaking and writing, is not as transparent as it evidently seems to be to a fluent child. There is more work in deciding what sort of puzzle it is. In the Introduction I stressed ontology; but the problem is broader than that. Where would one put 'naming' in a college curriculum?

If a theory of names and reference is conceived of as a chapter in epistemology, as it is for John Locke and Bertrand Russell, its findings are not likely to be the same as if it is taken to be a part of metaphysics, as it is for Charles Peirce and most semioticians, or part of behavioral psychology, as it is for W. V. Quine. What Alfred Tarski, Rudolf Carnap and their followers call 'pure semantics' is a mathematical enterprise that includes no theory of reference at all. The same is true today of linguistics done in the style initiated by Noam Chomsky. Theoretical linguistics is busy with semantics in the large (as a component of grammar), but has not come around to lexical reference (semantics of terms) except for anaphora.[1] So-called computer 'semantics' is basically syntax semantically interpreted by computer users, and includes nothing whatever relevant to naming.

The point is that conceptual frameworks from within which one might plausibly approach reference count very heavily in how the issues are construed and what the theory turns out to be. For instance, Gottlob Frege and Charles Peirce, both logicians, do not start from the same bases. For Frege, reference is an abstract relation he takes for granted. For Peirce it is a form of cognition, of abductive inference.

For reasons of this kind, to try to build a theory of reference on foundations established by Great Minds is hopeless. There is no foundation. But there is a tradition of thought on the subject that must be canvassed if we hope to make any inroads into it.

Most semantical theories found outside of computer semantics are either semiotical, causal, logico-mathematical, analytical or naturalistic, listed in approximately historical order. I say 'approximately' as there is overlap and heterochrony; the scheme of this list is more of paradigm than of history. Moreover, it does not classify people; it sorts theories or parts of theories. Bertrand Russell, for instance, can rightly be tagged as proposing a causal, logical or analytical theory depending on which stage of his thought one is looking into.

Here is a sketch of the five approaches to reference. Modern semiotical and causal theories stem from epistemological roots that are essentially medieval or Cartesian and presuppose that minds or ideas in minds are separated from the physical world by an epistemic gap, the world on the one side and the mind on the other. Reference is a relation between mental entities and the world, and poses about the same epistemological problems as perception and knowledge do. Reference of words derives from the reference of ideas, or other representations in the mind, to objects.

To the semiotician, reference of x to y is an object-directed correspondence running from the user z of the term x to the object y (the 'arrow theory'). There is, on this view, an entity in the mind that is a *natural sign* of the object; and this sign is conventionally expressed through the term x which refers to the object by dint of its association to the sign.

To the causalist, reference runs the other way, from the object y to the mind of the utterer z of the term x. On this view the object y causes an idea (or brain event) in z's head that is expressed by x; x refers to y by way of its conventional association to the idea.

Logico-mathematical theories abstract away from language users and natural signs and ideas in the head and construe reference as a map, in the mathematical sense of the word, from sets of words to sets of objects. They also concentrate on exact, formal languages, while semantical problems of natural language take a secondary place. The aim of a theory of reference here is to examine the relational structures built on a noncritically given semantical domain of words and objects of various sorts, much as abstract algebras or arithmetics are examined in pure mathematics.

Analytic theories are of two kinds. Ordinary language philosophers examine meanings of philosophically puzzling notions, such as 'reference', 'name' and 'truth', in terms of ordinary language concepts and practices – for instance by making explicit the correct use of 'reference' in English and digging into the implications of that use for semantics.

This stance exhibits an attitude completely different from that of the epistemologist or mathematician. The analyst is not directly concerned about the workings of reference in the mind–world economy or in abstract structures, but rather about the meaning of 'reference' in good philosophy (read *his*, typically); and he traces puzzles such as attend that of 'God' in our small theory (0) to linguistic confusion (and is surely right, in part).

The second kind of analyst, notably Bertrand Russell and W. V. Quine, resolve language puzzles, in particular of reference, by paraphrasing ('analyzing away') troublesome locutions in formal language terms, particularly in formal languages such as the predicate calculus. For both, good philosophical analysis is not grounded in carefully scrutinized natural language, but in the exact language of science and mathematics. Their work also falls in part under what I have called the logico-mathematical approach.

Naturalists consider semantics to be part of empirical psychology and linguistics. The naturalist is materialistic, not dualistic like Locke and Russell tend to be, and thinks of semantical phenomena as objective connections between users of language in a community and the world that all the talk is about, not as relations contemplated introspectively; it treats the epistemic features of reference as a part of natural science, not of a transcendent theory of knowledge.

Naturalists in the field of semantics tend to absorb insights and methods of the mathematical and analytical ventures, while at the same time keeping an eye on relevant developments in psychology, linguistics, artificial intelligence and neuroscience. Quine, already mentioned as an analyst, is also a naturalist, and in semantics the most influential; so is Peirce, although he is too odd to squeeze into any category or union of them.

In the remaining sections of this chapter I will discuss and then dismiss semiotical and early (Lockean) causal theories. All of them violate one or more of the Commandments given in Chapter 1 and fail to meet our tentative disquotation and existence conditions. Some of them suggest approaches to p-reference and the problem of linguistic role of terms; others, in particular causal Locke, do not. All of them, however, do suggest some kind of word–thing linkage which bare disquotation does not.

2. Locke's theories of names

Semiotical theories appear in medieval thought, Peirce, the IVth Book of Locke's *An Essay Concerning Human Understanding*, phenomenology and contemporary semiotic.[2] What these theories share is twofold: first, the idea that linguistic terms express the content of natural mental signs of objective things, and second, that these internal signs refer or apply in virtue of a natural ordering of the mind to objects. Locke's more familiar causal theory of Book III does not have these characteristics, for words in that theory are mere tags for ideas, and ideas are caused by, not signs of, objects.

Locke got snarled in the strands of an empiricist theory of knowledge which he tried to build over a Cartesian dualistic gap. The trouble of course is how to be an empiricist – all knowledge arises in sense experience – and at the same time to justify belief in an external physical world which he believes there is no direct sensory contact with. Ideas intervene. He tries two ways of extricating himself. As an empiricist, his official doctrine has to be that knowledge is the perception of agreement or disagreement of ideas (Locke 1760: IV, i, 2),[3] which are the sole contents of awareness. But as a realist he can be satisfied only with a view that knowledge is of an objective physical world, of God and of the Self.

The two theories of names, which correspond to the two strands, are not as explicit in Locke himself as one might want, so I will call the disclosed Locke 'Locke*' to evade accusations of bad exegesis.

In both theories the immediate objects of awareness are ideas. That is basic Locke. Names, both proper and common, mark ideas. The notion (ibid.: III, ii, 1) is very much like our stop-gap idea for nonbearing names, used in Chapter 1, of having terms refer to concepts. But the motivation is not the same. We were concerned about empty names being names nonetheless with respect to a given world, while Locke has no empty names, since there are no names except for the ideas already there to be marked. Words do not refer directly to external objects; but for Locke* they refer indirectly either causally or semiotically, i.e. intentionally, as I will explain.

It is also axiomatic for Locke that ideas are 'about external sensible objects, or about the internal operations of our minds' (ibid.: II, i, 2). The man's philosophical troubles revolve about 'about' and the two ways out of them are probed quite differently by Locke*.

Reference and application as relations sustained by words to things are parasitical on ideas. Locke makes no such distinction as we do between reference and application (his blanket term is 'signification'), but Locke* does. If you are Locke*, 'Shaftesbury' refers to Shaftesbury in virtue of its standing for the complex idea of Shaftesbury, which does have a putative relationship to Shaftesbury. 'Philosopher' applies to individual philosophers in virtue of marking the complex general idea of philosopher. As you rightly expect, the reference relationship is the source of major worry. It is causal when Locke* is running in the empiricist mode and intentional when he is being a realist.

Now the causal theory and its consequences go like this. Names have no direct signification except of ideas. The function of naming is solely to assist memory and to communicate our ideas to others (ibid.: III, ii, 2, 3). Inasmuch as names are tags only of our own ideas there is no guarantee that communication can succeed. I have knowledge of my ideas only, not of yours. So there is no basis, other than supposition, for believing yours are like mine or mine like yours; we are aware of just our own individual ideas. Locke puts it this way: speakers suppose that others using the same name refer to the same ideas; and they suppose they stand for things (ibid.: III, ii, 4–5).

As for things, there is more to go on than supposition. From Locke's basic doctrine against innate ideas it follows that they must originate from some source, as per the axiom of external objects. And so they do: 'they [ideas] are modifications of matter in the bodies that cause such perceptions' (ibid.: II, viii, 7). However, he nearly deserts this stance as he takes it: most ideas, he writes, are no more like bodies than the names that stand for them are like ideas (ibid.: II, vii, 7). So ideas are not like their causes. Of course this is significant for the point of disquotation, and we shall return to it.

With name-tags and externally caused ideas as objects, Locke* can explain 'reference' through a composition of the relation of tagging with that of causing:

> (1) 'Shaftesbury' refers to *o* means 'Shaftesbury' marks a complex Shaftesbury-idea that is caused by *o*.

Application is the same except that normally it applies to general ideas:

> (2) 'Philosopher' applies to *o* means 'Philosopher' marks a complex general philosopher-idea caused by some object, and agrees with the Shaftesbury-idea caused by *o*.

Presumably it is agreement which is a ground for the predication 'Shaftesbury is a philosopher'. The latter is a fairly thick gloss on Locke: abstract general ideas are 'nominal essences' of sorts of things; but there is no reason for concluding that *o*, although it causes a particular idea of the right sort, is itself of that sort or of any sort at all.

Such is an analysis by Locke* of Locke's notion of supposing named ideas are about things. The theory tells us what the linkage of word to thing is, and it tells us that the linguistic role of a word is to facilitate communication. The name expresses the idea that is in turn caused by a material body. The theory explains fictions, speculative reference and reference to past and future events via memory and imagination. 'Titania' refers in the full sense that 'Shaftesbury' does, for it marks an antecedently given, externally caused idea. However there is no justification for adding a proposition that a = Shaftesbury (1) since ideas are not like things. Causal Locke* does not support disquotation. (I am deliberately ignoring the primary–secondary quality distinction.)

Let us return to another interpretation of 'about' as this concept occurs in Locke's basic axiom of the origin of ideas.

At the very end of *An Essay Concerning Human Understanding*, in a passage warmly embraced by semioticians, Locke divides the sciences into knowledge of things in their 'own proper being', including matter, body and spirits; practical knowledge; and semiotic, the doctrine of signs. Semiotic as Locke conceives of it is to treat of ideas as signs of things, not merely as the furnishings of the mind brought about by unknown causes. Ideas are signs 'for understanding of things' in their proper being. '[S]imple ideas . . . must necessarily be the product of things operating on the mind in a natural way and producing therein those Perceptions, which by the Wisdom and Will of our Maker they are *ordained and adapted* to' (my italics) (ibid.: IV, iv, 4). Complex ideas also are ordained and adapted. Further, differing radically from the notion that words are mere marks, they are now signs of ideas in the same sense as ideas are signs of things, signs for conveying understanding of things or for 'conveying . . . knowledge' to others (ibid.: IV, iv, 4)

This new stuff is Cartesian, even medieval, and is far from the Locke of vol. II, viii, 7, who finds ideas to be totally dissimilar to bodies. The clergy had been busy.[4]

In medieval thought (with many variations) signification is a relation of a natural sign (a 'first intention') in the soul to a thing that is not a sign. 'A sign is something which, on being perceived, brings something other than itself into awareness.'[5] The idea of Russell in the mind brings him into consciousness. This notion that reference is a 'bringing into', natural to the mind, persists up to present day semiotic.

In its evident favor, the concept of natural sign seems indeed natural to unreflective thought. My cathode-ray tube impression is, I conceive, a natural sign of a cathode-ray tube on my desk. We do (I do) think of thoughts and words as directed toward things, or as bringing things into the mind and as being significant because of that power. Unless a reader of an engrossing story is distracted by an outer disturbance he is likely to be more aware of actors in the story than of print on the page. We perceive through signs; signs are signs of things, not of themselves. The same example shows how words can purport to be of things. They purport because they naturally express signs of things.

The semiotical notion can be summarized in a second Lockean* theory of reference:

(3) 'Shaftesbury' refers to *o* means 'Shaftesbury' is a sign of the complex Shaftesbury-idea which is in turn a sign of *o*.

Similarly for application as the role of words that mark general complex ideas, signifying things in turn.

There is not the slightest doubt that *o* = Shaftesbury, given God's ordination, and that the function of both natural signs (erstwhile *ideas*) and names is to bring things other than signs into awareness. Words are no longer mere tags; and ideas, which they represent, represent real things in turn.

Both semiotical and causal theories explain the linkage of word–thing. But the semiotical theory has the eminent advantage of meeting the disquotation condition since '*a*' refers to *a*, although the existence of *a* might be doubtful. Thus the causal theory guarantees existence, even of the bearer of 'Titania', but lapses on disquotation; while the semiotic entails disquotation, but not existence.

The role of communication gets played better in semiotic than in causal Locke* as it implies the common purport of names for everyone. The linkage is of natural sign to object, and words serve to communicate and enable human commerce; they signify the same things for everyone.

Unfortunately the notion of natural sign, which covers so much so easily, violates basic principles of individuation, which in this book are inviolable. Are the thoughts I have about Russell signs of Russell? Are Hume's weak sense impressions signs of Russell in the same sense? Is there a natural sign in the mind of the square root of −1? Of largeness? Or of serendipity? Are they like Russell signs? A good semiotician might answer that there are indeed many classes of signs (Peirce at one time reckoned sixty-six). But my point is one of identity. When is a thing a sign, and when not? Are signs material things? Mental things? Individual concepts or ideas? Universals post rem? Imageless thoughts? Phantasms? The list reads like an inventory of the accumulated conceptual impedimenta of two millennia.

Furthermore, to explain reference by means of natural signs is perilously close to explaining it in terms of itself (Commandment I). We do think self-reflectively of thoughts as bearing on things; but this is no explanation of reference. It just repeats the hard questions.

I hasten to point out that although Locke was influenced by the religious attitude of the times and his own Christian leanings, he need not have invoked God to order ideas to things. An alternative might have been a theory of human understanding in which the main players are *intrinsically* object-directed ideas.

3. Brentano's thesis

We owe an arrow-type theory of this direct kind to a turn-of-the-century German philosopher–psychologist, Franz Brentano (1924). In Brentano's psychology the concept of reference is central. All mental content is directed. Ideas, for instance, are object directed or 'intentional' in the medieval sense. Brentano's psychology, however, is closer to Descartes than either medieval philosophy or Locke since pains, emotions, vague yearnings as well as thoughts, beliefs and expectations have objects. Indeed mind is essentially the intentional, while Cartesian thought, for Brentano, is only one among many intentions. Some thoughts are about actual things, like Russell and rocks, and others are about objects like Titania that do not really exist or objects like propositions or meanings that are very obscure. Now although Titania does not exist, she might still be on your mind; and to have a thought about her is not the same as having a thought about nothing at all. In general all mental phenomena are about objects some of which might be inexistent.

In this philosophy signification is the central, primitive concept. The possibility that signs relate the mind to unactual objects is a two-edged thesis. That there are unactual, intentional objects is an ontological proposition not entirely foreign to Western philosophy.[6] That the mind is distinctively object directed, however, introduces an odd note into the late nineteenth-century world of rapidly developing physical and biological sciences. If Brentano is right, and if intentionality is the essence of mentality, psychology must be a far remove from the natural sciences. Here's why.

There are no physical relations without related objects. The physical relation of larger than includes all pairs (x, y) such that x is larger than y. However, mental relations might be partial. For instance, the relation *sign of* might include signs that are paired to no objects whatever. The object y does not exist, yet x is still a sign. Another way of putting it is this: a weathervane is a sign for us; but in the physical world it is merely a part of a causal complex and neither intentionally points nor does not point. There are mental relations that lack actual relata (is east a thing?) but still point; and this cropped relatedness distinguishes mind from body.

On Brentano's terms behaviorist and materialist psychologies are therefore doomed to failure since mental affairs could not possibly be reducible to the physical or to anything like S-R psychology. Physical things do not sustain relations without physical relata. Therefore the characteristically mental is irreducibly *mental*.

The doctrine that intentionality is the mark of the mental is known as 'Brentano's thesis'. It has been very influential in its negative import for the dominant philosophies of mind and psychology of the twentieth century. Aside from internal details, it is this exclusion of ordinary physical science from the precincts of the mind that separates Brentano from both the early semioticians and semiotical Locke. Certainly the medievalists saw no gap between logic and semiotic on the one hand and science (as they conceived of it) on the other. In Locke*, we saw that there is a rather weak tendency toward a semiotic distinct from natural science; but the idea emerges at the very end of *An Essay Concerning Human Understanding* and is not developed. Peirce, as we shall see in the next section, thinks of mind as Thirdness which is a category that transcends existence; but then semiotic phenomena are involved with, and inseparable from, science and mathematics as he thinks of them.

What is to be learned from Brentano is that reference is indeed intentional and, if he is right, is not explainable in purely physical terms. He gives us a dilemma: either reference is unanalyzably object directed (as are beliefs, hopes etc.) or there can be no semantics and, in general, no psychology. Beliefs, expectations etc. as well as referring, which may be 'about' Titania or Pegasus, are prima-facie nonphysical if by 'physical' we mean to imply complete relations and structures of minds and objects.

Negative feedback has been proposed as a model of the mental. Systems that incorporate feedback seem to be purposive and 'directed' to objects (Wiener 1948; Williams 1951). A thermostat setting is a goal for a heating or cooling system whose purpose is to attain and fix a comfortable ambient room temperature. A measurement of the distance of the actual temperature to the setting will be zero if the heating system is on target, and some nonzero quantity otherwise. If it is nonzero, a control turns on the furnace; otherwise the system stays in its present state.

Is this system object directed? Of course it is, but only if there is an object. In fact the object – the level of room temperature – drives the system. The example is a perfect one of what Brentano does *not* mean. He does not mean 'Titania' refers owing to the presence of an object. Contrariwise, the thermostat system 'refers' to a goal, but only in virtue of that very goal's causal participation in the drive toward it. I make mention of feedback because it has received considerable attention in the literature as a model of goal-seeking and intentionality.

If all we have got available is negative feedback or equivalent systems-theoretic ideas to provide a theoretical explanation for

Brentano, we are not likely to get an account of reference. But there are other ways, and Peirce might lead us to them.

4. Peirce: reference is inference

Charles Sanders Peirce (1839–1914) is often recognized as America's greatest philosopher to date. Whether this is true or not, his semantics (or 'Speculative Grammar' as he would call it, in his *Collected Papers*) is the most original and detailed of any writer I know of on reference.[7]

Unfortunately there is not much agreement on what constitutes his greatness. He is claimed by Scotists, Pragmatists, Mechanists, Hegelian Idealists, Functionalists and Cognitivists. Peirce revived the expression 'semiotic', which we know goes back to Locke and before, but from what I know of current semiotic, connections with Peirce are quite tenuous.

Peirce's central idea is that semiosis is *inferential*. I think this is right, although later we shall want to say it is *computational*. However, it is going to take some work here and later to show exactly what this means.

An inference is an act of drawing a conclusion from premises. A good example familiar to everyone is illustrated by this:

If Peirce is a logician, then he is a philosopher
Peirce is a logician
Therefore, Peirce is a philosopher

Looking back on the development of logic in the past hundred years or so, you can interpret the drawing of the conclusion from the premises in several ways. (a) The three sentences (which constitute the argument) can be understood as well-formed formulas in a sentential logic equipped with the rule of inference, *modus ponens*; this rule is just a certain recursive set of triples of uninterpreted formulas of which our three sentences are elements; or (b) the sentences can be interpreted as true or false; and if the premises are true, so is the conclusion, necessarily, by truth table, whence legitimacy of the inference.

Interpretation (a) is syntactical and (b) is semantical. The student of freshman logic learns the connections between (a) and (b) in his study of soundness and completeness of the logic; the logically true statements are precisely the ones that are provable. Neither (a) nor

(b) express Peirce's notion of inference, although the semantical way (b) does appear in Peirce's logic as an abstraction from his full semiotical doctrine, which is given below as (c).

(c) The argument represents a mental process which produces a licit derivation of the conclusion from the conjoined premises. The example illustrates a logical inference in accord with laws of thought that are real. This idea is not quite as traditional as it seems.

From standpoint (c) the sample argument has three parts: the governing logical rule, *modus ponens*; the sequence of three sentences that make up the argument; and an interpretation (in your mind and my mind) that the argument is a *sign* of the logical rule, a law of logic. What this means, simply, is that the three sentences on paper or sounded by a voice do not constitute an inference unless a mind interprets them as an instance of the logical rule of inference.

The inference is an example of a genuine triadic relation or 'third' which is not decomposable into dyadic relations of propositions. The premises internally mediate between the law of logic and the conclusion. A good analogy is betweenness, which is not a compound of simple dyadic relations (5.59ff); and like all other mediation its relation to the extremes is essential.

All semiotic phenomena, not just familiar arguments in spoken languages, are inferential. A *sign* (generalizing on the above) 'is something which stands to somebody for something' (2.228). The something it stands for is the *object*, and the 'somebody' in this case is *another sign* in the mind of an interpreter. So an argument, as a kind of exemplar of the relation, is a sign of an object that is interpreted (in more signs) as representing a law (e.g. *modus ponens*).

Generally and roughly, a sign signifies an object as *taken* in a certain way.[8] But to take, the taker must be itself a sign of the same object. In our terminology, 'Russell' refers to Russell who is taken by an interpretant sign as an actual object, Russell.

A *proper name* signifies its object *indexically*, i.e. by a causal connection with the object. Thus the story for reference is something like this:

(1) 'Russell' refers to Russell means 'Russell' *indicates* an object taken by an interpretant to be an actual thing, Russell.

Name types might also name possibles: 'Pegasus' *indicates* Pegasus taken as a possibility (II.254ff).

Similarly a common noun (a general term) is a sign (a symbol in English, say) of an object that is interpreted as a 'qualitative possibility', i.e. taken to be a sign of an attribute. A symbol for Peirce is not an index, as is a proper name or a demonstrative, but a sign that signifies by association of ideas or conventions (for symbols in ordinary language). So application is explained by

(2) 'Philosopher' applies to x means 'Philosopher' *symbolizes* an object taken by an interpretant to be an attribute, x is a philosopher.

As might be said in modern logical circles, 'man' is short for 'x is a man' where the blank x may be filled with a singular term. This is not far from Frege except for the locution 'interpreted as' (II.312). If the blank is filled in we get a sentence, which for Peirce is a symbol of a fact, e.g. that Russell is a philosopher.

Thus we have Peircean versions of the reference of proper names and application of predicates. In both cases the role of the interpretant is central, and resembles that of the agent in Chapter 1, §3.

The fundamental idea of a name referring in virtue of the inferring or 'taking' of an interpreter is a plausible theory of how reference works. There is an indexical connection of sign to thing for an interpreter that takes or concludes from the name to the concrete object. This is a long way from our initial theory coupled with a vague notion of an agent determining the identity of a referent. It satisfies the disquotation requirement that '*a*' refer to *a* if '*a*' counts as a proper name in Peirce's sense; it immediately provides a credible explanation of how names (in particular) might be names without having bearers. For, interpreting 'Titania' as directly naming an object is not the same as the interpretant *taking* Titania to be an object through the representation 'Titania'. The interpretant is an essential correlate of signification, not a tacked-on user of a prefabricated relation. This is no *ad hoc* trick for smuggling in purportedness, for the interpretant of a sign, any sign, is *essential* to its being a sign.

On the negative side, the basic idea of sign or 'thirdness' in terms of which 'name' and 'general term' (symbol) are defined is other than mere physical causality or iconicity, although it includes both.

Both symbolic signification, unless it could always be understood as habitual association, and taking-to-be-by-an-interpretant are conceived to be part of an irreducible triad. Interpretation, as the taking role of an interpretant, is certainly an intentional concept on a par with Brentonian content.

The theory is conceptually fuzzy on crucial points. Since the interpretant is a sign, it must have an interpretant (as Peirce of course claims), and so on *ad infinitum*. Signs spread out in a continuum; and this sign-stream coursing 'according to the laws of thought' is Mind. Human (or other) minds are individuated by proneness to error. Inferential process, which informs all thought, is objectively real. This Hegelian streak is a feature of Peirce that any naturalist will find dispensable. We should be inclined to frown on both infinite regresses and commerce with Hegel.

Finally, even eschewing the heavy metaphysics, the theory is still stuck with a very unclear distinction between an interpreter and an interpretant. In ordinary English the first must be an agent or mind or processor of some sort – in short an operator – and the second a product or operand. This distinction – in logic, between a prover and a proof – did not become clear until well into the twentieth century in the work of A. M. Turing which we shall avail ourselves of in Chapter 10, §2.

5. From mind to logic

Brentano and Peirce (who are rarely paired in the same breath) in their diverse ways show what word–thing linkage might be (it seems to involve both the causal and intentional, for Peirce anyway) and bring front and center a good idea of what any theory of reference should deal with. They sustain our own view that directedness (our purportedness) is the main thing. Human acts are intentional, both in the ordinary sense and in Brentano's sense. We attribute beliefs, desires, hopes, expectations and plans to others in order to predict their actions, and to get them to accept what we want to do to or with them. We attribute referential use of words to them for the same reasons. This estimate of the psycho–social role of intentional attitudes is widely held in theories of language today by many who do not identify themselves with Brentano.

The trouble is, according to Brentano's thesis, no such theory is forthcoming on strictly naturalistic, physical grounds. If you want semantics, you need a full-blown, irreducible psychology of intentions.

There is a counterpart in modern logic of the thesis of irreducibility. The language of physical and biological science is largely *extensional.* It can be formulated (approximately) in the familiar predicate calculus. The language of psychology, however, is *intensional.* For the moment it is good enough to think of an *intensional* sentence as one containing words for *intentional* attitudes such as belief.[9]

Roughly what the counterpart thesis means is that important features of extensional, scientific language on which inference depends are not present in intensional sentences. In fact intensional words and sentences are precisely those expressions in which certain key forms of logical inference break down.

(a) In an extensional language, all compound sentences are truth functions of the elementary sentences. The easy, familiar, example is sententional (propositional) calculus. But truth functionality (ideally enjoyed in all scientific, logical and mathematical practice) does not hold for belief. For example, 'Schmid believes that Russell is an Hegelian' is an intensional sentence; its truth value does not depend on the part of the sentence 'Russell is an Hegelian'. For supposing the whole sentence is true of Schmid, it would remain true whether 'Russell is an Hegelian' is true or false. It could be that most of what poor Schmid believes is false.

The same obtains if we suppose the report is false of Schmid. Maybe he does not believe Hegelianism of Russell, while it be true that Russell is indeed an Hegelian. Exactly the same point can be made about sentences reporting desires, hopes, expectations etc. that express intentional attitude. The sentences are not truth functional; if 'Jane desires that it snow' is true, that truth is not altered by either its coming to snow or not.

(b) A familiar principle of logic, essential to scientific reasoning, is substitutivity of identity, which reads as follows:

(1) $a = b$ implies that . . . a . . . if and only if . . . b . . . .

For instance if $y = 7$, then $x + y = 12$ if and only if $x + 7 = 12$.

However, (1) does not hold in intensional, e.g. belief, sentences. To illustrate this we note that

(2) If 'a' refers to c and 'b' refers to c, then $a = b$.

If 'Hesperus' refers to Venus and 'Phosphorus' refers to Venus, then Hesperus = Phosphorus. In general, if '*a*' and '*b*' co=refer, then *a* = *b*.
  Combining (1) and (2) we get

(3) if '*a*' and '*b*' co-refer, then . . . *a* . . . if and only if . . . *b*
    . . . .

(3) helps us see what it means to say that one can 'plug in' one name for another in a formula of high-school algebra, say.
  Now consider the example,

(4) 'Russell' and 'the junior author of *Principia*' co-refer

Therefore, from (3),

(5) Russell wrote the *ABC's of Relativity* if and only if the junior author of *Principia* wrote the *ABC's of Relativity*.

However, the following *does not* hold:

(6) Schmid believes that Russell is an Hegelian if and only if he believes that the junior author of *Principia* is an Hegelian.

He might not believe 'Russell' and 'the junior author of *Principia*' co-refer even though they do, by hypothesis; moreover, even if he does believe they co-refer, if he is not rational (whatever that turns out to mean), (6) could still be false.
  Evidently the truth of the premise 'Russell wrote the *ABC's of Relativity*' depends on the referent of 'Russell' being indeed Russell. It does *not* depend on the name, for 'junior author' serves as well. However, the truth of the premise 'Schmid believes that Russell was an Hegelian' depends on something other than just the reference of 'Russell' (although it does depend on the reference of 'Schmid'). That something is the meaning or intension of the name 'Russell', possibly, or of the underlying intentional attitude – to put the matter psychologically rather than semantically.
  (c) These examples show that substitution in belief sentences involves more than reference. In other cases names do not refer at all, not because they are empty, like 'Pegasus', but because reference cannot be inferred. We cannot infer from 'Schmid likes the cat next door' that there is a cat, although there might be one identified on other grounds than Schmid's belief. We cannot infer there is no cat either as some of the things Schmid likes are really cats.

(d) It is said that we may not (without other information) 'quantify into' attitudinal sentences such as belief or reference sentences (Quine 1966; 1981). For instance, from 'Schmid believes something is in the attic' we may not infer 'there is something Schmid believes is in the attic'. Reference is intensional in precisely this sense. Take ' "Pegasus" p-refers to Pegasus'. We frown on the inference of 'there exists an x 'Pegasus' p-refers to'. In fact the last sentence is a short history of our troubles with the Deity back in Chapter 1, §2.

If you think of a science as characterizable by idiom, you might say Brentano's thesis asserts that psychology can never get outside of its circle of intensional terms, the intensional idiom, which means the logical procedures just discussed will not work in it. There is no explaining away of 'belief', 'desire' or for that matter 'reference' in terms outside the circle. It is as if sciences of the mind had their own closed lexicon (cf. Quine 1960: 221) and consequently their own restricted logic.

It is widely claimed today by philosophers of logic that intensional sentences cannot be equivalently rephrased or replaced by extensional sentences. Thus Brentano's thesis reflected in linguistic terms asserts that psychology cannot be framed in the extensional terminology of mathematics, physics or biology. Inasmuch as 'reference' is intensional, the denial applies to it as well.

Of course we let the question remain open – otherwise we would have to close this book now. We have learned that to satisfy condition (*R*) of the last chapter we must deal with the intentionality of reference. After a long excursion, it is going to turn out that causal Locke is close to being right, as is semiotical Locke and Brentano – reference has both causal and intentional elements – and that a good way of discharging the intensional element is through an inferential theory not unlike that of Peirce.

CHAPTER 3

Sense and Reference

1. Frege's semantics

From the logician's point of view few thinkers have had as great an impact on the theory of reference as Gottlob Frege.

Frege's semantics is an extension of his work in logic and the foundations of mathematics. The mathematician's working concepts reduce, as Frege himself showed, to individual objects, sets of objects, identity and functions. Frege's greatest achievements at the foundations were the reduction of arithmetic to logic (Frege 1884) and the invention of predicate calculus (1879) interpreted (as we would say today) over this ontologically simple domain. His reduction of arithmetic to logic as later developed and refined by Whitehead and Russell (1925) and others suffices in principle for all of mathematics. Frege's inquiries into semantics all derived from his inquiries into the foundations of mathematics.

Frege's theory is best seen, I think, as the study of an abstract structure consisting of linguistic and nonlinguistic objects of various sorts that are functionally related. The human user who knows the structure grasps a ready-made system of language, semantics and all, and is in no way part of the mechanisms of reference and application. The user is not constitutive of reference as he is for Locke, Brentano or Peirce, but wields a prefabricated language-world system for mathematical ends. Even natural language, as we shall see, is viewed in this abstract way, for the most part. Unlike Locke, for instance, Frege has no truck with ideas in the head, with natural signs, with Peircean inferences or with interpretations of a semiotical mind. English, for instance, is like a piece of sculpture. Understanding it does not require understanding the sculptor.

43

To put the point another way, reference is a direct connection between name (Frege uses 'name' to include proper names, complex names and descriptions indifferently) and object. Application is a functional mapping, expressed by a predicate, from a named object to a truth value. Contrasted with Locke, there is no tagging or marking of an idea with a linguistic sign and no puzzle as to the relationship, either causal or intentional, of idea to thing. Reference is a direct, abstract relation, word to thing.

As many writers have put it, Fregean semantics does not presuppose epistemology: it presupposes neither acceptance of epistemic priorities nor solutions to thought-world puzzles. And it is founded on no special theory of mind, except for attribution to the intellect of a power reminiscent of the Platonic *nous* to grasp objective meanings, concepts and thoughts.

Semantics is a part of logic, that is to say, a part of a theory of truth, validity and inference, and quite derivatively a theory of meaning, understanding and communication of natural language. Naming enables the picking out of objects that are to be subjects of discourse. Logic sets conditions for passing from true thoughts about things thus selected to other true thoughts about those things. For instance, the truth of an atomic statement depends on who or what is mentioned. 'Russell is a philosopher' is true, that truth depending on the named object being Russell. 'Bush is a philosopher' is false, that falsity depending on the named object being Bush. Furthermore, the truth or falsity of more complex statements depends on that of the component statements. So (temporarily ignoring quantification) truth ultimately depends on the reference of the proper names occurring in the simple parts and secondarily on its illative dependence on other statements.

The first and chief problem of reference is to explain this. Frege's seminal notion, which probably could have occurred only to a reflective mathematician, is that the dependence of truth on bearers of names is best construed as *functional*. Before taking up this idea I wish to promote a separation of formal from natural language.

In common with other logicians, Frege's initial interest (I do not mean this in an historical sense but in a theory-building sense) was in languages with an exact structure, and this essentially means the formalism of a predicate calculus. This commitment is disappointing; for instance, he sweeps the problem of nonreferring names aside, as a 'carefully constructed' language will not include nonbearing names. Indexical terms also have no place. This does not mean Frege was uninterested in natural language – to the contrary – but it does mean that he does not bring up questions of nonreferring names and indexicals in his studies of exact language. English or German come later.

2. Exact languages

Even in fairly formal Frege there is a rich ontology and a vocabulary to go with it. There is a domain of individuals including physical objects in the world, numbers, functions and still other objects that will appear as we proceed; on the linguistic side there are the basic categories of symbols of a first-order theory (Frege's predicate calculus is actually second order as he uses predicate variables; but for this discussion I will treat them as if they were dummy symbols): constants (proper names), individual variables; connectives, 'if – then' etc.; arithmetic operation symbols '+', ' · ' etc.; predicates, including '=', quantifiers and parentheses.

Since the language is well constructed, all names have bearers (if they did not, some sentences would be neither true nor false, as we shall see) and all predicates apply to subsets of the given objects. Many names refer to the same object, e.g. '5 + 7' and '12'. However, all names are univocal; no name refers to two objects. Similarly many different predicates apply to the same things: e.g. 'is divisible by 8' and is 'is divisible by 2^3'; or 'is human' and 'is a political animal'.

Complex names (names with name-parts) have objects that depend on the objects of the parts. '5 + 7' has a reference, for example, that depends on the reference of '5' and '7'; and there is a principle of substitutivity of names that applies: $10/2 = 5$, and therefore '$10/2 + 7$' refers the same as '5 + 7'. Similarly 'the statue of Lincoln in the Memorial' has a reference that depends on 'statue', 'Lincoln' and 'Memorial'. On the other hand 'the statue of Venus in the Louvre' is an empty name, not permitted in the exact language, since the part-name 'Venus' is empty (unless, of course, one were to take statue-of-Venus as a simple name without parts).

Given the built-in semantics, reference and application satisfy relations (1) and (2) in Chapter 1, §2, which express necessary conditions; and Frege's further task is to explain the semantics of sentences. There is for him no antecedent problem of explaining what is meant by a name or by nonreferring, or of what a singular term or predicate expression is. Names etc. are given for a theory that then proceeds to explain their semantical roles in larger settings.

The first thing to understand is Frege's generalization of the idea of a function: predicates or general terms express functions. Anyone who fails to understand what is meant by this fails to understand Frege.[1]

To begin with the familiar, an arithmetical function is a relation of whole numbers or pairs (or triples etc.) of numbers to whole numbers. For example, the successor operation (′) is a function that maps each number n into its successor n'. Its domain is the set of whole numbers and its range is again the set of whole numbers, excluding zero. Another example is addition, which is a function from pairs of whole numbers to sums, which are again whole numbers. And so multiplication, exponentiation etc.

Function is a primitive notion for Frege. You have to think of a function as a rule or law or 'mapping' for passing from objects of one set to those of another, not as a set of ordered pairs. One of Frege's great insights was to liberate the idea from its tie to numbers and to open it up to arbitrary domains including physical objects and people.

The first step in generalizing the idea is to include functions whose values are either the True or the False. True and False are two new objects in Fregean ontology; they are the referents of sentences. A true sentence 'refers' to the True and a false sentence to the False. It is well to keep in mind that truth values are not predicates of sentences (as they are generally regarded to be today) nor predicates of thoughts.

All of this is clear enough if we change our way of thinking about predicates as expressing properties of things to thinking of them as expressing functions that map individuals (bearers of names) to the True or the False.

Consider '1 = 1'. Treat = as a function of two variables and write '= (1, 1)'. Think of this expression as a *name*, in this case a name of True; and write '= (1, 1) = True'. This should be read as: the value of the function = for the object 1 in both argument places is True.

A better example is the true statement that the successors of any two distinct whole numbers are distinct. Write this 'If $n' = m'$ then n

= *m*, for any *n* and *m*'. Now if we eviscerate the numeric variables and drop the quantifiers, we get the complex predicate 'if . . .' = '____', then . . . = ____'. To simplify matters write this '*S*(. . ., ____)'. Then write, '*S*(*n*, *m*) = True' for any *n*, *m*.

Note that here the function *S* (expressed by the complex predicate we just abbreviated to '*S*') comes out to have the value True for any numbers, as indicated by quantification over *n* and *m*. By analogy to the example 1 = 1, we might read this as: the value of the function *S* for any *m* and *n* is the True. Finally for a false case, using '*L*' for 'less than', *L*(3, 2) = False and, for any *n*, *m*, *L*(*n*, *m*) = False.

This strategy generalizes the notion of function from the realm of integers to a range including True and False. A further step is to accept functions whose *domain* is the set {True, False}. This idea of functions from truth values to truth values, which is in effect just the idea of truth tables, is not quite explicit in Frege, although it is clearly there.

Today functions from arbitrary domains to the range {True, False} are often called *propositional functions* and those from {True, False} back to {True, False} are *truth functions*.

Next Frege takes a still further step toward a semantical theory by allowing functions of any individual objects whatsoever and, in particular, of nonarithmetical bearers of proper names. An atomic sentence '*F*(*a*)', to begin with the simplest case, expresses the value of a function *F* for the argument introduced by the name '*a*'. Note that Frege is thinking here of predicates as expressing functions, not attributes or properties in the more usual sense. Again, the value is either True or False. In our favorite example, we obtain Philosopher(Russell) = True. Russell is of course the referent of 'Russell', and is mapped by the *function* philosopher to the True.

Similarly a dyadic atomic sentence '*G*(*a*, *b*)' is to be thought of as expressing the value of *G* for the ordered pair of objects named '*a*' and '*b*'. If '*G*' is 'older than' then, for instance, *G*(Whitehead, Russell) = True, and *G*(Russell, Whitehead) = False.

Functions of one argument to the range {True, False} are *concepts*, and they are expressed by monadic predicates. Functions of two arguments are *relations*, e.g. less than or older than, and are expressed by dyadic predicates (general terms). All such functions from objects to truth values are collectively termed propositional functions in modern logic.

Sentences express propositions, or for Frege, *thoughts*. A thought is the meaning of a declarative sentence. Thus 'Russell is British' and 'Russell is an earl' have the value True (are materially equivalent), but express different thoughts or propositions.

In all, 'F' expresses the concept F; 'a' names a; $F(a)$ is the output of a mapping of a by F and is either True or False; '$F(a)$' is a sentence that refers to the True or the False; and '$F(a)$' expresses the thought that $F(a)$. There is already a lot of paraphernalia here for furnishing a semantical structure.

No one in her right mind is going to change his or her practice of reading 'it is true that Russell is a philosopher' in this strained way, but that is beside the point. The point is that Frege has here made a step toward explaining the pretheoretical notion of both predication and of how truth depends on the referent of a name. And he manages this using a fairly conservative repertoire of things – individual objects and functions, which are already central in mathematics, and of course the adjoined True and False – but no subjective ideas or natural signs or anything of the kind.

What about compound sentences? 'If Russell is a mathematician, then he is a Swedenborgian' is false. According to Frege the concept mathematician maps Russell into True, and the concept Swedenborgian maps it into False. Then (If True then False) = False, by the truth functional property of if – then. So the ultimate functional dependence is on reference of names. Similarly for other truth functions.

Let us also illustrate how truth of a quantified sentence in a well-constructed language is handled. Consider the rather unlikely statement, 'for every x $F(x)$'; if this is true, it means that the concept philosopher maps every individual object in the domain onto True; if it is false, it does not map every individual object in the domain onto True, i.e., there is an x in the domain that F maps onto False.

The 'x' of the predicate expression may refer to objects of any kind, but it is supposed to refer to them one at a time; and then application of a quantifier means the predicate says x is true of all objects thus taken one at a time. The concept maps any individual of a given domain, not only those picked out by names. Such an understanding of quantification is known as the 'objectual interpretation' because the universal (or existential) quantifier ranges over individual objects, and is indifferent to naming.[2]

Inasmuch as all sentences of the well-constructed language can be generated by a recursive procedure beginning with atomic sentences and using truth functional connectives and quantification, the truth of sentences ultimately depends on the references of proper names or, in quantification, on mappings from unnamed individuals. We shall see this line pursued even more precisely in Tarski's work. Sentences of this type of structure and the languages comprising them such as the predicate calculus are extensional (see Chapter 2, §5).[3] Thus Frege's theory has the merit of explaining substitutivity – co-referring names can be swapped since they introduce the same argument for a function-concept to map to True, False.

Thus the semantics of names, so far in the Fregean story, is that they refer to objects, and their semantic value is to be found in their role in thought or, in the linguistic mode, in their contribution to the truth or falsity of sentences. If empty names were allowed there could be sentences that refer to neither True nor False, which would violate the idea of a well-constructed language. For instance 'the greatest whole number less than 0 is either odd or even' is neither True nor False because 'the greatest whole number less than 0' does not furnish an object for either odd or even to map to True or False; and the OR truth function is defined only for pairs of the two truth values.

Perhaps Frege's distinctive philosophical bent is economy of ideas. The ontology – individual things, functions, thoughts and True and False – is neat and the linguistic apparatus is canonical: singular and general terms (names and predicates), connectives, quantifiers, variables and complete sentences.

A little reflection should reveal, however, that what he has built using the ontological elements from one store and linguistic elements from another is a relational structure in which both the elements and the relations are abstract and primitive. If you do not already understand what a name is, what a predicate is and what is intended by 'reference' and 'expresses', you will be lost because Frege does not say. And although some connectives can be defined in terms of others and some of the ontological elements can be reduced to others, reference itself is just what is given in the name-bearing pairing and expression of a concept by a predicate is ineffably intuitive. Frege does not get beyond our lists in this regard, although there is more machinery or 'linkage' in his view of words to things, as we have just seen.

The True and the False are entities used to complete the idea that concepts are functions. Construed as such the best handling of these things is to get rid of them, which can be done by making a switch of 'True' from a value of concepts to a predicate (not an object) of sentences, and then defining 'true' contextually in a schema, 'a sentence *S* is true if and only if . . .'. I shall explain this in Chapter 5. But revamping True and False would be a gross distortion of Frege: they are also the objects of sentences; and the thoughts sentences express are ways of understanding the True, of understanding reality. I shall return to the topic of Frege's realism in the next section. In Frege's theory, True and False stay.

3. Sense and reference

Frege is widely known to students of philosophy of language, if not to every schoolgirl, as the author of 'On sense and reference' (1892b) which promotes a distinction between the objects a term or sentence refers to and the content or meaning expressed by it. Fregean 'sense' is quite close to 'meaning' which was dismissed in Chapter 1 as a term unfit for theory without some careful explication. Indeed the fate of 'sense' in the reckoning of §5 of this chapter will be in part that of an object-lesson for faithful followers of the Commandments, and in part a comforting compensatory reminder of semantic issues Frege must be credited with identifying.

'Sense' is on a footing with the intension, connotation or ground of general terms, which have histories associated with Leibniz, John Stuart Mill and Peirce respectively. Intension, for instance, is typically contrasted with the extension of a predicate, the latter being the set of objects the predicate applies to and the former being the attribute a thing has (or is thought to have) that makes it eligible for membership in the extension. Frege, however, also recognizes senses of singular terms and sentences.

All terms and sentences (except empty names and sentences) have both a sense and a reference. The aim of Frege's article is to show why both are needed in an adequate theory of language.

In Chapter 1, §1 and §2, we were already struck by the contrast between 'Russell = Russell' and 'Russell = the junior author of *Principia Mathematica*' which are different identities about the same object. Examples such as this one and Frege's own contrast between '*a* = *a*' and '*a* = *b*' (if true) exhibit differences in cognitive value that everyone would acknowledge. '*a* = *a*' tells nothing, while 'a = b' might contain a surprise. There are also cases of substitution wherein 'a' cannot go for 'b', despite co-reference. Remember Schmid and his belief that Russell, but not the junior author of *Principia*, was an Hegelian. So differences in information conveyed as well as differences in illative power in some contexts are not explained by nominal reference alone.

We suggested that nonreferring terms such as 'Pegasus' might still count as names because they are meaningful, but then rejected meaning for the time being as it is less clear than reference itself. But now it appears that postulation of referents for each name is not enough of a theory to account for simple cognitive contrasts. It appears, therefore, that we have a new reason for wanting to resurrect meanings: not to guarantee reference of singular terms (we saw that it does not back in Chapter 1) but to help account for cognitive distinctions.

In earlier writings Frege took identity to be a relation between signs, not objects. If this were correct, the differences in cognitive impact could be explained by the disparities in physical shape of the tokens of 'a' and 'b'. However, for reasons we take for granted today, this is not a good interpretation of identity. But both cognitive value and substitutivity can be explained by variation in the ways we take signs to refer.

'Russell' and 'the junior author . . .' have the same semantic value, but different *cognitive value*. The force of the latter idea is this: the referent of a name is given in a list of name-bearer pairs; but the sense of a name 'contains the mode of presentation' of the object. It is by following the sense of it that a name picks out its object. Thus the two names present one and the same person, Russell, in different ways.

Complex names provide good examples of what Frege seems to mean by mode of presentation. For example, $\int_0^2 e^x \, dx = 6.39$ is True, which of course just says that '$\int_0^2 e^x \, dx$' and '6.39' refer to the same thing. But the modes of presentation are radically different and in fact illustrate sharply the significance of sense versus reference in mathematics. '6.39' refers by disquotation – just look: the reference is 6.39 – while – '$\int_0^2 e^x \, dx$' refers by way of a conceptual path open only to those who understand mathematical analysis. Perhaps Frege's own example is better: 'Let a, b, c be the lines connecting the vertices of a triangle with the midpoints of the opposite sides. The point of intersection of a and b is the same as the point of

51

intersection of *b* and *c*' (Frege 1892b: 57). The two descriptions present the point in different ways.

These nicely illustrate what is intended by 'mode of presentation' in a way that is lacking or faint in straight proper names. The philosophers' favorite example is the pair 'Hesperus' and 'Phosphorus', which both name Venus but carry different senses, one intimating something about evening and the west and the other about morning and glowing in the east.

The sense of 'Hesperus' is what it is that we grasp when we understand the word; but grasping does not seem to be a mode of presentation. 'Titania' has a graspable sense, but can hardly contain a mode of presentation of its bearer since there is no object Peaseblossom to be presented. What Frege means by different mode of presentation is not really clear, and more will have to be said about it in the context of our discussion of natural language.

Many definite descriptions of things such as 'the point of intersection of *a* and *b*' quite literally spell the reference out in perceptually compelling ways. 'The junior author of *Principia*' spells it in terms of other objects and concepts remembered. Russell held that grammatically proper names are usually abbreviations of definite descriptions; and, as we shall see, a case can be made that if this is true one might dispense with senses of names altogether. However, Frege advocates no such idea. Descriptions are just to be numbered among proper names, for him, and there is no explicit doctrine in his writings of a principled reduction of names like 'Russell' to descriptions.[4]

With the notion of sense introduced into the theory we obtain means of explaining both the information-carrying quality of '*a* = *b*' as opposed to that of '*a* = *a*' and the anomalies of substitution. '*a*' and '*b*', which are two numerals in Frege's example, contain different modes of presentation, and the fact that these modes produce the same object is informative. Also, adverting to Schmid, the reason we may not substitute 'the junior author . . .' for 'Russell' in 'Schmid believes that Russell was an Hegelian' is that the names do not have the same sense. The semantics of names does not work in intensional sentences as it does in extensional ones.

Frege was a staunch foe of 'psychologism', which is his label for the philosophical habit of taking senses, thoughts and concepts to be subjective things in the mind. To him, every ontological item (as it figures in his theory) is as objective as a physical thing or set of things. When I heed your utterance of 'Ottoline' I understand the sense of the name exactly as you do, and 'Ottoline was Russell's friend' expresses the same thought for both. In fact, the senses of terms in the sciences and mathematics are held in common by all who can grasp them, otherwise there would be no science. However, images and subjective ideas (Locke, for instance) are uncertainly associated to words, and a difference for one person might be a similarity for another. Senses cannot be subjective entities such as images or vague memory impressions.

Frege's antipsychologism appears to be prima-facie right. In the cases we cited there is little doubt that sense is objective. Understanding $\int_0^2 e^x \, dx$ to be 6.39 is radically unlike understanding 6.39 to be 6.39, and the difference is real; understanding one presentation of a point in Frege's example is not the same as understanding the other. But even if objective senses are needed to explain cognitive values, positing them does not explain them. We shall worry about this more in due course.

Relative to predicates, the notions of sense and reference are unclear in Frege as well as in the writings of his commentators. The idea of a referring predicate does not fit his semantic scheme, nor does that of the 'sense' of a predicate if that is meant to be any more than the concept itself. In 'On sense and reference' Frege himself explicitly places general terms outside the range of discussion, since concepts are not objects. Only proper names and sentences refer to objects (1892b: 57).[5] However, our earliest intuitions, bred in elementary logic, recognize predicates that have different senses but the same extension, such as '___ lives in Ohio' and '___ lives in the seventeenth state'. So predicates have sense, while the notion that they refer is problematic. To settle things for the time being, it seems to me that it is not too far-fetched to think of the sense of a predicate as a mode of presentation also. 'Jones is a resident of Ohio' and 'Jones is a resident of the seventeenth state' express different thoughts because the sense of the predicates construed as just the functions they express compute differently. ___ is a resident of Ohio and ___ is a resident of the seventeenth state, however, map exactly the same subset of objects to True and the rest to False. This is an interpretation of Frege, but I think we can make it stick and we shall try to do so in Chapter 10.

The sense of a sentence is a thought, as we have known all along. Frege has two arguments in support of his view that thoughts are not the same as the True or the False. The first is that different thoughts can enjoy identical truth conditions; 'the morning star is a body illuminated by the Sun' and 'the evening star is a body illuminated by the Sun' express different thoughts, yet both are True, indeed True under exactly the same objective conditions.

The second argument is that a thought is still a thought if the expressing sentence contains empty names. 'Odysseus was set ashore at Ithaca while sound asleep' expresses a thought; and yet since 'Odysseus' is empty the concept-function, set-ashore-at-Ithaca-while-sound-asleep, has nothing to map to a truth value. So the sentence is meaningful but neither true nor false.

Thoughts are the only complete senses, as the senses of referents are only modes of presentation or ways of understanding a name; and the sense of a predicate, the concept itself in my interpretation of Frege, is incomplete or unsaturated and becomes complete only in the full sentence. The relation of the sense of a sentence to the senses of the component parts is analogous to that of the truth value to individual objects. The thought depends on the senses of the names and predicates contained.

Adverting to our earlier comments on True and False, there is a theory of science embedded in this theory that is free of the epistemological baggage carted around in most of modern philosophy. One grasps reality through the thought which is expressed in a sentence and this is a way of understanding or presenting the True or the False. True thoughts constitute science. This is no correspondence theory of proposition to fact as appears in the medieval notion of *adequatio* and in semiotical Locke. The scientific thought is the sense of the mapping of objects to True. Reality is true thought, and like Platonic ideas is there to be grasped.

4. Natural languages

The empty name puzzle draws attention away from well-constructed languages over to natural languages where shifting reference, ambiguity, vagueness, speculation and fiction are no longer exceptional, but central. Frege meant for his theory of sense and reference to apply to untamed natural language, and pursued a plan, still the established one in the philosophy of language, of transporting the insights accrued in the semantics of exact languages over to the natural languages, making adaptational changes as necessary on the way. The trouble is that some notions do not transport easily and tend to break loose.

For instance, basic Fregean doctrine has it that an extensional sentence in English containing an empty name is neither true nor false. But there is an infinite number of sentences of the sort '____ does not exist' for which this rule fails. 'Titania does not exist' is true for a Fregean as well as for everyone else despite the emptiness of the proper name.

This old chestnut can be warmed over starting from 'Titania exists'. A Fregean might counterclaim it to be without truth value, as the concept 'exists' maps only physical objects to truth values, and 'Titania' is empty. There is no object to map; the function is undefined there. So then the negation must be without truth value, and the sentence denying Titania's existence is *not* True; your intuitions are wrong. No Fregean would accept the sentence as true.

But again (for one not willing to yield on the truth of the nonexistence of Titania), 'exists' is not a Fregean concept-function. And if it is not, 'Bush exists' does not exhibit a mapping from an object to True any more than 'Titania does not exist' does. With or without objects to map, truth does not always depend on reference and mapping of names.

This criticism does not end the matter except, I think, for Frege, and we shall witness a resurgence of it in the next and later chapters.

However, there is another half-hearted Fregean rejoinder which goes like this. Natural languages contain sentences without truth values, such as the one about Odysseus, as well as imperatives, questions and exhortations, and in particular some of your sentences about existence. Many declarative sentences, moreover, might be expressed without 'advancing to a truth value'. Users use sentences in *judging*, and also in *making assertions*. But a judgment is just the grasping of a sense or a thought, while an assertion advances the truth value of a thought.[6] Expressing the thought that Titania does not exist is not the same as asserting that Titania does not exist, so the judgment can be made without commitment to a truth value. The allegation that a Fregean would assert the sentence has to be modified to say only that he could make a judgment without intending to assert.

The trouble with this is that it makes truth a question of pragmatics while Frege holds that truth values depend on reference of names, which is a matter of semantics. Moreover it smudges the Platonistic image of Frege: semantic relations are there to be grasped, not constructed. Language users do not *establish* reference, even to the extent of advancing to a truth value. If the sentence's truth is independent of the user using it, the judgment-maker entertains the whole thought, truth and all, when he understands it. Assertion does not add anything, but puts a stamp on what is already there in thought.

Natural language is full of truth-value singularities, but Fregean theory does not adequately explain them. A companion problem concerns sense. In natural languages there are, on Frege's account, empty names whence empty sentences; however, such sentences, other things being equal, express thoughts. Two such sentences are those just cited that contain occurrences of 'Odysseus' and 'Titania'. So we might have sense without truth.

But wait! If the sense of a name is the mode of presentation of an object, how can an empty name have a sense? 'Titania' does not pick out anything, and it seems you cannot have a mode of presentation of nothing to present. If the thought expressed by a sentence is a function of the senses of the names in it, then 'Titania does not exist' not only lacks truth value, it lacks sense. It is meaningless. Despite our seeming understanding of 'Titania . . .' or 'Odysseus . . .' there are no thoughts to understand! This consequence of the theory is not tolerable.

A solution might be found by looking around in Frege for some other notion of sense. Indeed, such a notion is provided for by construing sense as an object of indirect reference of a name. If the sense of a name is an object enjoying ontological status independent of the bearer and is not (or not only) a mode of presentation, then perhaps an empty name could have sense without reference. This does, I think, add to Frege, but let us see how the idea of sense qua object works.

Names can be used to talk about names as well as things, which is the name of the game in logic and theory of reference. 'Russell' names Russell, ' "Russell" ' names 'Russell'. But Frege claims that they can also be used to talk about their senses. 'Russell' can be used to refer in the usual way to Russell, or, in certain contexts, to its own *sense*. The former is the familiar direct reference, and the latter is *indirect reference*. Similarly, sentences which ordinarily refer to the True or the False can be used to 'refer' to *thoughts*.

Such reference is also said to be *indirect*. And the contexts which compel indirect interpretation of reference are called 'oblique' by Frege.

The notion of indirect sense appears to provide a good way of making the semantical oddities of intensional sentences intelligible. A mark of intensional sentences is that their truth values are independent of the values of at least some of the component sentence-parts (cf. Chapter 2, §5). But now, using the notion of indirect reference, there is a way to understand the semantical involvement of the belief clause: the sentence 'Schmid believes Russell is an Hegelian' is true provided that 'Russell is an Hegelian' be understood as 'referring' to its own sense, that is to say, to Schmid's thought. His belief is a thought, and that thought is one of the objects mentioned in the belief sentence. Another way to put it is that the truth or falsity of the whole, in such sentences, depends on the direct reference of 'Schmid' and the indirect reference of the subordinate clause. Hence Frege can still claim that the reference of a sentence is a function of the reference of the parts, but only under a construal of some referents as indirect, as senses.

Now canonical Frege, even in the realm of natural language, teaches that the sense of a sentence depends on the senses of the parts. Clearly if a name in a sentence is exchanged for one having the same sense the sense of the whole will be preserved, while if it is exchanged for one having a different sense, the sense of the whole will change. Consequently, if 'Russell' is replaced by 'the junior author . . .', which is not synonymous, then although the terms co-refer, their indirect references are not the same. This is why substitutivity fails in sentences expressing intentions.

Therefore, in intensional contexts the substitutivity principle has to read that the indirect references of '*a*' and '*b*' must be the same for a substitution of one for the other to be correct. That is to say, in oblique contexts, 'it is not permissible to replace one expression in the subordinate clause by another having the same customary [direct] reference, but only by one having the same indirect reference, i.e. the same customary sense' (Frege 1892b: 67).

This theory, if right, supports the basic principle that the sense of a sentence depends on the senses of parts, even in the intensional cases, and we obtain an extended principle of substitutivity. Unfortunately the scheme depends crucially on *synonymy*, on sameness of sense. Frege assumes both that it is a clear idea – that there is a way of deciding when a name or description '*a*' has the same sense as another one '*b*' – and that all speakers of English know the right way, which is just to assume the doctrine of anti-psychologism. However, this is highly questionable, and must be so even to the most dauntless objectivist. Suppose that some name 'R' other than 'Russell' itself is a synonym for 'Russell' (for the life of me I cannot think of an 'R'). It clearly does not follow from 'Schmid believes that Russell is an Hegelian' that Schmid believes that R is an Hegelian. I would not bet on it, and you would not either. Furthermore, I see no reason to think that if Schmid believes that R is Russell he also believes that R is an Hegelian, at least without assuming that Schmid (or indeed anyone) is a rational believer. The most a Fregean can hold is that synonymy is a necessary condition for carrying out substitutions in intensional contexts.

Assuming indirect naming, nevertheless, let us return to empty names. The indirect referent of 'Titania' is a different entity than the sense qua mode of presentation of an object; or, if not different, is a mode of presentation hypostatized, a transitive element of thought made substantive.

If the idea of indirect sense is credible at all it seems it might afford a way of understanding how empty names can be names nonetheless. Sense construed as mode of presentation does not help explain namehood, as it seems that if there is no object there is no presentation – as previously remarked. But here we have an object even in the absence of a direct object. Such a way of taking 'sense' would overcome the objection that 'Titania' is not only neither true not false but meaningless. It has sense, even if there is no object to be directed to.

Further, why not characterize purported reference in terms of objective sense? A singular term purportedly refers if it has a sense taken in this objective way. Thus all proper names and descriptions, but not the indexicals and demonstratives, purportedly refer in virtue of their sense-objects.

I like none of this, for reasons I have discussed earlier and will review in the last section; but it does indicate some of the underlying subtleties in an instructive way.

Yet almost all of our writing and talk is counterfactual, speculational, futuristic and fictional. 'If someone else had been President, . . . then'; 'the center of the solar system in 5000 AD . . .'; 'Hamlet was Shakespeare's favorite character, not King Henry IV';

'if it is raining on this day in 1994, we shan't go'; and so on, are snippets of everyday nonreferential utterances of one sort or another that include purported names of many kinds. All are somehow about this world and none are meaningless. If a theory of meaning and reference throws up a bar to explanations of how language in this full richness works, it is a bad theory.

Frege was aware of this and besides having a theory of sense he had a theory of fictions of sorts, 'a cover-up' (Evans 1982: 28), to deal with it. Names that lack semantic value, i.e. do not fulfill the role of names as names, are 'mock' proper names. Even perceptional slips, reports such as 'that lime tree' where the designation is empty, is a slip 'into the sphere of fiction without knowing it' (ibid.: 28).

But this is more than evasion, for it tends to assimilate questions about speculative language to the fictional. The practice of science (I do not mean formalization of hard results) is not even possible without positing objects that later investigation show to be nonexistent or having other properties than those attributed to them *ab initio*. Supposing that there are tachyons, for instance, is a far cry from writing about Peaseblossom. 'The neuronal group correlated to rough-edged images reacts to input with a lag time of half a millisecond' is possibly false, if there is such a correlated fiber, or empty if there is no such fiber. But the sentence is heuristic and is scientifically meaningful even if factually open or indeterminate at a given time.

Any adequate theory of reference has to explain how purported reference is possible, and Frege's does not seem to, except for the theory of exact language semantics. There, reference implies purported reference: ' "a" refers to b' implies ' "a" p-refers to b'; and if $a = b$, it implies disquotation. But there is no extension of the theory for empty names.

We have so far seen no way of incorporating indexicals such as 'I', 'you', 'here', 'now' and demonstratives such as 'that' and 'those' into a theory of reference except for issuing a notice to the effect that they are not disquotable. The indexicals or 'token-reflexive' terms have reference depending on the utterer or place or time of utterance of an instance of a term, and the demonstratives have reference depending also on pointing, nodding the head, or otherwise boosting the semantic power of the word in order to single out an object of discourse.

According to Dummett (1981: 83f), there is no systematic treatment of indexicals to be found in Frege's writings, except for scattered remarks. Frege notices that one and the same sentence (syntactic type) can express different thoughts. An example, in which the phenomenon depends on personal pronouns, is 'I love you' sincerely uttered by Mary and shortly thereafter by her lover, John. But then 'I' and 'you' have different senses in the two sentences, contrary to our own earlier surmise and to canonical Frege himself, who holds sense to be independent of utterance.

An opposite situation arises in the example of the sentence (token) 'it is raining today' uttered on Tuesday and the sentence 'it rained yesterday' uttered on Wednesday. These are two different sentences that say the same thing. But a Fregean analysis can handle it if we allow reference to depend on circumstances of utterance: 'today' uttered on Tuesday has the same referent (a determinate time interval) as 'yesterday' uttered on Wednesday.

These points bring important problems to attention; but the whole question of indexicals is foreign to Fregean treatment (of course not to Frege, who I presume treated whatever he wanted to) if he really meant that reference and sense are fixed and objective and independent of use.

5. Sorts of sense

Frege's contribution to mathematical logic, the invention of quantification theory, earned him a position of great eminence in the history of the subject. On the semantical side, the idea of functional dependence of sentences on names is central to an understanding of exact languages in science. They make extensionality and substitutivity clear; the notion of concept or property as function, including truth function, ties together the underlying strands of significance and syntax in logic, and provides the elements for analysis of truth, validity, consistency and completeness. Even the notion of sense, especially taken to be a mode of presentation, at the very least points up the nature of cognitive value in computational mathematics. The notion of an effectively computable function, for instance, depends on the idea of presentation (Nelson 1987; Shapiro 1980). Equation solving – which, semantically speaking, serves to demonstrate that several names or descriptions have the same referent – can make the difference between hitting Venus with a probe or not.

A weakness (if it is a weakness) in his treament of exact languages is that the basic vocabulary on both the linguistic and the ontologic sides is taken for granted. Reference is an unexamined relation of name to thing, no names being empty. And except for the notion of application of a predicate as expressing the mapping of an individual to a truth value, there is no hint of semantical linkage.

There are mixed consequences of this free-wheeling use of unexamined vocabulary when it comes to reference and sense in natural language. Semantical terms cannot be fixed by edict as they can in logic.

The doctrine of sense, it seems to me, is hopeless, especially the sense of a name as an abstract entity. Frege never says what sense is nor what the sense of a particular expression is.

There are quite a few uses of 'sense' in Frege, but I do not know whether they signify various entities or only one entity bearing distinguishable marks or subject to several perspectives (whatever that could possibly mean). Three uses of 'sense' are: mode of presentation of the object named; way of understanding the name; and object of indirect discourse.

'Cognitive value' in the sentence ' "$a = a$" has a different cognitive value than "$a = b$" ' seems to me just to express that the two equalities do not mean the same, in our ordinary pretheoretical speech. I cannot see that it illuminates or is illuminated by saying the expressions have different sense. 'Sense' as cognitive value is a violation of Commandment I. Sense qua way of understanding, although supposed to be other than a mode of presentation, is equally sterile.

Evans suggests that the sense of a name is displayed in disquotation (1982). In ' "Cicero" refers to Cicero' the sense of 'Cicero' *shows* whereas in the equally true ' "Cicero" refers to Tully' it does not. I think there is something to be said for this interpretation of sense, although if accepted as true Frege, synonymy reduces to orthography: for instance, 'Shakespeare' is not synonymous with 'Shakespere'; this might not apply to disquotation of descriptions although I do not pretend to know how to tell.

Frege uses indirect reference in order to explain how a thought can be preserved under substitution of names. The substituent must have the same sense as the substituend. However, in intensional contexts this condition appears to be neither necessary nor sufficient as Schmid abundantly illustrates.

In this book, a demand on any theory of reference is that it explain purported reference without which you cannot explain the linguistic significance of empty names. None of the notions of sense, except possibly that of mode of presentation, is of the slightest help in accounting for the namehood of empty names. To say, for instance, that a condition of namehood is having an indirect sense or being understood in a way peculiar to that name is of no help as the conditions are not identifiable except to intuition, and I claim this is just appeal to the pretheoretical idea that any empty name is a name nontheless and may be used essentially in human communications, including science, and not only in fiction.

CHAPTER 4

Naming and Describing

1. Philosophical analysis

Bertrand Russell's main work on philosophy of logic, 'On denoting', written in 1905, is often regarded as the greatest piece of logical analysis to date. It began a movement that led to logical empiricism and taught that much bad metaphysics is traceable to bad logic and defective language.

In terms of styles of approaching reference, which I described in Chapter 2, §1, Russell's work falls under theory of knowledge, and in it there is a causal strain in the British empiricist tradition running close to Locke. But as one of the foremost logicians of all time, he is also reductionist; he views science pretty much as he does mathematics – as expressible in principle in the language of *Principia Mathematica* which is his version of a Fregean exact language.

Differing on a crucial point from Frege, Russell seeks analysis of reference, not uncritical acceptance of it as a factor in meaning and truth. For him, reference is a problem, not a given primitive component of grammatical structures. In this respect he is an analyst.

Russell's concept of reference continues the line of British empiricism from Locke through Mill. Reference is based on the acquaintance a person has with the objects of his immediate experience; it is a word-to-object link established by a knowing subject's acquaintance with the world. Hence reference theory is a department of theory of knowledge. Similarly, meanings are not Fregean senses grasped by an understanding mind, but are constituents of experienced objects. 'Red' signifies the quality red of the actual world, for instance, and not a concept that maps individual, named objects to a truth value. Objective meaning is (most often) a mark of Russell's thought and figures markedly in present day thought.

Russell's logically proper names are 'this', 'that' and indexicals such as 'you' and 'I'; they are Frege's wastebasket cases. Demonstrative words pick out the particulars of immediate experience, and *that's* your basic reference. Russell scotches the whole idea of Fregean (and almost everyone else's) reference of words such as 'Venus' or 'the point of intersection of two lines' and discards any idea of the dependence of sentential truth on objects picked out by ordinary names and descriptions. Neither 'Abel' nor 'the junior author . . .' nor any other items on our list in Chapter 1, §1, are logically proper names. In Russell's theory they do not name at all, except in a certain secondary, indirect way.

The ends of inquiry are different. Frege was interested in the semantics of sentences and sentence parts and in the role inference plays in logic, while Russell pursued all of that and also sought in reference of demonstratives and in quantification the contact points with reality for the knowing mind.

The difference shows up strikingly in two theories of truth. For Frege, the True is the value of composite mappings – reference of words to objects; concept-mapping of objects to truth values; and truth-functional mappings of truth values to truth values – which mappings are independent of individual minds. If truth is construed as some sort of correspondence, it is one of thoughts to the True. Russell, on the other hand, proposes a full-blown correspondence, a similarity of structure between the sentence and the real world. This contrasts with Locke also, since truth for Russell is not agreement or disagreement of ideas but agreement of language and expressed thought with objective fact. Language is no mere Lockean instrument for communicating knowledge, but constitutes knowledge, when true.

Russell's methods are directed both to founding a theory of knowledge and to analysis of natural language, mainly with an eye to avoiding ontological sin committed in arguing from logic to being. He forbids unactualized possibles for empty names to bear and third truth values for sentences that are neither true or false. Russell's aim is not only arid semantics of logical languages, but applications of logic to conceptual puzzles, to the economy of ontology and to questions of life and morals.

In Russellean lore a paradigm of his analytical style is his no-class theory. If a mathematician wants to, he may construct at will any class of things he can list, or else characterize by an attribute: the class of things on his desk, of red things, of transcendental numbers or of non-Aryan languages. This suggests a question whether there might be restrictions to observe in specifying classes. Does anything go? The answer is 'no' if we want consistency.

In 1901 Russell discovered that free-wheeling use of arbitrary conditions to define classes leads to trouble; this is known as Russell's paradox. For instance, the class of abstract objects might itself be a member of the class of abstract objects, while the class of cats would not be a cat, that is to say, a member of the class of cats. So it seems reasonable to say that the predicates 'things that are members of themselves' and 'things that are not members of themselves' are both plausible defining conditions of classes; they appear to have extensions.

But in the second case an object would be a member if and only if it were not a member; more formally, let A be the class of things not elements of themselves, defined by the expression

x is an element of A if and only if x is not an element of x.

Let x be A. Then

A is an element of A if and only if A is not an element of A.

So A is both an element of A and not an element of A. This is Russell's paradox.

This famous result was disastrous for Frege (to whom Russell communicated it in 1904), since he had to assume all predicates (Fregean concepts) had extensions to get his arithmetization of logic under way. Russell wanted to avoid Frege's fate, and so invented the 'no-class' doctrine. Eliminate classes altogether from the notations and ontology of mathematics – no classes, lower risk of contradiction.

The key idea is that notations for classes are *incomplete* symbols, symbols having no meaning outside the context of sentences. If a symbol occurs in a sentence that can be rephrased in a new equivalent sentence free of the symbol, then that symbol and any ontological commitment attaching to it shall have been shown to be dispensable and illusory, respectively.

Consider the class of red things, called 'Red'. Now the sentence this apple is a member of the class Red

can be paraphrased to read simply

this apple is red.

where the class of red things has simply disappeared. In this example, 'Red' is called an incomplete symbol because it does not refer to anything; this is shown by the equivalence of the first to the second sentence, in which the symbol does not occur. Assuming this analysis is quite general (it is not), all reference to classes can be eliminated in carefully framed classless discourse: simply replace '*a* is a member of *X*' by '*a* is *P*' where '*P*' is the predicate used to define the class *X*.

Russell's method of logical analysis by paraphrase, as in the foregoing example, marks more than anything else his philosophy of language and knowledge. His theory of reference uses the same style of analysis and enables one to eliminate empty names like 'Pegasus' or 'Santa Claus' as incomplete symbols while still allowing significant talk.

2. *Logical atomism*

The theory of reference can be best understood as a part of Russell's metaphysics and epistemology. The metaphysical theory, which he shared pretty much with Wittgenstein's *Tractatus Logico-philosophicus* (1925), is *logical atomism*; and his epistemology is a sensationalist version of empiricism – *the theory of knowledge by acquaintance and description.*

The scheme of atomism is suggested by Russell's philosophy of mathematics. The basic formulas of predicate logic are atomic expressions like '$F(x_1, x_2, \ldots, x_n)$' where the individual variables range over arbitrary but fixed objects, while 'F' is a variable which ranges over properties and relations sustained by these objects. Mathematical content emerges in the definitions of classes, numbers, relations, functions etc. in terms of the atoms plus logical vocabulary, and disappears in the reverse process, i.e. 'unpacking' – taking definientia for definienda. Such (very approximately!) is the technique of *Principia Mathematica*.

Empirical science builds on primitive atomic sentences parallel in syntax to those of pure logic, but having real content. Ideally, science has the extensional quality of logic and mathematics, which in effect is just to say that it is expressible in a language ideally like that of *Principia*. Complexity is built up using connectives and quantifiers and scientific predicates are either defined from primitives (that is Russell's goal, anyway) or shown to be dispensable. Thus linguistic complexity in an ideal language can be analyzed (decomposed into simples) in a way harking back to Frege. But the ultimate residuals are the empirical atomic premises.

Excepting his youthful fling with Hegelianism, Russell was a realist and held that truth is a correspondence of belief with fact (1912: 121).[1] Logical atomism is a metaphysical theory of the ground of that correspondence, which is a structural similarity of facts to sentences of a language.

In order to understand him we have to grasp what Russell means by 'fact' and 'atom'. Logical atoms are altogether different ontological items than physical atoms. A logical atom is an ultimate ontological simple, an individual object or a simple attribute such as a connected patch of color. Logical atoms, but not physical atoms, are the ontological images, so to say, of the components of atomic sentences '*a* is *F* ' (1918b: 194). So a hydrogen atom, for instance, is not a logical atom since it is not a reductum of logical analysis. Atomic facts such as this being *F*, which corresponds to the belief that this is *F* (or the sentence '*a* is *F* ') are epistemically primary and comprise the building stones of all knowledge. Facts are ultimate constituents of the objective world, which is everything that is the case (Wittgenstein: 1925): the world consists just of all the facts. The ultimacy of atomic facts entails that they are logically independent of each other – for instance, the fact of being red is independent of the fact of being a round spot or, indeed, of all other atomic fact. This is not as clear in Russell as it is in Wittgenstein, to whom Russell is in part indebted for his atomism. But no matter; we shall assume it is sufficiently clear.

Facts are the truth conditions of sentences. For an atomic sentence '*a* is *F* ', if the thing referred to by '*a*' is an *F*, then the fact of its being *F* makes the sentence true, and if not *F*, false. For other sentences the factual conditions might be extremely complex. Russell never had a complete theory of truth to deal with them although he often says that a correspondence theory is possible in principle.

Russell defines 'proper name' in terms of 'atomic fact', 'predicate' (in the sense of an objective attribute, *P*) and 'is a word for', which I will render 'refers to'. First,

> particulars are terms of relations (including one-place predicates) in atomic facts.
>
> (1918b: 199)

For example, in the atomic fact *a* is *F*, *a* is a particular, and in the fact *a* is *R* to *b*, *a* and *b* are particulars; and so on for relations of any number of correlates.

Second,

> proper names are words for particulars.
>
> (1918b: 199)

The proper name '*a*' is a name for the particular *a* in the fact *a* is *F*.

Assuming that 'atomic fact' is primitive and does not have to be explicated in terms of 'atomic proposition' (which is doubtful) this defines 'proper name' (in effect defines 'singular term' as we shall see) in terms of reference and predication much as we did in Chapter 1, and is open to similar objections. However, these definitions are basic Russell, and for our purposes need emendation, if any, only from the standpoint of the theory of acquaintance. Notice that these definitions attempt to analyze the very concepts Frege took for granted without analysis.

The basic theses of logical atomism – that the world is a plurality of independent atomic facts which declarative sentences are true or false of – serves as an abstract frame for Russell's epistemology. To go further he must give it content. Is a factual thing a physical object? A sense datum? Are attributes universals? What is correspondence? Russell's answers are found in his theory of knowledge by acquaintance and description, a close companion to logical atomism.

3. Knowledge by acquaintance and description

Acquaintance is a relation between a knowing subject and directly experienced facts, reportable in atomic sentences like 'this is a lamp', 'this is an angry tiger', 'that is a hard problem', 'that person is in a hurry', 'you look tired' and 'I am hungry'. Notice that all the subjects of these sentences are indexicals.

Knowledge by description, on the other hand, is of facts *under-*

stood but not directly *experienced*, such as are reported in sentences like 'Titania is a fairy', 'Bhutto is President of Pakistan', 'the other side of the moon is hemispherical', 'the solution to this puzzle is on page A' or 'all motion is governed by forces'.

As shown in the examples, descriptions and ordinary names are used to talk about objects outside the range of immediate experience or of impressions or thoughts brought up from memory. Not all particular things we can think of, such as experiences of others or the inside of the earth, have ever been or can occur in direct experience. There are things we know beyond the immediacy of sense data (Russell 1914: 138; 1918a: 214); but these facts are not identified by this's and that's. 'The man in room R' does not mention this man or that man or indeed any man present, but describes an individual whom none of us here see, hear or touch. So the grammatical subjects in sentences that report indirectly known facts are descriptive, not demonstrative 'that' or 'this' – which occur in acquaintance only.

This does not explain 'Titania' and 'Bhutto' which appear not to be descriptive. But these terms are not indexical either. 'Bhutto' is about a certain person, but does not point to her. With exceptions that I will presently note, ordinary names such as 'Bhutto', 'Bush' or 'Titania' are considered by Russell to be *abbreviations of definite descriptions* as we shall see.

Thus a central semantical distinction in theory of knowledge is between logically proper names, which are indexicals and refer to particulars in acquaintance, and definite descriptions and ordinary names – the proper names of traditional grammar – which describe but do not refer to the world outside of immediate acquaintance.

Logically proper names fall into the class of singular terms we divided off in Chapter 1 from those subject to disquotation. We also have in consequence that disquotation for items such 'Abel' or 'Bach' is meaningless. 'Abel' does not refer to Abel since it is not a referring word. Only indexicals refer. It perhaps still counts as a singular term, because in ordinary speech it combines with a predicate to form a meaningful sentence. However, this point is not clear in Russell and later on I shall simply suggest that 'Abel' and its kin 'Lady Ottoline' etc. *purportedly* refer.

It follows that disquotation is not a reasonable necessary condition for proper naming or else that Russell's theory is unreasonable. Of course it is not unreasonable given his epistemological preferences. I am not one to try to decide this; but our discussion does show that relation (1) of Chapter 1, §2, has more content than appears on the surface.

Presumably this theory covers ordinary names of objects or persons met face to face. If I introduce Susan to you saying 'this is Susan', the 'is' is the identity and the token 'Susan' names the object of the demonstrative 'this'. However, with the exception of such occasions, ordinary names are most often used for persons or objects not in one's field of immediate awareness and not called up in an inner sensory image, and therefore do not refer.

Being true of or false of is not reference. Therefore sentences do not refer, as Frege thought. Reference is a relation sustained by logically proper names only. Correspondence of sentence to fact, whatever it is, is not reference.

A predicate 'F' does not name but describes; or, as already discussed, applies in virtue of our being aware of the universal F, as we shall see presently.

Therefore reference is left only to indexicals and demonstratives or to ordinary names that co-refer with demonstratives in acquaintance. This theory is almost a total reversal of Frege for whom all significant terms refer in one way or another, except for indexicals, which to him present special cases in natural language.

The immediate objects of knowledge are sense data, including particulars and the qualities they bear, for example the sense impression of a dog. A short inventory of other objects of acquaintance (Russell 1912: 46–52) includes – in addition to impressions of physical things – items drawn from memory, awareness of awareness itself (introspection – e.g. awareness of the hardness of a problem), other people and one's self, perhaps only as a cluster of introspected images and ideas.

Inasmuch as atomic sentences are true of objective facts the doctrine of acquaintance leads to major, tri-partite quandary: (a) . . . are the particulars named by logically proper names sense data or objective facts? (b) are the meanings of sentences the facts, or entities in the mind, or both? (c) truth is correspondence to what and how can it be objective if each individual knows only what he is aware of ?

Our principal end is to understand reference, so my discussion of (b) and (c) will be summary.

(a) The mind is aware of sense data, not physical objects (ibid.: 52). This is pure Locke and presents the same problems. However, it is not either unfair or shaky exegesis to state that in Russell all of the following hold:

> atomic sentences are about objective facts;
> atomic sentences are never in error;
> the object of acquaintance, which is the referent of a singular term in the atomic sentence, is the sensum, not the outer object.

This is not a credible view,[2] but it is Russell's, and we shall not deny him it.

The problem applies to naming as well since names make the links with fact. A name can be 'a word for' a particular only (by the official definition) and yet you cannot name anything you are not acquainted with. And because the mind is aware only of sense data, we must conclude, in order to keep going, that naming sense data gets through to particulars in virtue of some very strong equivalence of sense data and objects, as canvassed in note 2.

The same treatment has to be given to predicates and to what roughly corresponds to application. Russell is a realist, not a nominalist, and holds that the mind grasps or, as he puts it, 'is aware of', universals (ibid.: 52). Thus in analogy to item (2) in Chapter 1, §3, the agent as a knowing mind determines that an attribute applies to an object owing to his capacity to grasp universals, not to match for similarities, in Berkeleyan style. In this wise universals occur in facts, and they are the meanings of predicates; meanings are objective. So just as names link to objective fact, universals apply to the facts in virtue of apprehension of them in the data of immediate sensory acquaintance.

(b) 'Meaning' has many meanings in Russell and he also takes words for things and things for words quite often, all of which makes for very hard going for the reader. However, it is clear that logically proper names do not have Fregean senses. The meaning of a logically proper name is its bearer and nothing else. Proper naming depends on context of acquaintance and the persons doing the naming. For instance 'this' obviously can have no fixed sense.

'This' in situation *S* is not the same name as 'this' in situation *S'*.

Ordinary names like 'Abel' and definite descriptions like 'the inventor of . . .' do not refer, as we have seen. Neither do they have meaning in some sense of 'meaning' other than reference, since they are incomplete symbols, as I shall explain. However, in everyday speech they are meaningful in the context of speech.

In cases where ordinary names do refer (as was the case with 'Susan') they do not have sense. Using Frege's famous example, '*a* = *b*' is as much a tautology for Russell as '*a* = *a*' and carries no more information. If '*b*' is a definite description or a substitute name for one, then '*a* = *b*' (for instance, '*a* = the author of *Principia*') is simply meaningless as the definite description does not refer. I will say more about this theory below. For the rest, predicates and sentences are meaningful in both natural and logical languages.

The meanings of linguistic items that do have meaning are not things of the mind, but the components of facts. This is official atomist doctrine.

> [T]he components of the fact which makes a proposition [sentence] true or false, as the case may be, are the meanings of the symbols which we must understand in order to understand the proposition.
>
> (Russell 1918b: 196)

This is not very compelling except possibly for the meaning of items in direct experience. To understand 'red', Russell says, you 'do not have to know, concerning any particular "this" that "this is red", but you have to know the meaning of saying that anything is red' (ibid.: 205). Obviously he is alluding to awareness of universals. Whether this awareness is itself direct (which would be consistent with logical atomism) or of a mental representation of the universal (which is a departure) is a further issue closely related to that of propositions (in the nonverbal sense) as neither sentences nor facts.

It is tempting, therefore, to say that sense data and conceived universals intervening between knower and object are meanings grounded in the objective facts (ibid.: 289ff). However, belief sentences have meanings other than the sense data, images and concepts in the mind. These meanings are nonlinguistic propositions and the introduction of them into Russell's ponderings about meaning seem to be required by the facts of false belief.

Suppose, for a moment, that the meanings of belief sentences are just the facts or the data reflected in the mind, through which we are acquainted with the facts. Now perceptual sentences are without error (see (c) below). They are true of necessity. But one can have a false belief even though a correspondence holds between sentence and fact. Schmid, as we have long known, can hold unerringly true sentences to be false. So whatever the sentence he expresses his belief in is about cannot be a veridical image or concept. This strongly suggests that there are propositions (ibid.: 304ff) that can be true to, or false to, the facts.

The trouble with this view for the atomistic scheme is that it intrudes a new semantical element whose object is not a sentence (which we know Russell persistently terms a 'proposition') but is a mental entity with propositional content. It imports a meaning (in another sense of 'meaning') for sentences over and above the objective facts that make them true or false. In later work (1948) Russell distinguishes between the truth value of a sentence and its significance (which resembles the Fregean notion of thought as the sense of a sentence); and beliefs are then said to be inner mental representations that express propositions. We shall encounter the same idea in contemporary cognitivist theories of mind. Much of what remains to be discussed here revolves around the issue, easily marked in Russell's work, of whether meanings are objective, as in atomism, or in the mind as representations of outer things.

(c) Returning to the idea of correspondence, sentences about immediate experiences are indubitably true or false of facts, so that truth value is determinate in perception, which is always veridical; it is not 'liable to error' (Russell 1918b: 223). Here the sentence is a picture of the fact, and the picturing is the true.[3] This sanguine doctrine seems to extend to all sentences that express human knowledge, for ideally every sentence 'which we can understand must be composed wholly of constituents with which we are acquainted' (Russell 1912: 58). This includes knowledge by description. Knowledge of both particulars and universals is often conveyed to us by description, but 'is ultimately reducible to knowledge concerning what is known by acquaintance' (ibid.). Of course this is impossible unless there is indeed a principled scheme of reduction of theoretical, descriptive concepts to terms of acquaintance. He never did this, it has not been done, and it is generally regarded as infeasible today.

Quite clearly truth in the limit, so to say, is a question other than the practical one about private sense data, communal knowledge and belief. Russell's nominal definition of the true is correspondence, but the epistemic mechanism needed to construct it in scientific practice is a different matter. There is more to be said about communal knowledge. But I want to get on right now with the question of names and descriptions.

4. Reference and denotation

Bertrand Russell was perhaps the first philosopher in recent times to consider seriously puzzles about empty names and sentences in natural language. The puzzles sprout in all frames of linguistic use except on occasions of acquaintance (for Russell, since acquaintance is sure). Frege does not face the question for logically perfect languages, as we have seen. But Russell wanted to show how empty locutions can be explained in terms of exact ideas, or at the very least, explained away. This is a vastly different enterprise than that of Frege who threw up his hands and relegated everything empty in natural language to fiction.

Consider, once again, 'Titania does not exist', which we insisted is meaningful, even true, contrary to Frege. Now if 'Titania' is a genuine name, the sentence says something that exists does not exist. Russell's way of avoiding this is to deny that 'Titania' is a name.

Given logical atomism wherein facts are one to one with basic sentences, ideally, there can be no exceptions: no particular, no name. However, this does not provide a *criterion* for proper namehood, which the following argument does.

'This exists' is meaningless. 'This' is indeed a proper name and refers to a particular in acquaintance. The meaning of a sentence, we just saw, is nothing but the components of the atomic fact; but 'exists' is not a component. Again, if 'this exists' were meaningful, 'this does not exist' would be; but the latter is not meaningful, as 'this' is a name of an actual thing.

In contrast, 'Romulus existed' is quite meaningful, and consequently 'Romulus' is not a proper name. If it were, 'the question of existence could not arise . . . because a name has got to name something or it is not a name'. In short, 'Romulus existed' is as

meaningless as 'this exists', unless Romulus is a disguised description (Russell 1918b: 241–3). But the same holds of ordinary names,
excepting the direct ones like 'Susan' in 'this is Susan'. They
abbreviate definite descriptions.

For Russell, as for Frege and later logicians, it is meaningless to
express that a thing exists save as satisfying some property or other.
'This exists' is meaningless, Russell says, as 'exists' is not a
predicate. On the other hand in the sentence 'there exists a red
thing' the quantifier essentially 'completes' the propositional function, ___ red thing, making a general fact out of it. So existence
applies to propositional functions, but not to objects of names.

Russell's solution to the various puzzles about names and
existence hinges on an eliminative technique using a fundamental
distinction between reference and denotation. As we know very
well, reference occurs only in immediate acquaintance with objects.
Denotation is a new, vague relation he introduces into the theory in
order to acknowledge the significance of reports about objects and
affairs outside of present experience. Russell's strategy depends
upon replacement of names by denoting phrases and then analyzing
the latter in terms of quantified expressions.

Russell explains what he means by 'denoting phrase' by the list: 'a
man, some man, every man, all men, the present King of England,
the present King of France, the centre of mass of the solar system,
the revolution of the earth around the sun' (Russell 1905: 41). All of
these intend objects more or less indirectly, but of course do not
refer. We may exclude here everything but definite descriptions as
the others, 'every man' and the rest, can be expressed in terms of
quantifiers in familiar ways.

Denoting phrases are such in virtue of their form. Russell means
that their logico-grammatical significance, not their specific deno-
tations, depend upon form. They may not denote anything (e.g. 'the
present Kind of France') or they may denote one definite object
(e.g. 'the present Queen of England'). Of course we know they
function denotatively in the descriptional knowledge of things, for
instance as in 'the center of mass of the solar system' or 'the last
tachyon to enter the tube first'.

Consider the sentence 'the father of Charles II was executed'. The
denoting phrase is 'the father of Charles II'. This phrase is not a
proper name and does not refer to anything. But it does happen to
denote a person. However, it does not denote save within the

context of the whole sentence. So it is an incomplete symbol, on all fours with 'class'. Russell shows this in the following way.

The sentence asserts there was an x who was father of Charles II and was executed. Since 'the' involves uniqueness, the sentence also asserts no one else but x was the father of Charles II. These two imply that someone x begat Charles II and x was executed, and any y who begat Charles II is identical with x. More formally this reads,

(1) $(\exists x)[(y)(y$ was father of Charles II if and only if $y = x)$ and x was executed]

where '$\exists x$' is the existential and 'y' the universal quantifier. Note that the description has been dissolved away in favor of quantifiers which express unique existence; and this dissolution shows the incompleteness of the denoting phrase 'the father of Charles II'.

Now let us see how this theory can settle problems of emptiness and truth value gaps. In our ordinary way of thinking every declarative sentence is either true or false, by the law of the excluded middle. So 'the present King of France is bald' must be true or false. However, there is no present King of France. There are two old ways of handling this, plus Russell's.

According to Frege, since there is no such king the sentence is neither true nor false, but is still meaningful: it expresses a thought. There is a truth value gap.

For the ontologically nonfastidious a *possible* present king could be whomped up, thus allowing us to hold the law of the excluded middle. The sentence is true of a possible kind.

For Russell, on the other hand, the sentence is to be rephrased, using the theory of denoting applied to 'the present King of France'. What we get is 'there is one and only one King of France, and he is bald':

$(\exists x)[(y)(K(y)$ if and only if $y = x)$ and not $B(x)]$

where 'K' is 'is King of France' and 'B' is 'is bald'. Inasmuch as there is no present king of France we may negate this paraphrased version, getting the true sentence

not$(\exists x)[(y)(K(y)$ if and only if $y = x)$ and $B(x)]$.

This agrees with intuition that the original unanalyzed sentence is in fact false, not meaningless.

Now if there were a king of France, but he had hair, we would simply negate the second conjunct of the first expression, denying of the king that he is bald

$$(\exists x)[(y)(K(y) \text{ if and only if } y = x) \text{ and not } B(x)].$$

This analysis makes clear that the definite description in 'the present King of France is bald' can be negated in either of two ways. In the first, the description is said to have a *secondary occurrence* since it is a constituent of a larger sentence the whole of which is negated. In the second, the description has a *primary occurrence* as it is outside the scope of negation. All primary readings are false, since there is no such king.[4]

The same analysis applies to ordinary names in the subject position. For instance 'God is good' becomes on replacement of 'God' by a standard description of God as the Creator, 'the Creator of the Universe is good'; and analysis yields, 'there is one and only one Creator, and He is good'. Denial results in either 'It is false there is one and only one Creator who is good'; or, 'There is one and only one Creator, but He is not good'. Therefore the sentence is either true or false in either the primary or secondary readings. Similar treatments apply to all speculative entities as well as to the fictional.

In this way the theory of descriptions moves around the puzzles of reference and existence: how can we say of a thing that it does not exist? Answer: analyze a description corresponding to the ordinary name of the thing in terms of an existentially quantified statement in the canonical form above and negate it.

Russell also thought his theory of descriptions dissolves puzzles about substitution. His favorite example of an intensional sentence is 'George IV wished to know whether Scott was the author of *Waverly*'. Now if 'Scott' was the author of *Waverly*' is true, then if we allow the substitution of 'Scott' for 'the author of *Waverly*' we derive the absurd conclusion 'George IV wished to know whether Scott was Scott'.

But this substitution is blocked when we see, on rephrasing, that 'the author of *Waverly*' is not a name and in unabbreviated form 'does not contain any constituent for which we could substitute "Scott" Russell' (1905: 52). So there is no counterpart in Russell's theory to the Fregean idea that substitution in oblique contexts requires synonymy of names, not merely co-reference. The theory goes further – to complete elimination of the idea that what looks like a referential context is one, even for indirect reference.

It turns out, however, that Russell waffles on the most crucial issue: are all occurrences of definite descriptions incomplete, not names, and hence not open to subsitution? The answer is 'no', and comes in two parts as we shall see in §6.

5. *Reference and use*

Originally a British phenomenon, ordinary language philosophy entered into the historical stream we are following here with P. F. Strawson's criticism of Russell's theory of denoting. Frege and Russell were almost entirely absorbed with philosophy of mathematics and epistemology, and the analytical tools they used were borrowed from formal logic constrained, in Russell's case, by his logical atomism. Neither one was much interested in daily language usage, communication, the role of the listener or the intentions of the speaker. There was a sharp preference in both thinkers for exact, formal languages both as objects of study and as sources of working concepts.

Strawson (1950) reverses this attitude. Truth depends on use, he maintains, and the key to it is to be found in the ordinary ways of speaking and writing English, not in abstractions borrowed from mathematical philosophy. Truth is a function of the use of expressions, not of expressions themselves.

Now relying on a pragmatic stance, as Strawson does, to launch an attack on a theory grounded in quite other presuppositions is just the thing for generating heat. His essay 'On referring' (1950) appeared forty-five years after Russell's article. In it Strawson strikes right out, asserting that Russell's 'essay embodies some fundamental mistakes' and the theory of names is 'logically disastrous' (ibid.: 186). This is strong stuff; but Russell, being occupied elsewhere at the time, took no notice. Eventually (at age 87) he got around to a warm reply (1959: 238) writing that he was 'totally unable to see any validity whatever in Mr. Strawson's arguments'.

1905 to 1950 is a long time, during which Russell was considered the first word in logical analysis, and perhaps the elapse shows he was more closely followed than understood, if Strawson is right. Whether he is or not, Strawson is more responsible than anyone else, except possibly Carnap, for the 'pernicious error' (Quine 1987:

211) of separating semantics from pragmatics (see Chapter 6, §2). Let's see what's what.

According to Russell, grammatically good declarative sentences are either true or false, depending on the facts, while according to Strawson this is completely wrong. None but *asserted* sentences – sentences used to make statements – can be true or false. No one who uses English correctly asserts sentences about nonactual kings or winged horses. In particular 'the present King of France is bald' would never be asserted by anyone who reads current news.

A key feature of Strawson's diatribe is this: in ordinary speech or writing one and the same sentence can be used on different occasions with different intent, an observation that depends on the distinction between sentence-type and sentence-token. Consider 'the president of the USA is George Bush'. Both you and I might utter a token of it on the same occasion and make the same assertion, ask the same question or whatever depending on the common use we have in mind. But one of us could utter it in 1987, making a false statement, while the other could utter it in 1990 or 1991 making a true one. Similarly the description 'the president of the USA' would refer to different objects at different times by different speakers, one and the same term-type being used for Reagan, Bush and Abraham Lincoln.

Strawson claims neither the full sentence 'the present King of France is bald' nor the description 'the present King . . .' refer to anything; the sentence in itself is not the sort of thing that can be true or false and the name in itself does not name. Persons, not sentences, refer to objects and say things that might be true or false. Sentences can be asserted, thus making statements, and names can be used by human agents to refer. But except under use, language is referentially mute. 'The present King of France is bald' is a significant sentence and is understood by any English speaking person, but it has no truth value unless it is put forth. Russell's first mistake is to suppose that the law of the excluded middle applies to unasserted sentences.

Second, for a subtly different point, even if one asserts 'the present King of France . . .' meaning to make a statement, the assertion is neither true nor false. In general, all assertion is neither true nor false unless the person making it is talking about something (Strawson 1950: 182), and this is not so in the King of France example. There are gaps, as in Frege's theory, in truth values of asserted sentences, some of which contain empty singular terms. Having truth values presupposes actual objects.

But note (here's that point) that truth value indeterminacy or hiatus in the domain of assertions is not the same thing as indeterminacy of truth values of sentences. Unasserted sentences are categorically the wrong items for making *any* truth value assignments. In analogy, an electronic switch might be on or off, or neither – a 'don't care' gap – whereas it is nonsense to say of a rock that it is on or off, although it no doubt could be used or in some way described as a kind of switch. If this is right, Russell cannot get his theory of denoting and definite descriptions off the ground unless he tacitly assumes phrases 'the such and such . . .' are used to refer, in which case one can go on to assert 'there must be at least one and not more than one thing such that . . .'. I will return to this point.

Unasserted, 'The present King . . .' is nonetheless understood by speakers of English. Questions of meaning and significance should not be mixed with questions of truth and reference. Meaning is a function of the name or sentence while reference and truth are functions of their use. This rough approximation to Fregean sense versus reference indicates different psychological facts about engagements with language. 'The table is covered with books' is English-wise significant to the reader now; but it is absurd to ask what object the sentence is about because it is just being used as an example of what it is to be significant. Knowing what the description 'the table' means is just knowing how to use it; but knowing how to use it is not the same as using it. Similarly, until it is used in a situation as asserting something it is neither true nor false. What you have to know to understand significance of words and how to use them is distinct from the using of them on occasions (ibid.: 182).

Searle, who is a disciple of Strawson, puts it this way (1969: 17): speech is governed by rules of syntax, meaning and naming; the study of these is part of semantics; the other main part, pragmatics, is the study of speech *acts*. Semantics without heeding speech acts is like studying 'baseball . . . as a formal system of rules and not as a game'. Language can be understood only when set in the arena of communication where there are speech acts: conveying of information, persuading, avowing, expressing feelings and so forth.

Now Russell mistakenly thought, says Strawson, that a name without a bearer is meaningless, and thus overlooked the above distinction. In Russell's theory, if names are meaningful, they must refer, and the sentences in which they occur must be about the facts, i.e. be true or false. Hence no distinction can be drawn between assertion and uncommitted expression, and no question can arise of one expressed token of a type being true and another of the same type being false. At the heart of Russell's problem is his identification of reference with meaning. Assimilation of meaning to reference leads to the notion of incomplete symbol and the ensuing analysis of descriptions.

But the mistake here is Strawson's as he ignores the crucial difference between reference and denotation. 'The present King of France' is not a logically proper name and neither are names like 'Scott', which are usually disguised descriptions. It is a denoting phrase and is meaningful but incomplete. It is not true for Russell that meaningfulness implies reference.

Russell even supplies a kind of demonstration. It is axiomatic in his (as well as Frege's) thought that sentences of the sort '[logically proper name] exists' are meaningless: 'exists' is not a predicate, but a functor[5] that combines with predicates (Russellian propositional functions) to form new expressions. But 'the present King of France exists' is false, not meaningless; and therefore 'the present King of France' is not a logically proper name. The description is a meaningful, denoting phrase, in context, although it does not denote. The expression is said to be an incomplete symbol for this reason, not for the mistaken one that it is without meaning.

This misunderstanding stems from Strawson's using the phrase 'having a uniquely referring use' which he adopts as replacement for both 'logically proper name' and 'definite description' (1950: 178, 181f), completely ignoring the background distinction between acquaintance and description which I maintain Russell never really dropped (cf. Russell 1948, pp. 85–8). We must not lose sight of the fact that the theory of descriptions, although introduced in terms of logical puzzles which might obtain even in mathematics, is essential to the theory of knowledge. Russell needs to bridge from empirical, perceptual input to knowledge and language far from the perceptual. Description theory plus the principle of reducibility of knowledge to acquaintance gives the means.

Strawson does not pay any attention to this. Reference for him is a problem in the logical analysis of ordinary language, not one of epistemology. So he directly criticizes Russell's theory of descriptions – as if it stood in isolation from his epistemology – essentially on grounds that the theory is idle as soon as you see that assertion is not merely entertainment of sentences. Descriptions are as uniquely referring in Strawson's view as proper names or demonstratives. If they do not refer, their including sentences are without truth value, but are not therefore meaningless.

However, recalling the logico-epistemological stance, logically proper names (later called by Russell 'egocentric terms') occur only in sentences expressing the facts of immediate acquaintance; there is no difference between a sentence and an asserted sentence in acquaintance since only in an asserted (or otherwise used) sentence does a logically proper name function at all! Russell never meant 'this' to have reference, purported or otherwise, outside of its use in acquaintance. This is the gist of Russell's reply to Strawson in 1959. 'This' occurring in the atomic sentence 'this is red', for instance, has no purport whatever other than what it has in assertion (which, incidentally, is why it did not appear on our disquotational list in Chapter 1).

Equally, a companion observation holds for the sentences of mathematics and theoretical science. Unlike situational statements where truth value depends on who is speaking, where they are speaking etc., if Strawson is right, every asserted token of a mathematical or physical (except experimental) sentence has the same value as any other. So the distinction between a sentence type and an uttered token is, as regards applicability of truth values, a distinction without a difference. Again, in mathematics one would normally prove that a sentence type is true before asserting it. (However, this is often disputed by intuitionists – see Chapter 5, §3.)

Nevertheless, it does seem that in daily use and in the biological, geological and social sciences Strawson is right (although there are alternative views of the matter, as we shall see in Chapter 7, §3). Truth and falsehood are of statements – sentence tokens – and reference (in a loose sense) is time and place bound. Of greater importance is his (and other ordinary language philosophers) stress on the pervasive use of sentences in communication for question-asking, making demands, avowals and other utterances. In such speech acts there is usually no claim to truth or factuality. 'Shut the door' or 'I do take this woman . . .' are not statements and are not intended to be so.

Even so, I shall later (Chapter 6) want to argue that this insight needs qualification because understanding is cognitively prior to assertion. In Strawson's own terms, assertion presupposes reference, but not the other way around. 'To refer is not to assert, though you refer in order to go on to assert' (1950: 186). Moreover, assertion entails belief and beliefs are true or false although in most cases they are tacit. Intentional attitudes underlie all 'illocutionary' acts, such as questions, avowals etc. as well assertions; so even in other speech acts truth or falsity is implied.

Meanwhile, more or less independently of Strawson's criticisms, it has become increasingly evident that Russell's theory of ordinary names will not stand up. In natural language, names do not always correlate uniquely with descriptions. There could be many, good, nonsynonymous descriptions that fit Russell.[6]

Keith Donnellan (1966) claims that descriptions are often used to refer. On the street you might talk of Schmid saying 'the drunken bum on the curb' while I use 'the guy in the stained lederhosen', and we would be communicating perfectly well. Such situations put still more strain on the thesis that names are substitutes for descriptions that faithfully attribute identifying marks. We will return to Donnellan's point in Chapter 6, §2.

Returning to flaws in Strawson, how might he manage our old chestnut 'Titania does not exist' ? I claim that anyone unspoiled by deep thoughts would assent to it, owing precisely to the fact that 'Titania' does not name anything. Russell's reduction is just the ticket provided there is an appropriate definite description close at hand. But on Strawson's accounting the assertion is neither true nor false because 'Titania' is 'not about anything'. This will not do.

On the Strawsonian assumption that meanings are one thing and reference another, proper names have something like a Fregean sense, and by availing ourselves of this point we might show that the sentence is true, not valueless. This is Searle's plan.

The idea is to go along with the Russell-Frege idea of existence as a 'second-order' concept, that is to say, a quantificational concept, and then, in order to apply a quantifier to 'Titania', to construe the name as expressing a *concept*, i.e. a Fregean propositional function of one variable (Searle 1969: 165). If this is done, 'Titania' is not used to refer (which of course would presuppose her existence by Strawson's and Searle's principle), but in virtue of its having sense, can contribute to the complex predicate expressing the cocept.

Using this somewhat unclear idea our puzzling assertion is rendered 'there does not exist an x such that x = (the concept) Titania', which we might all assert as true. The trouble with this analysis is that it is open to all the criticisms we made of Fregean senses, although it does seem to be Strawsonian in spirit.

A simpler way is just to construe proper names as predicates that apply to one case, if at all. Predicates, as I commented earlier, normally apply but do not refer (Chapter 1, §3). Then 'Pegasus exists' becomes the false sentence 'there exists an x such that x is a pegasus [or x pegasizes]' and 'there is no x such that x is a pegasus' is true. This was Quine's (1953: 7f) way of handling such cases twenty years before Searle wrote. I shall return to it later.

6. Glosses and objections

Russell was one of the first to define the basic notions of a theory of reference. There are four extensional word–thing relations, and one (with some fudging) meaning relation.

(a) Reference is a relation of logically proper names to particulars, and logically proper names are precisely the nondisquotable singular terms.

(b) Quantification is indefinite reference (syntactically, it is an operator on sentences) exemplified by 'a man', 'some man', 'any man', 'the men' and so forth.

(c) Denoting is a fuzzy relation between definite descriptions and unspecified objects. Descriptions are incomplete symbols, have meaning only within contexts, and are eliminable in favor of quantified sentences. Ordinary names are substitutes for definite descriptions and they denote, but do not refer. They are not logically proper names since they do not refer in immediate acquaintance. Ordinary names and descriptions are disquotable. Denotation of descriptions and ordinary names resembles purported reference.

(d) Correspondence is a relation of sentences to facts; correspondence is not reference as sentences are not proper names and have no objects.

In view of the theory of denoting, these four reduce to three: reference, quantification and correspondence.

Reference of demonstratives in acquaintance is essentially causal (Russell 1948: 114). This is the closest Russell gets to a theory of the connection of words to things.

Application of predicates to particulars is, in Russell's atomism, double-sided. Russell is a realist, not a nominalist, and the components of facts which are correlated to predicates are universals grasped by the mind. So application may be understood as in (2) of Chapter 1, §3, including an agent. On the other hand, from a strictly atomistic point of view, application is just correspondence of a sentence containing the predicate to some fact in acquaintance.

Correspondence of sentence to fact is semiotical. I do not know how else to construe the Wittgensteinian metaphor of picturing; Russell himself says the relation is based on a structural similarity of sentence to fact, which is a kind of iconicity. If so, sentences are signs, a theory which leads to some confusing conjecture about false facts in order to avoid the topic of belief. This faintly Lockean quandary gradually forces the notion of belief into the open in Russell's epistemology.

Meaning, in Russell's atomism, is found in the atomic fact, a theory similar to a current view that meanings of sentences are truth conditions (Davidson 1967). Definite descriptions and abbreviating ordinary names are analyzable in quantificational terms. And, keeping in mind the principled reducibility of knowledge by description to acquaintance, the meanings (in virtue of which they are meaningful) are components of objective facts (see §§ 2 and 3).

This suggests a recasting of Frege's idea of the sense of terms. The sense of an ordinary name might be thought of not as a psychological entity (although the mind grasps it in understanding the word); and not as an abstract platonic entity. Sense is an ingredient of the conditions that make a sentence, in which the name is represented as an analyzed description, true to facts.

If Frege were to adopt such a notion, and if he were consistently to take names to be abbreviated descriptions, the result would be a variation of the idea that sense is a mode of presentation of an object, the mode of presentation being precisely the checking out of naming conditions expressed in a description.

The central criticism of atomism is its circularity. A fact is just what corresponds point-to-point to an atomic sentence. This is as pretty a piece of arguing from logic to reality as exists in philosophy – ancient, medieval or modern. It violates Commandment II: it assumes much of what is at issue in both reference theory and theory of knowledge in one fell swoop.

The same tendency shows itself in the theory of descriptions, which is supposed to show why you cannot substitute at will in belief sentences: 'Scott' for the 'author of *Waverly*' in the belief sentence 'George IV wished to know whether Scott was the author of *Waverly*'. If the description is analyzed there is nothing to substitute for. Russell thinks this affords an adequate *syntactical* block to illicit substitution.

However, this is false, as it turns out that the reasons you cannot make substitutions, for Russell, are really semantical and intuitive, not syntactical. Here's why.

Proposition 14.15 in *Principia Mathematica* allows substitution for unanalyzed descriptions; for instance, substitution '*b*' for the description 'the *x* such that *F(x)*', yielding '*F(b)*'. This is just Russell and Whitehead's formalization of common mathematical practice. Why not allow the same in belief sentences? The quantificational analysis 'there exists an *x* such that for every *y* etc.' does not nicely lay out a term to substitute for, as Russell says. But why not substitute directly for 'the *x* . . .' in the description? Why all the fuss? There is nothing in the *syntax* to prevent substitution for belief sentences any more than there is in sentences in mathematics. The trouble is the intensionality of belief, which is not a syntactical trouble.

In 'On denoting' itself Russell says (1905: 32) that substitutions can be made for definite descriptions that have primary occurrence (see the discussion following (1) in §4) in belief sentences, while not the secondary. But this is a semantical distinction with no grounds other than intuition. Descriptive phrases are complete in primary occurrence, they *name*: and in this respect they match their completeness in mathematical logic. Take 'George IV wanted to know of the author of *Waverly* whether he was Scott'. Here the description has a primary occurrence, and the substitution 'Scott' is allowable. The result is 'George IV wanted to know of Scott whether he was Scott'. There is nothing strangely trivial about this sentence as there is about 'George wanted to know whether Scott was Scott'.

The upshot is that substitution gets blocked when the user becomes aware of an intensional or opaque (or oblique) context in his belief reports, not when he sees that a Russell type of analysis would dissolve the subtituend. Russell gives no explanation beyond that of ordinary intuition. An intensional context is an intensional context, so be wary of substituting into it. We are to use the puzzling intensionality to explain the intensionality. Do not substitute if you cannot substitute![7]

If truth in a reductive, atomist framework is correspondence, there can be no error. In acquaintance, immediate perception must be infallible. This does not square with the psychology of perception; error there cannot be explained by correspondence to false facts, which is a wholly unintelligible idea.

What can be false, however, is perceptual belief. This is exactly the position to which Russell is pushed in later writings (1940, 1948). Truth and falsity attach to beliefs. This greatly complicates the possibility of a correspondence theory. But truth aside, Russell's switch to belief heralds a matching switch in puzzles about intentional attitudes. Let me explain.

Syntactical or other analyses of belief sentences might be supplanted by an analysis of belief. Issues presented by belief sentences such as substitutivity get shifted over to psychology. While the objects of belief, for Russell, are still external facts, belief itself, he claims, is a mind/brain state or assemblage of states (1948: 145). This is no theory, but it suggests, even promises, another way of looking at belief and hence possibly of p-reference itself. We shall pursue this possibility later after clearing some ground.

Finally the description theory of ordinary names will not stand up, as Russell himself saw (1948: 77–9). Most of our knowledge is by description, and we describe things in different ways. 'Piccadilly', for instance, does not name any simple factual constituent (we know it is not a logically proper name) and has a different significance for you than it has for me. Words are ambiguous: 'When one person uses a word, he does not mean by it the same thing another person does by it. . . . The meaning you attach to your words must depend on the nature of the objects you are acquainted with.' If he holds firmly to the view that descriptions are the only meaningful designative expressions (logically proper names and names except as abbreviations of descriptions are meaningless), this already compromises Russell's doctrine of definite descriptions. 'Piccadilly' simply does not have the same associated description for you as it does for me.

Names are not abbreviations of descriptions to which they

correspond uniquely. 'The dull Bavarian . . .' and 'the drunk in the street . . .' perhaps both describe Schmid only. Examples of multiple descriptions abound, and we shall exhibit some of them as we go along.[8]

Couple the collapse of the simple picture theory of truth with that of the descriptional theory of names and the sharp split Russell made between logically proper names and others gets fuzzy. Perhaps many names (such as I suggested in 'that is Susan') are immediately demonstrative, or perhaps, even, all of them are Strawsonian, or uniquely referring terms. If so, we would recover disquotation, but of course lose the striking qualities of several phases of Russell's thought.

The biggest loss of all is perhaps the ingenuity of Russell's methods for 'Pegasus': 'Pegasus' might be empty while yet 'Pegasus does not exist' be true.

CHAPTER 5

Truth Without Reference

1. Semantics and paradox

According to Frege, reference and truth are fixed entities grasped by a passive user of language. In Russell's theory, reference is grounded in acquaintance with sense data and truth is a picturing of the fact. For one, truth is a correlate of an abstract semantical relationship, as is the object of a referring term, while for the other the connections are epistemic. Neither offers an analysis of 'truth' or of 'reference' (Russell's treatment of 'denotation' is not an exception as denotation is not reference).

In Tarski's remarkable theory (1931) we get truth in terms of a spare ontology that avoids both suspect objects and gratuitous epistemology. His semantics, like Frege's, is limited to exact, formal languages; but he restricts himself to extensional concepts. Functions, for instance, are not concepts but ordered n-tuples out of a domain of individuals. The True and the False disappear. Truth is a predicate of sentences, not an object, and like reference it is disquotational; roughly, 'S' is true if and only if S. In its application to mathematics his semantics is metaphysically neutral; but as one interested in philosophical problems of science, he insists that truth is grounded in the actual physical world.

Rudolf Carnap, that great champion of logical empiricism, continues a Tarskian type semantics for Fregean ends, and attempts to reduce the senses and thoughts of Frege's repertoire to nonsemantical terms. Unfortunately he has little to contribute to reference, and fails to capture everything intensional. However, there is more to be learned from his lapses than from the pallid successes of many others.

As to Tarski, two initial constraints on his theory are (i) to avoid

89

epistemological traps, in particular ineffable correspondences between sentences and facts or states of affairs; and (ii) to eliminate all undefined semantical and intentional notions such as meaning, belief etc. Truth and the rest are to be explained, not assumed.

There is no good way not to violate (ii) right at the outset, since we are going to need a working idea of reference in order to follow the way to the concept of truth. It is best to keep disquotation in mind as a model despite the fact that we have no nonsemantical analysis of it. We shall probe the idea somewhat more deeply than heretofore in §3.

How can a notion of truth be reached using a stingy set of concepts constrained by (i) and (ii)? Tarski's answer is this: by availing ourselves of the tools of logic itself plus Aristotle's dictum:

> To say of what is that it is not, or of what is not that it is, is false; while to say of what is that it is, or of what is not that it is not, is true.

> (Metaphysics Γ, 7, 27)

Thus the idea is that to say a sentence or proposition is true is just to say it. A couple of readings of this dictum among others that might come to mind, using Tarski's favorite example, are:

(0) it is true that snow is white [saying it is true] is the same as [just saying] snow is white

and

(1) 'snow is white' is true if and only if snow is white.

(0) and (1) are intuitively faithful to Aristotle and informally say about the same thing. What they say is not a theory; but the simple idea that saying a sentence is true is just saying it reveals the spirit of the theory. It affords a characterization of truth by cases and a truth criterion as well. What could be clearer than the condition of being white snow as a criterion of the truth of 'snow is white' ?

The first has certain advantages, one of them being that if truth and falsity are of propositions we shall not need a truth theory for each language, English, Chinese, set theory etc., for presumably they all express the same propositional content one way or another. But the second avoids propositions or any hint of intensions, which we gladly accept as a boon. Relation (1) exemplifies Tarski's Aristotle, the version we shall study.

90

Let us attempt to generalize from 'snow is white' to any sentence S in English:

(2) 'S' is true if and only if S.

Superficially this has the mark of a definition already (note it is a form of disquotation on a par with p-reference) and has the pleasing advantage of relying on no notions other than sentence, name of sentence and a logic connective. 'True' is entered as a predicate of a sentence whose subject is the name of a sentence on the left; and the sentence on the right of the equivalence is the explicans of 'true' in context. No epistemic gap, propositions, concepts, correspondences or acquaintances are involved. Will it lead anywhere?

Assuming it does, I hasten now to warn of peril lurking in (1). As it stands, without safeguards additional to (i) and (ii), the infant theory will be inconsistent.

Suppose we confine our energies to English and allow any grammatical expressions of it including semantical terms. Thus sentences like 'some statements in psychology are true, but not all are meaningful' is well within the linguistic repertoire of ordinary users. Suppose, further, that (2) might enjoy some restatement such as 'Tarski's favorite sentence is true if and only if snow is white'.

But now we sense trouble, and the trouble is in allowing 'true' and 'false' to be terms in the same language as the one for which we are seeking a theory. Our laxity leads to the paradox of the liar.[1]

In stark form the paradox takes the following shape. Consider the sentence below labeled (S) in which 'false' occurs and is predicated of (S) itself.

(S) (S) is false.

By disquotation, (2),

'(S) is false' is true if and only if (S) is false.

But since '(S) is false' is just (S), we get

(S) is true if and only if (S) is false

which is contradictory.

This unwholesome result is a consequence of (a) allowing the terms 'true' and 'false' to apply to sentences in which the terms themselves occur; and (b) allowing self-reference: '(*S*)' is the name of a sentence that is about itself in (*S*).

Now the paradox evidently can be blocked by proscribing inclusion of semantical terms, in particular 'true' and 'false', in the language for which we are seeking a concept of truth. We are to allow no expressions to say of themselves that they are true or false.

So let *L* be a fragment of English. Ban item (*S*) from it, together with all other sentences that include 'true' and 'false'. The effect is that if you cannot say or write 'true' or 'false' at all in *L*, you cannot say it or write it in sensitive spots; hence a truth value term can do no logical harm. Semantical terms including 'true' and 'false' are to be available only to the language used to talk about *L*.

L is called the object language and the language we use to talk about it is the metalanguage.[2] Call this language *M*. By habit we already observe a basic practice of marking off the mention of an expression from its use by flying single quotes or by syntactical descriptions like 'Tarski's favorite sentence'. These conventions are enough to remind us of what is talking about what and of where to draw the line not to be crossed by 'true' and other semantical terms.

By contrast, although (*S*) is about a sentence (namely itself), the object language–metalanguage distinction is not observed: (*S*) allows a forbidden occurrence of 'false'. So does the contradictory sentence.

As we shall soon see, *L* must be an exact, formal language. It might be a phrase structure language closer to actual English than the predicate calculus, but never mind this suggestion for the moment. *M* will include translations of all of the sentences (purged as heretofore ordered) of *L*, the means for expressing both semantical and syntactical facts about *L* and a deductive apparatus at least as strong as that of *L*. In this chapter I will not refer to *M*, but simply use it, understanding that it is English and meets the foregoing requirements.

Disquotation of each individual quoted sentence of *L* already provides both a translation and a truth theory of sorts. Simply enumerate the metasentences of *M* expressing truth conditions for sentences in *L*, imitating the listing of proper names and descriptions of Chapter 1. All that is necessary is that we are able to generate the expressions of *L* and tell which ones in the generation are declarative sentences. For exact language this is easy; for natural languages it is not. But let us try.

'Abel is a man' is true if and only if Abel is a man
'Lady Ottoline is pretty' is true if and only if Lady Ottoline is pretty

Each one of these sentences is 'valid' (Tarski 1933: 404), i.e. true intuitively, and might be considered by some (but not by Tarski) to be analytically or logically true.

As a theory, this one is not fancy and is not a theory at all unless you are willing to count an unstructured system consisting of an infinite list of axioms as a theory. Each item is an axiom in itself as it is a priori and valid.

But since we have got disquotation might we not rest with (2) as a theory of truth in imitation of the theory of p-reference in Chapter 1, §2? A requirement of a definition of this sort is that it adhere to the Aristotelian dictum. What this means is that every sentence in the metalanguage such as (1) – every one of the original 'axioms' in the initial 'theory' – become a theorem of the sought-after theory. Tarski (1931) expresses this requirement as a *material adequacy* condition: any adequate theory of truth must entail all instances of the following pattern:

   (T) X is true in L if and only if S

where 'S' is replaced by a sentence in L and 'X' is a name of it in the metalanguage. Note that here 'X' and 'S' are not quantifiable variables; they are schematic letters that stand for places one can insert sentences (like 'snow is white' for 'S' and ' "snow is white" ' for 'X'). Note that all the replacements made in (T) come out like (2), that is to say, they are disquotations. To see the significance of this suppose (T) were annotated this way: 'where "X" is a name of a sentence of L and "S" is a translation of it into the metalanguage M'. Then if L were French and M English, we might have

'La neige est blanche' is true in L if and only if snow is white.

And again, we might have (L being English)

'Snow is white' is true in L if and only if columnar ice crystals are white.

In the first case we have a translation, which presupposes a notion of sameness of meaning; and in the second we have something like indirect disquotation (Chapter 1) which also presupposes synonymy. Instead, the official annotation forces literal disquotation.

Thus strict disquotation sidesteps the semantics of 'same meaning' (following constraint (ii)) but of course restricts M to be English, or whatever, if L is.

2. *The concept of truth*

Tarski's fundamental idea in the theory of truth is *satisfaction* of predicates which is essentially the same as application of predicates to objects as in (2) of Chapter 1, §2: *a* satisfies '*Fx*' provided that *a* is *F*. To get at 'true' and 'false', he extends 'satisfies' to all sentences in steps that accord with their constituent structure. He then defines 'true' and 'false' explicitly by way of satisfaction: a true sentence is satisfied by all objects and a false sentence by none. Finally, he shows that the definition implies all instances of condition (*T*).

This overall attack calls for the familiar syntactical chore of describing the logical grammar of L in M. The definition of 'sentence' is recursive, and the definition of 'satisfaction' of sentences by objects follows the inductive pattern imposed by the definition of 'sentence'.

L is to be the language of a first-order predicate calculus typically studied in logic I (logic clothed in English). Its basis is a fund of symbols: of individual variables, $x_1, x_2, \ldots$; of constants (singular terms), $a_1, a_2, \ldots$; predicates (general terms of any finite number of places), $F, G, H, \ldots$; and logical symbols: (,), – (not), ∨ (or) and ∃ (existential quantifier).

Sentences S of L are defined in the usual way: Individual variables and constants are *terms*, and are the only terms. An *atomic sentence* is an expression '$F(t_1, \ldots t_j)$' where each '*t*' is a term, and *j* is the number of places of '*F*'. An atomic sentence is a *sentence*; if S is a sentence, its negation $-S$ is a *sentence*; if S and T are sentences, their disjunction $S \vee T$ is a *sentence*; if S is a sentence, then $(\exists x_i)S$ is a *sentence*; nothing else is a *sentence*.

The universal quantifier is defined contextually in the familiar way as are the other truth functional connectives. A variable is *bound* if it is within the scope of a quantifier, and *free* otherwise. A sentence having no free variables is *closed*, otherwise *open*. Note in particular that an atomic sentence can contain both free variables and constants.

I shall suppose the reader is familiar with all these concepts.

Unlike Frege's (1879) presentation of predicate logic this one is formal; it makes no use of semantical terms in the definitions. Terms and predicates are displayed in lists, as above, not in terms of a presupposed semantics.[3] We have here no unanalyzed notion of reference of name to object or of predicate to concept. Of course we do have intended meanings of these symbols in mind which we might as well suppose are given by disquotation, but only as aids for tracking the technicalities. *L* is ultimately about some universe of objects called the *domain D*. Its symbols are interpreted to refer or apply to these objects under some relation *R*, the *interpretation*. We are supposing these matters have been or can be fixed temporarily by disquotation.

Now on to satisfaction. We need to be able to discuss satisfaction of sentences of arbitrary complexity. This is not quite straightforward owing to variation in the number of occurrences of free variables in sentences.

Informally, the object Russell satisfies '*x* is a philosopher' (equivalently, '*x* is a philosopher' applies to Russell) because, according to the sense of the *dictum*, Russell is a philosopher. The pair of objects Plato and Aristotle satisfies '*x* is older than *y*'; the triple Chicago, Des Moines and Cleveland satisfies '*x* is between *y* and *z*'. To manage cases where the number of predicate places goes up to *n*, we use infinite sequences.

To illustrate the idea for a sequence of objects $\sigma = o_1, o_2, \ldots$, suppose the predicate being discussed is 'between(x_5, x_1, x_{90})'; then what we have to explain is what it means for this infinite sequence σ to satisfy a three-place (finite sequence) predicate. This is done by picking out the right o_i's from the infinite sequence according as their subscripts match those of the *x*s. Thus the fifth element o_5 of the sequence matches 'x_5', o_1 matches 'x_1', and so forth. Matching of this sort is an *assignment*. So we say 'σ satisfies "between (x_5, x_1, x_{90})"' just in case o_5 is between o_1 and o_{90} (that is to say, just in case the objects assigned to the variables are in the relation of betweenness to each other)'. In particular if o_5 = Chicago, o_1 = Des Moines and o_{90} = Cleveland, the sequence satisfies 'between'.

The strategy does not include constants and the objects they map into under the interpretation. If '*a*' is one of the constants, we do not wish to give it an assignment according to a sequence σ as above, but one that accords with a prior interpretation, whatever that might have been. If '*a*' is interpreted as *o*, its bearer, then *o* is assigned to '*a*'. Given disquotation, *a* is assigned to '*a*'. Assignments to variables will vary with the sequence σ, while constants must be fixed to their objects as set up in the interpretation, independently of σ.

The technique can be summarized by using a function σ ', for each σ, from terms to objects defined as follows:

> If a term *t* is a variable 'x_i', then $\sigma '(t) = o_i$.
> If a term *t* is a constant 'a_i', then σ '(*t*) = the object associated to 'a_i' in the interpretation, specifically a_i if the relation is disquotation.

This assignment arrangement, given an interpretation of constants, is a *reference scheme*.

Now the definition of 'satisfaction' – which, you will note, is done without sneaking in any semantical terms. Let *F* be the interpretation of the predicate '*F* '.

(a) A sequence σ satisfies '$F(t_1, \ldots, t_n)$' if and only if ($\sigma '(t_1)$, . . ., $\sigma '(t_n)$) is *F*;

(b) σ satisfies a sentence −*S* if and only if it does not satisfy *s*;

(c) σ satisfies *S* ∨ *T* if and only if it satisfies *S* or it satisfies *T*;

(d) σ satisfies ($\exists x_i$)*S* if and only if there is a sequence τ that is identical to σ, except possibly in the *i*th place, such that τ satisfies *S*.

Clause (a) differs from the other clauses in that it is really a summary of a finite number of clauses, one for the monadic predicates, one for the dyadic predicates and so on. Term (b) on the other hand is quite general, and so are the others.

Note that if '*F* ' in (a) has no occurrences of variables, then the first part of the definition of 'σ '' is simply not used.

Clauses (b) and (c) explain themselves.

Clause (d) can be explained in terms of an illustration. Suppose that a sentence is '*F*(. . . x_i . . .)' where '*F* ' might be very complex (not atomic) and the ellipses mark places for any assortment of free variables and constants. Then if τ satisfies '*F* ', even though the *i*th object in it might not be the same as the corresponding object in σ, σ satisfies '(x_i)*F* '. For example, the object sequence τ = 2, 1, . . . satisfies 'greater than (2, x_2)' and therefore the sequence σ = 2, 99, . . . satisfies '(x_2) (greater than (2, x_2))'.

In brief, a sequence satisfies a sentence if and only if the result of substituting a symbol representing o_i for each free variable x_i in the sentence is intuitively true (this is an informal explanation, not a part of the definition). If S has no free variables (is a closed sentence) then it can easily be shown that any sequence you pick satisfies S, if S holds (Tarski 1931: 194ff). As an example, if an atomic sentence contains only constants in its argument places it is satisfied (or not satisfied as the case may be) vacuously by any assignment of objects to variables, since for any sequence σ, σ' will have no variable arguments.

Finally, a sentence S (without free variables) of L is *true* with respect to the interpretation over D if and only if every sequence σ over D satisfies S.

A sentence S of L is *false* with respect to the domain D if and only if there is no sequence that satisfies S.

From this theory one can show that condition (T) is satisfied, if reference is disquotation.

Using only the assumption that D is nonempty, it is possible to show that every sentence is either true or false (law of the excluded middle), that not both a sentence and its negation are true (law of noncontradiction), which of course depends in part on the language being semantically closed, and so forth (Tarski 1931). In short, truth and falsity have been explained in a way that allows them to play the roles we want in logic.

Thus Frege's True, False and his idea of a predicate expressing a function in intension are all tamed; they fall to analysis in terms of a syntactically defined language and a metalanguage which absorbs extensional semantics into the concept of satisfaction for a given reference scheme.

3. Where is reference?

Now what about reference? Tarski's own answer, as interpreted by Field (1972) in a very influential article, is that reference is disquotation of names. Will this simple account of reference be any good for truth theory?

A curious thing about Tarski's theory is that it has come to form a basic chapter in pure mathematical logic, while his intention in 1931 was to give a definition consistent with logical empiricism. Tarski evidently wanted to serve both purposes at once, although he was certainly aware of the distinction. He indeed had applications to logic in mind (see my note above as to his demonstrations of the laws of logic); yet he also saw his work as explaining truth in science and as being compatible with extensionalist philosophy, including the doctrine of the unity of science.[4]

To put the matter quite plainly, the topic of reference is irrelevant in mathematical logic; and, it turns out, unexplained disquotation is inadequate for philosophy of science, i.e. to the purpose of explaining the semantics of reference and of illuminating language, mind, and epistemology: Tarski's version provides no account of the linkage of word to thing. Here's why I say this.

We said that given a domain of objects D, an interpretation R is a function from constants and predicates to objects and classes of objects. R is total, i.e. there are no empty names or vacuous predicates for any language to which a Tarskian truth theory is to be applicable. Writers use 'interpretation' ambiguously, and so shall I, sometimes for the pair consisting of D and R, and sometimes for R alone.

There are two avenues to interpretation, one with an eye to logic and the other with an eye to empirical science (see Tarski 1931: 199; Tarski and Vaught 1957: 82). On the second, L (a fragment of English squeezed into predicate calculus notation) has its ordinary significance; or, if not ordinary, a *fixed* significance, whence the treatment of L just given in the truth definition should be considered to be an abstraction from a language-world whole. In such wise, disquotation, which I earlier asked be kept in mind to avoid our getting lost in the technicalities, is in some sense the 'correct' interpretation for English. Without it you cannot satisfy convention (T). For instance, if 'a' refers to b and a is not b, then a sequence satisfies '$F(a)$' if and only if b is F, which is no instance of (T).

A definition of truth for a language under a fixed interpretation, presumably the correct one, is said to be *absolute*.

Taking the other avenue, for logic, L has variable significance, which means it is subject to interpretation of various sorts at various times. If you think of a language in this way it is separable from nonlinguistic domains, but may be linked up to objects *suppositiously*. For instance if the constant 'a' is 'Russell' we might conceivably want to have it name Plato or the number 1 or a 90° rotation of a rectangle. '=' could be interpreted as identity, congruence, loves or father of.

A definition of truth of a language given one of several intended interpretations is *relative* to the interpretation. An interpretation in which the sentences come out true is a *model* or *possible world* for *L*, of which more in due course. Relative interpretations figure strongly in Quine's views on reference, and we shall return to them in Chapter 7. At the moment our focus is on Tarski's absolute concept of truth.

We, too, may think of our *L*, being a formalized part of English, as having an interpretation in the actual world: 'philosopher' about philosophers, 'Russell' about Russell and so forth. If so, the theory we just presented is also absolute.

An absolute theory must entail all instances of condition (T), and this is an extremely important mark of its difference from relative truth.

Now reference is a semantical concept (but only degenerately so in model theory) and by constraint (ii) it cannot be assumed in an unanalyzed listing for a semantical theory of truth. Listing syntactic terms is formally computational (see note 3). But listing disquotations is not arbitrary. There is good reason to list ' "Russell", Russell' rather than ' "Russell", George Bush' or ' "Russell", Mt Whitney', for the idea is to conform to real English.

Tarski proposes to explicate 'reference' in terms of satisfaction. The reason, we should say, is to reduce the idea in a way that presupposes no semantical notions; and at the same time to capture standard English. The basic idea is that a name *N* refers to an object *o* if and only if *o* satisfies a predicate of a 'particular type', namely '$x = P$', where '*P*' is *N*.[5]

Thus, for illustration, suppose there is one monadic predicate, '*F*' in *L*; then the definition says that a name *N* refers to *o* if and only if *o* satisfies '*x* is *F* and "*F*" = *N*'. Combining this with the definition of satisfaction, we get that *N* refers to *o* if and only if *o* = *F* and '*F*' is *N*.

The full definition for *L* with a finite number of names (Field 1972) is

(1) To say that *N* refers to *o* is just to stipulate that either *o* is Abel and *N* is 'Abel', or ,. . ., or *o* is Russell and *N* 'Russell' . . ..

We thus get disquotation via satisfaction, a clause for each name, parallel to writing a clause for each predicate in (a) on page 96 –

and tantamount to our (1) in Chapter 1, §2, with the substitutional existential quantifier dropped in favor of a list of alternatives.

It is not absolutely clear that (1), under any construal of Tarski's 'particular type', succeeds in eliminating the intentional component in reference alluded to several paragraphs back, since the definiendum simply summarizes linguistic practice. There is no trace of purporting, which we phrased into our condition (*R*). If purporting is implicit in the original listing, his constraint (ii) is again violated since it is still in (1); if it is not covered in the explication Tarski has missed the pre-analytic idea of reference.

Field mentions an analogy between a theory of valence in chemistry that defines 'valence' by a list,

> the valence of chemical x is the number y if and only if x is a and y is n (where a is an element and n is a number), or x is b and y is m or . . . or . . . etc.,

and a disquotational theory. Both definitions are extensionally adequate, but neither the chemical nor the semantical tell a thing about the anatomy or the nature of the phenomena involved. A useful definition of 'valence' should tell what valence is; and Field's view (and mine) is that a theory of reference is hopeless without saying what it is, and this must include the constitutive user as agency of linkage and p-reference.

This puts us back to square one. However, there is some gain of insight into truth. Suppose we had a theory of truth that entailed all sentences of the kind instanced by the following:

(2) 'Russell is a philosopher' is true if and only if the object named by 'Russell' belongs to the class determined by the predicate 'is a philosopher'.

(Davidson 1979: 298)

It seems obvious (to me, anyway) that this should qualify as a correspondence theory as it makes truth of a sentence consist in parts of the sentence referring and applying to nonlinguistic objects in the actual world. Now assume disquotation. Then we can derive from (2) an instance of Tarski's condition (*T*):

(*T*) 'Russell is a philosopher' is true if and only if Russell is a philosopher.

Field (1972) points out that the opposite holds; so (1) follows from

(*T*) under the assumption of disquotation and vice versa. Therefore, given disquotation, correspondence truth and Tarski–Aristotle truth seem to be equivalent. The linkage of sentence to fact is thus to be found in disquotation, and with the latter in mind condition (*T*) is far from trivial or empty.[6]

Tarski's account of truth has come under fire from Michael Dummett on grounds related to Strawson's points. If truth applies to statements, not to sentence types, then the semantical concept of truth applied to ordinary language does not catch what is meant by pre-analytic 'truth' (Dummett 1958) Conditions given by truth tables, for instance, do not succeed in representing assertion conditions of compound statements in all cases. According to the usual truth table treatment of 'and', '*A* and *B*' is true under the condition that both '*A*' and '*B*' are true, and this accords with one of the meanings of 'and' in ordinary language, for you can assert '*A* and *B*' when and only when you can assert '*A*' and assert '*B*'. But asserting '*A* or *B*' has a different meaning than asserting '*A*' or asserting '*B*' (ibid.: 54), for you can exercise the former without being committed to the latter. You can assert that it is snowing or raining without asserting that it is snowing or asserting that it is raining. This strikes at the heart of Tarski's recursion clauses for 'satisfaction'. Of course one might want, as we shall see, to keep the matter of truth separate from assertability.

A deeper point is that truth and falsity as predicates of assertions can be assigned only 'in virtue of something of which it [a statement] is either true or false' (ibid.: 66). This something is not an abstract condition but a state of affairs, a fact of the world that justifies the assertion. And to be so justified in making a statement we must have a method that warrants assertability of it.

I take this to mean that truth of a tokened sentence, unlike truth of a sentence type in logic and mathematics (see Chapter 4, §5), depends on assertability; and the latter involves conditions that justify. Consequently no truth without justification.

This view adverts to a concept of correspondence which can be interpreted variously in either Russell, Field's Tarski or any other style indifferently. But the main thing is that the very idea of truth in natural language contains that of justification. One does not justify an assertion by declaring it true, but one declares it true in virtue of a method of justification. A statement can be asserted only when it is effectively decidable, i.e. when its truth or falsity can be established by a mechanical or algorithmic method. In due course I shall attempt to reconcile a Tarskian type of theory of truth with Dummett's viewpoint.

Although disquotation still remains incompletely analyzed as an account of reference, I still want to follow Hill (1987), insisting that disquotation is a necessary part of any theory of normally used names. Condition (*R*) still holds, and the quality of purportedness will turn out to be closely related to decidability.

4. Carnap and logical truth

Two attitudes have been taken toward reference from within a Tarskian framework. One is to keep reference as a conventional, analytic relation and treat semantics as a kind of pure mathematical theory related to natural language semantics as mathematical physics is to descriptive physics. This attitude, which goes back to Rudolf Carnap, comes in for brief review in this section. A descendant of Carnap's pure semantics, 'California semantics', is reviewed in Chapter 6.

The other attitude is to drop Tarskian truth and reference altogether except as an instrumentalist thesis. This is W. V. Quine's view, and will be taken up in Chapter 7.

In Rudolf Carnap's great work in semantics (1942, 1956) a minor goal, though major for us, is explication of reference as an *a priori concept* in pure semantics. The fact is, however, that Carnap wavers in the face of his task, opting, in some passages, for a picture of disquotation as an analytic relation, while in the end falling back on a list wherein reference is tacit and unexplained. However that might be, reference is not his great mission. Carnap's aim is nothing less than to found a complete semantics of idealized languages. The concepts of reference and truth form the basis of a theory meant to explain meaning, including propositions, predicate intensions, sense, belief, the analytic and paradoxes of identity, among other points, using extensional tools only.

As a deductive science Carnap's pure semantics is analytic while empirical studies of language are synthetic. Until recent times the distinction of analytic from synthetic, following Hume and Kant, was based on matching or not matching meanings in the mind; but in Carnap and logical empiricism it becomes one of logic, the analytic sentence being true by rule and convention and the synthetic by agreement with fact.

A germane example is disquotation. The apriorist would claim that each disquote ' "*a*" refers to *a*' is analytic because referring-to-*a* is part of the meaning of '*a*' understood as a name. Most philosophers of language would deny this; if the apriorist is right, however, he has an easy answer for us and a gap-filler for Tarski (who denied the analytic–synthetic distinction).

In his early thought Carnap (1937) took logic and mathematics to be purely syntactic, concerned with uninterpreted symbols and concatenations of them according to effective rules of formation and transformation. Even problems of metaphysics were to be replaced in a formal mode of talk, showing them up as either trivial or syntactically senseless.

But under Tarski's influence, Carnap's analysis (1942) became semantical analysis. Objects – individuals, properties and sets – come crowding in where pure syntax kept them out. For many questions in philosophy of logic and language are not syntactical. Truth is not, as Tarski showed; reference, application and meaning are not; and inductive logic, on Carnap's own approach (1951), is concerned with the confirmation of scientific hypotheses by evidential sentences, and 'confirmation' is a semantical term – roughly on a par with 'logical implication' in semantically interpreted deductive logic.

That semantics attracts objects is scarcely a novel perception, but for Carnap it is more than routine; for him it means trouble. Semantics, pure or not, deals in objects as well as words, and the real being of objects appealed to in a theory of meaning could undermine the positivist cause. How can he justify his appeal to abstract objects if ontology is forbidden as pseudo-philosophy?

His answer is in part instrumentalist and in part reductionist. His warrant for entertaining meanings as objects, for instance, is a principle of free choice, constrained in its exercise only by practical success in thought – with no metaphysical regrets. Thus if Carnap thinks his theory needs a concept or an object he uses it, provided only that it enable the theory. His ontology is purely pragmatic, not a discipline of the real. I shall call this Carnap's principle of choice. The principle will be amply illustrated later on. The reductionist part of the answer is displayed in the following program.

The characteristic feature of *Meaning and Necessity* (1956) is

Carnap's use of the concept logical truth for explicating inten-sionality. The lapses in execution of this program, as you have been groomed to expect, occur in his indecision about reference in particular and analyticity in general.

He presents the theory using an illustrative language S_1 (among others) which is about the same as our L of the last section. Carnap is not concerned with users or situations in his pure semantics. There is a metalanguage M, careful English, in which theory is expressed, and he assumes it satisfies Tarski-type conditions.

However, the semantical concepts of reference and truth for S_1 are not Tarski's, strictly speaking; and it is in the divergence from him that our interest in Carnap arises in this book. Reference is falteringly disquotational, and truth is defined in terms of it but without any use of the idea of satisfaction since all variables in S_1 are bound.

There are two initial sets of semantical rules, rules of *designation* and rules of *truth*. The domain of the language is given implicitly in the rules and consists of ordinary objects of daily life and their properties. He presents the rules of designation by example:

(1) (a) For constants (names): 's' is translated by 'Scott'
'w' is translated by 'Waverly'
etc.

    (b) For predicates: '*Hx*' _____ '*x* is a human being'
'*RAx*' _____ '*x* is a rational animal'
'*Fx*' _____ '*x* is featherless'
'*Bx*' _____ '*x* is a biped'
'*Axy*' _____ '*x* is an author of *y*'
etc.

It does not take deep logical insight to see that (a) is not disquotation and (b) is not application.

The rule of truth is not given fully, but only exemplified for simple cases:

(2) (a) An atomic sentence is *true* if the individual referred to by the name has the property referred to by the predicate;

    (b) 'True' and 'false' apply by truth tables to sentences compounded of atomic sentences in the familiar way.

There is no clause defining 'true' for quantified statements (however, see note 7 below).

Carnap needs a special clause for identity expressions:

> (c) If a term '*x*' refers to *o* and if '*y*' refers to *o'*, then '*x* = *y*' is *true* if and only if *o* = *o'*

As the reader may check, a complete statement of the basic clause (a), including truth for *n*-ary predicates, would obviate a separate clause (c). Observe also that 'refer' in (a) and (c) is used instead of the official 'designate' of rule (1), but this is not yet the time to worry.

Now on to the crucial idea of logical truth.

A condition parallel to Tarski's condition (*T*) but this time for '*L*(ogical)-truth', is Carnap's version of analyticity:

> (*L-T*) A sentence is *L*-true in a semantical system if and only if its truth follows from the semantical rules without any reference to fact.

> (1956: 10)

For example, tautologies are *L*-true because their truth follows from truth table rules and not from contingent facts.

Carnap points out that (*L-T*) could not itself appropriately be used as a basis for the definition he seeks since it is expressed in a metalanguage once removed from *M*, the *metametalanguage MM*. 'True' is defined for S_1 in *M* by (2); by contrast, if (*L-T*) were used, '*L*-true' would come to be defined within *MM* for a sentence of *M* that expresses the truth of a sentence of *L* (cf. Carnap 1942: 84). One of Carnap's expressed aims, of course, is characterization of 'analytic' for the language S_1, not for its metalanguage *M*.

An acceptable concept to this end is that of a state description *D*. A state description describes a possible state of affairs. One such description is the actual world, which consists of all the atomic facts (think of Russell, Chapter 4, §2, and Wittgenstein). Another description might describe a possible, nonactual world in which the properties red and green, say, are permuted; or brothers in our world are not brothers in the new; and so on.

Suppose that a collection of names with their objects and predicates with their sets is given for S_1 that is sufficient to define atomic sentences like the following: '*Fa*', '*Fb*', '*Fc*', '*Qa*', '*Qb*', '*Ra, b*', '*Sbc*') . . . .

A *state description* is a set of sentences of S_1 which contains for every atomic sentence of S_1 either that sentence itself or its negation, but not both, and no other sentences. For illustration, suppose that a system is limited to the atoms

Fa; *Fb*; *Qa*; *Qb*; *Ra, b*; *Rb, a*;

this assumes there are just the names '*a*' and '*b*' and the predicates '*F* ', '*Q*' and '*R*' in the system. Then a set consisting of just these elements themselves is a state description. Another such set is

Fa; -*Fb*; -*Qa*; *Qb*; -*Ra, b*; -*Rb, a*.

Next we want to explain what it means for any sentence of S_1 to 'hold' in an arbitrary state description *D*. This can be done inductively, but Carnap is content with examples and not a full definition. An atomic sentence *S* holds in *D* if it is an element of it; the negation of –*S* of a sentence holds in *D* if *S* is not in it; *S* ∨ *S'* holds in *D* if either one does; and so forth. A quantified sentence '(*x*)*Fx*' holds in *D* if all of the atomic sentences '*Fa*', '*Fb*' etc. hold in it.[7] A neat way to think of holding is this: *S* holds in description *D* if and only if the conjunction of the sentences of *D* implies *S*.

Exactly one state description contains atomic sentences true of the actual world (by clause (a) of (2)); this one is called 'the true state description'.

We are now ready for '*L*-true':

(3) A sentence *S* of S_1 is *L-true* if and only if *S* holds in every state description.

In simple terms, an *L*-true sentence is true no matter what conditions are the case. An *S* is *L*-false if it holds in no *D*, and factual if it holds in some but not all.

Relation (3) satisfies condition (*L-T*) and is properly rendered, as required, in *M*, not in a metametalanguage.

The chief tools in Carnap's reconstruction of extension and intension (the counterparts of Frege's reference and sense) are truth and *L*-truth. Briefly, Carnap analyzes 'same extension' for sentences, predicates and constants without relying on an a priori concept of extension. Thus two predicates '*Fx*' and '*Gx*' have the *same extension* if the universal sentence '(*x*) (*Fx* ≡ *Gx*)' is true, where '≡' means 'if and only if'. Next, by the principle of choice, an entity, the extension of a predicate, is identified as the class of all *F*-things.

Similarly, sentences have the same extension if they are true or false under the same truth condition, and the extension (object) of a sentence is its truth value, T or F, following Frege. Two names, 'x' and 'y', have the same extension if '$x = y$' is true; and the extension is just the individual object.

'Same intension' is defined in M for S_1 in a similar way using a concept of *L*-equivalence. Thus,

> A sentence S is *L-equivalent* to R just in the case where $S \equiv R$ is *L*-true.
>
> A predicate P is *L-equivalent* to Q just in the case where $P \equiv Q$ is *L*-true
>
> A name 'x' is *L-equivalent* to 'y' just in the case where '$x = y$' is *L*-true

This explicates analytic or necessary truth, necessary identity etc.

A term or a sentence has the *same intension* as another term or sentence in the case where they are *L*-equivalent. Thus the sentence $S \vee (R.S)$ has the same intension as $(S \vee R).S$: that is, by the above, $S \vee (R.S) \equiv (S \vee R).S$ holds in all state descriptions. In a system more complex than S_1, say arithmetic, any two true sentences such as '5 is a prime number' and '5 + 12 = 7' have the same intension, for both are *L*-true – their truth follows from the rules of the system – and hence they are *L*-equivalent.

Now to say two sentences have the same intension is one thing, while to say what that intension is, is another. Again using the principle of choice, *propositions* are selected as the intensions of sentences. Hence the sentences of the last paragraph having the same intension designate the same proposition.

The predicate 'human x' has the same intension as 'rational animal x', and both refer to the same *property*. Properties are the entities chosen to be intensions of predicates.

Note – an extremely important point – that synonymy of predicates is more than same intension or *L*-equivalence. Carnap says (1956: 15) we have to understand, from English, that 'Hx' and 'RAx' have the same meaning. This is no semantical rule of S_1. Therefore, there are *two* ingredients in sameness of intension read as 'synonymy': (a) *L*-equivalence and (b) synonymy of the terms in ordinary English. Using the abbreviations given in the rules of designation, (1):

(a) '*Hx*' is *L*-equivalent to '*Hx*'

and then since

(b) '*Hx*' is synonymous with '*RAx*'

the right-hand occurrence of '*Hx*' can be replaced by '*RAx*' yielding

(c) '*Hx*' has the same intension as '*RAx*'.

Expression (b) and the replacement of synonyms are informal and extralogical; they are not part of the formal apparatus of S_1.

Similarly, there are two ingredients in the same intension of names: logical truth and an informal synonymy. The shared intension, by the principle of choice, is an *individual concept*. Thus 'individual concept', like 'property', is an amalgam of 'same intension' and 'synonymy', the latter imported from outside the system S_1. To illustrate (for names it is easier to do nonsynonymy than synonymy): 'Cicero' is *L*-equivalent to 'Tully'; but the names are not intuitively synonymous, and therefore do not have the same intension.

Parallel to Frege's sense and reference of terms and sentences we now have individual concepts and individual objects; properties and classes; propositions and truth values. Going back over the recent definitions, we see that the ideas are developed extensionally, including that of state description, true state description and intensional sameness, at various linguistic levels. An uneasiness attaches (or should attach, perhaps) to the use of alien sameness of meaning or synonymy in (b), for predicates and names, and to the *ad hoc* admission of intensional objects. But discounting the latter lapses from strictly pure semantics, Carnap thus indeed explains sameness of extension and intension on the basis of the primitive semantical rules S_1 and the concept of state description.

An advantage of Carnap's extensional approach, if it would only work as intended, is that he can manage substitution in intensional contexts without falling back on such devices as Frege's indirect objects, Frege's senses as bearers in opaque settings.

Carnap needs no such device; for him, substitution term for term in intensional sentences depends on the sameness of intension (ibid.: 46–52). But sameness boils down to *L*-equivalence (overlooking the synonymy problem) which, in turn, is ultimately a purely extensional question of verifying the identity of ranges of sentences, i.e. stated descriptions. In Frege's philosophy, however, the legitimizing of substitution has to fall back on an intuitive matching of indirect objects.

Now let us worry specifically about alien sameness of meaning and, finally, about designation and reference.

Alien synonymy, as I have been calling it, is a topic of Quine's (1953) now classical criticism of the analytic–synthetic distinction. Let us assume that *L*-truth and *L*-equivalence are unassailable notions, (a) above, and look at the additional element of the synonymy of '*Hx*' and '*RAx*', (b) above. If (c) is true because the predicates mean the same (Carnap 1956: 4) and if it is claimed that same meaning is guaranteed by a definition, we have not really pinned down intension. For, Quine points out, the definition as written by the lexicographer is an empirical report of English usage. So 'same meaning' is explained by 'same meaning' and, to get out of the 0-radius circle, we are going to have to explain synonymy in 'terms relating to linguistic behavior' (Quine 1953: 24).

There is an issue here between acceptance of logical insight into ordinary language, i.e. taking the pre-analytic as self-justifying, and of insistence that there is no clear notion of 'same meaning' to be grasped or analyzed. It might be argued that alien sameness is a perfectly sound, commonly understood concept, and that an explanation in some sort of psychological terms is not impossible. So Quine's objection is not conclusive against the idea of synonymy. He must go further and show that no linguistic, psychological or other explication is possible in principle. He does, and the up-shot is his doctrine of indeterminacy of meaning, discussed in Chapter 7, which has extremely grave negative implications for the entire enterprise of semantics.

5. Is reference a priori?

What about the question of the analyticity of reference? To begin with, note that 'designation', Carnap's rule (1) in the last section, is not the same as 'reference' in his rule of truth for S_1, rule (2) in the last section.[8] (1) says nothing of objects, while (2) speaks of 'truth' directly in terms of objects. Neither (1) nor (2) is disquotational.

So, as a third notion, consider disquotation, ' "*a*" refers to *a*'.

From time to time Carnap claims the sentence is analytic: '. . . any expression of the form " '. . . designates . . .' " is an analytic statement provided the term ". . ." is a constant in an accepted framework' (1956: 217).[9] Moreover 'designates' in a certain coordinate language Carnap discusses (ibid.: 75ff) is evidently (informally) disquotational; but he never gives it an official definitional stamp. In a certain language S_2 Carnap (1942) explains designation by enumeration, essentially Field's construction of Tarski.

But on reflection Carnap sees that, if it is analytic, disquotation cannot be explicated in terms of L-truth, which applies to true sentences of S_1 (or the like) only. Quite simply, ' " 'a' refers a" is analytic' is in the *metametalanguage*, as is the condition $(L\text{-}T)$ above for L-truth in Carnap's system. So if you want analyticity, it must be on pre-analytic terms. But then negation of disquotation is *not contradictory*, has been shown in our discussion of causal reference as it appears in Locke's *An Essay Concerning Human Understanding* and in Russell's atomism. What Carnap settles for, then, is a list of translations (1) of constants into the metalanguage when writing in his official idiom, since disquotation cannot be construed as L-true. And what he gets in rule (1) is safely analytic (in the metalanguage M) since it is merely abbreviational. However, he shifts to reference in writing his rule of truth (2, a) for atomic sentences, and again in his rule for identity sentences since mere abbreviation, although indicating same reference (if any) does not introduce 'reference'.

It is moderately instructive, while also leading to my punch line, to see that it does not make any difference how Carnap conceives of reference so long as he uses the same word–object pairings (tacitly or not) for S_1. This does not mean truth is relative or that he is working in model theory wherein interpretations come and go. His semantical systems are word–object coupled units, so to speak, and reference is fixed, as in Frege. His languages are all pure and abstract and do not fuse with the world.

Further, one could simply eliminate clause (a) for the truth rule, choose one of the state descriptions as the true one, construe quantification as substitutional as we did in note 8, and rid pure semantics of reference altogether. For a truth definition in a system with quantifiers taken substitutionally needs no preliminary theory of reference (cf. Kripke 1977).

These reflections lead me to suggest that Carnap's pure semantics has nothing whatever to do with reference even if it is construed, as it is in some contemporary versions, as modeling actual natural language (see Chapter 6, §3). Reference (but, once again, not arbitrary mappings in model theory) is an empirical, synthetic relation.

CHAPTER 6

Reference and Speech Act

1. Understanding and use

From a naturalist's point of view, a good account of reference will be empirical, and that means a part of cognitive science. A good theory will entail instances of purported reference – items on our initial list in Chapter 1, §2, of disquoted names – and will explain the linkage of word to object. None of the theories we have examined, from Frege onwards, comes close to explaining this phenomenon. They all abstract from language as characteristic of people and societies to a stark, two-way, word-to-thing relation.

A block to deeper inquiry, even when the presence of people is acknowledged in studies of referring, meaning or asserting, is confusion of two semiotical roles. In Chapter 1, §2, I suggested 'user' for the person as repository of semantical knowledge, and 'user*' for him as a linguistic performer.[1] Purported reference and demonstrative reference reflect the distinction, for the one is marked by attitude and the other by act. Understanding a sentence *versus* asserting it (Strawson), and interpreting a sign versus using it (Peirce) also reflect the distinction.

The confusion comes of imagining that the notion of the active user* covers all there is of human involvement in referring. A large body of theory written during the past forty years takes reference to be a question of speech act, not of the inner intention of a user; or, less radically, that the intentional user role can be put to one side, as a minor part in a staged show.

As a consequence the very concept of reference is impoverished; the user is left to languish in the shadows of something called 'semantics', or otherwise is assimilated to the locutive user* in 'pragmatics'.[2] What happens (I shall exhibit the happening) is this:

semantics is left aside as a motley of rules and conditions that enable speech acts, rules emanating from a linguistic empyrean, not from a society of human users. Pragmatics is pushed center, its speech-actors the only players on the scene.

This is no parody. Susan Haack (1978) writes of a semantics deprived of users, who are the exclusive property (identified as users*) of pragmatics. Semantics, she suggests, has to do with what expressions 'do', and pragmatics with what persons do (ibid.: 70). She goes so far as to promote a slogan to the effect that words *denote* and persons *refer*. This slogan, taken seriously, not only discourages studies of linkage and intention in reference, but blocks interesting and perhaps even correct distinctions. I am thinking of our attempt in Chapter 1, §3, to fix the distinction between nominalism and Aristotelian realism on a linguistic agent. I claim the distinction is basically one of reference of a user, not of ontology. Haack's semantics does not allow it.

A different disposition of the user is made in pure semantics. David Lewis (1972a: 170) gets rid of him, while Richard Montague (1974) deflates him. Lewis advocates separation of abstract semantics from theories of language and thought, and claims 'only confusion comes from mixing the two . . .'. The effect of his advice, if followed, is to purge pure semantics of any business with mind and cognition, that is to say, of the live user.

In Montague's pragmatics (also known as 'California semantics'), which is Carnapian semantics with users factored in, reference is claimed to be relative to contexts (times, people) of interpretation, not to models alone. The user in his theory is an element of an abstract index set, and so is neither a straight user nor user*. For this idea I will write 'user[a]', meaning 'user in the abstract'.

Opposing both British pragmatics and pure pragmatics, W. V. Quine sees the separation of semantics from pragmatics as a 'pernicious error' (1987: 211). Other naturalists, including myself, see the same and are anxious to put reference theory back on track, in particular to explain purported reference.

To continue this pursuit I see no alternative to politely showing the friends of speech act theory and abstract pragmatics the door. I do not mean to imply users* or users[a] do not have roles in linguistic affairs or in the theories of them; they certainly do. But I do mean to reclaim the *primary user* and I do not see how to ring the others into a single, unified theory in this book or in a shelf of books.[3]

113

2. *Language users, silent or banished*

Where they touch on language, the psychologies of Locke and
Brentano quite explicitly include a user, and ideas in his head are
either causally or intentionally related to objects. There must be
underlying user-activity in the conventional association of words to
ideas or to inexistent objects, but otherwise the user is passive –
reference is simply there, not made. But the main thing is that the
mind of the user is intrinsic in reference.

For Peirce no signs are signs unless they are interpreted. The
interpretant sign (or sign-stream) is the user. Peirce's user*, whom
we did not pursue, shows up in his theory of scientific practice, e.g.
in rules for acceptance of hypotheses. Peirce is the only philosopher
we have discussed for whom a user is an explicitly constitutive
element of reference.

For Frege, word–object relations subsist as structures in a
Platonic semantic domain and are grasped by one who knows the
language – indeed, knowing the language is precisely that grasping.
Although there is no definite allusion to a user (except in brief
passages where Frege mentions assertion) we imagine a person to
be there. But take him out and canonical Frege still goes. There is
no pragmatic element in the theory of sense and reference, and the
same is true of Tarski. There is no hint in Tarski of the connection
of his theory to people (which of course is the gist of Dummett's
criticism, noted in Chapter 5, §3).

Russell's epistemology of language is less psychological than
Locke's. Knowledge by acquaintance is no theory of perception,
but rather an anchor for epistemology of science (in Russell's
atomism). Reference is strictly deictic, and meaning is embodied in
atomic facts to which sentences correspond when true. We imagine
a user who knows language, has acquaintance with things, and can
describe things. But he is pretheoretical, and plays no more a part in
Russell's analysis than the occasional asserter does in Frege's. The
difference is that Russell's user grasps facts; Frege's, Platonic ideas.
Neither user fashions the tools of reference.

In late Russell, however, the user is endowed with beliefs, which
perhaps lends him more character. The objects of belief are
propositions and the beliefs that intend them are mental or physical
states, depending on Russell's theory of mind at the moment (see
Chapter 4, §6). Thus there is a believer who is a fairly full-blooded

user, some of whose linguistic practices express the content of belief states.

The role of an asserter, referrer, in short of user* , enters our account with Strawson in Chapter 4, §5; but there seems to be no separate, distinguishable user role in the sense I am concerned to bring out. For Strawson, sentences are meaningful independently of assertion by a user*. But sentences, not persons, mean. Meanings are not objects in the mind or attitudes logically prior to use*. Assertion presupposes reference, even intended reference (Strawson 1950: 184); however 'intended' does not imply an intender or an internal state or an intended object juggled in the head.

Names, for Strawson as for Russell, are disguised descriptions (1959: Ch. 1) But his analysis of knowledge of descriptions (beyond elaborate discussion of ways and conditions of describing) remains pretheoretical. Using Haack's slogan, descriptions refer; but persons use* them.

Strawson (ibid.: 102ff) construes 'intending', 'believing' and other attitude-words – his '*P*-predicates' – as ascribing behaviors or dispositions to behave to people; the words do not mark hidden faculties of a substantial mind, either spiritual, physical or functional. They indicate capacities or skills of the person, not mentalistic entities.[4] Given this stance we might say semantic role is accounted for by the disposition of a user* to behave in speech, listening, communication etc. situations in certain ways and not others. If you count a bundle of dispositions-to-use* as a user – mildly contravening the 'words denote' view of semantics – then Strawson has a user. But, unlike Quine (Chapter 7, §2) who uses behavioral tests in thought-experiments to look into reference and meaning, Strawson merely ascribes to the user* what his theory of assertion and speech act requires and lets it go at that.

In John Searle's estimable work (1969) meanings and conditions of use* get far more play than they do in Strawson, and there are allusions to a semantical user who knows the conditions.

Searle's theory of speech acts is three-tiered. Language, he strongly emphasizes, is a social phenomenon; and he recognizes within communicational situations an important difference between meaning something by what one says to others, and something having meaning. Following Grice (1957), to say a speaker means something by *N* is to say that his utterance of *N* is intended to produce some effect in a listener. If I say to you 'it is raining', and if we are standing by a door ready to go out, what I no doubt mean is something like, 'get your umbrella' or 'put on a coat'. The *utterance* does not entail either it is raining or not raining. In general, meaning something by *N* is not the same as the meaning of *N*. Here we can distinguish the speech act and its intended practical effect (two of the tiers) from the meaning of the expression *N* itself.

Now in referring, there is the speech act of using* a name within a sentential utterance that means something in the Gricean sense of having an intended effect on a hearer. Underlying the act are the rules and conditions of reference – the meaning of the name (Searle 1969: 43) – that in effect guide the user* to a successful act. Among these is a rule of identification: the listener must be able to identify the object from hearing the speaker's utterance (ibid.: 82). For proper names, this means the identification must be a kind of shorthand description (ibid.: 163). And if the intention of the user* (as in the 'it is raining' example above) is not to utter a true statement, but to urge action of some sort within a situation, the utterance must in principle supply other means of identification of the object – pointing and fitting a description to the scene.

In this interesting theory Searle even alludes to a plain user. The rules of language must be 'somehow realized' (ibid.: 40), which might suggest something more than rules defined by behavioral ascriptions.[5] But although having rules internalized in mind might account for purporting and intentionality, his theory in the end is concerned with the speech act. The paramount psychological problems are hinted at in talk of meaning and intention, but not directly faced. Moreover, the idea that reference depends on known descriptions probably does not hold water. Russell doubts it (Chapter 4, §6); Donnellan, in the sketch below, doubts it; and so do the causalists discussed in Chapter 8, §1. However, the issue at the moment is users, not the reference-fixing means used*, whether they be descriptional or causal.

In Keith Donnellan's 'Reference and definite descriptions' (1966) there is no notion of reference outside of use*, even with Russell's (or Haack's!) denoting. Opposing Russell and Strawson, Donnellan argues that definite descriptions can be used* either to attribute or to refer. For instance, suppose Smith has been foully murdered, but no one knows who the murderer is. On being shown the mutilated body of the victim Brown exclaims 'Smith's murderer is insane'. Brown does not have a definite person in mind in using* 'Smith's murderer', but only utters the phrase to attribute insanity to a killer, whomever it might be.

Later, suppose Jones (you need not know Jones is named 'Jones') is charged with the murder. Having her in mind, Brown utters the same sentence, 'Smith's murderer is insane'. The description now picks out Jones; it does not ascribe insanity to someone or other, but precisely to Jones. In this situation the description is referential.

Now a description could refer, even if wildly false, if it were analyzed in Russell's way as the one and only such and such. In the example, suppose Brown says, in the presence of Jones in court, 'the fellow in the leather jacket is insane'. He might very well succeed in calling attention to Jones although Jones is really wearing a plastic jacket. Referential descriptions can work without being attributely faithful to the object intended.

If this is right, not all descriptions can be supplanted by names since referential descriptions might make false attributions and yet succeed in picking out an individual. So the descriptional theory of names applies, if it does, only to attributive descriptions, which denote only if true.

Now the clincher. Against Russell, Strawson and Searle, Donnellan argues that you cannot tell in advance of use* whether a descriptive expression is attributive or referential. There is just one syntactical sequence of symbols; but several semantical interpretations emerge in use*. Therefore you cannot tell whether a description that is proposed as an abbreviation of a name is attributive or not outside of that use* (ibid.: 44). It follows that names cannot be abbreviations of definite descriptions. And of course (incidentally) the argument threatens Searle's distinction between meaning something by an act and an expression's meaning.

If names do not link to their objects via descriptions, how do they? Donnellan asks this question from within the framework of a speech act, user*, concept of reference: 'what is . . . the appropriate relation between an act of using a name and some object such that the name was used to refer that object'? (1979: 229)

His answer is that 'successful reference will occur when there is an individual [object] that enters into the historically correct explanation of who it is that the speaker intended to predicate something of'. Reference ties to the object in the speech act if and only if it (the relation, I think we should say) has a true history.

This is no theory of a user* referring from knowledge of rules.

There aren't any a priori rules, and hence there is no knowing user of them, as in Searle's theory, although there are intentions somehow connected with a history.

Donnellan's historical condition of reference is third-person (ibid.: 230f). The inquiring, 'omniscient' observer, not the first-person user* himself, need know the history of the linkage; or if the user* does know, Donnellan does not tell us how knowledge of it guides reference*. In fact he makes a point of denying there is a direct, causal tie – a 'dubbing' event – of object to speaker at 'one end of the historical connection' (ibid.: 233). So the right link of word to thing is something of a mystery, although of course that does not mean the linkage is totally irresoluble. It just means that Donnellan's chief concern is not purported reference.

3. *Pure pragmatics*

An influential group of linguists and philosophers have much to say about users in the abstract, but nothing about reference.

Pure pragmatics, which stems from Carnap, attempts to carry forward the work of obtaining a theory of intensions in extensional terms, and also to incorporate the insight, going back to Strawson at least, that truth, reference and meaning, in natural language, depend on context of use – time, place, speaker etc. (whence 'pragmatics'). The move is in two steps: (a) a shift from Carnap's state descriptions to possible worlds, and (b) incorporation of index sets into the concept of reference. My steps (a) and (b) correspond to a received distinction, often made, between *structural* and *lexical* semantics (Partee 1979).[6]

(a) Carnap (1963: 910ff) drops state descriptions for possible worlds, which may be understood as the systems of atomic facts the atomic components of state descriptions are about. A possible world (or, closely enough, a 'model' in the sense of Chapter 5, §3) is an alternative interpretation of a formal language such as Carnap's S_1. As such, a world is an extensional object, a set of individual objects and sets. Worlds are equal if and only if they comprehend the same facts. Among the worlds is the actual world, which corresponds to the true state description in Carnap's first scheme exhibited in Chapter 5, §4. One can think of the other worlds – corresponding to other state descriptions – as contrary-to-fact variants of the actual.

At one stroke this idea enables one to introduce intensional objects in terms of possible worlds. A proposition as the meaning of a sentence in a formalized language such as our *L* is no longer an entity injected *ad hoc*, as in Chapter 5, §4, to provide a common meaning for logically equivalent sentences. Instead, a proposition is explicated as the set of possible worlds the sentence is true in; alternatively, as a map from worlds to truth values. This idea seems to match our intuitions pretty well, for it just says that sentences have the same meaning if they are true in identical imagined circumstances. So here we reclaim propositions for extensional semantics; the meaning or sense of a sentence is now extensional, a set of possible worlds.

Other intensions are introduced in a similar way. The intension of a predicate '*F*' (or property expressed by the predicate) is a function from possible worlds to subsets of possible individuals. Thus if *w* is a world, F_w is the set of individuals that are *F*. F_w is the extension of '*F*' in *w*. Again, an individual concept in early Carnap turns out to be a function from possible worlds to individuals in the new semantics.

These ideas are developed with great elegance, originally in Kripke (1963) and in formal treatments of English in Montague (1974). They apply to intensions including belief (Montague 1974; Hintikka 1969) and to questions of modal logic, which are out of our reach. For the most part, the development of intensional semantics of formalized English is structural semantics, for Montague, and goes far toward completing the reduction of Fregean semantics to extensional terms.

(b) Now on to the user[a]. Here the situation is basically the same as the one we left with Field at the end of our discussion of Tarski. In canonical Frege and in model theory, reference is a relation from name or constant to object in an interpretation. If we think of Tarski semantics and reference schemes (Chapter 5, §3) as standard, the big move is to change over to the notion of a *set* of reference schemes, one for each user[a]. The result of the change is 'pragmatics'. It relativizes reference to contexts of use. For instance, reference might not be the same relation for Steve as it is for Peter, and this is especially so of descriptions. If English is formalized we might have expressions such as ' "Russell" refers for Steve, now, to Russell' instead of ' "Russell" refers to Russell'. Here the pair (Steve, now) is an index on a par with indicator words such as 'I',

119

'now' etc. Similarly we might have ' "Russell" refers for Peter, then, to a certain piano-playing comedian'. The inclusion of indexes for individuals (or times, places etc.) is the reason for calling the subject 'pragmatics'; and when these notations are dropped you are back in 'semantics'.

Note that the user[a] is an abstraction drawn from the idea of user*, as the aim is to model contexts of actual speech behavior with actual objects. Therefore pragmatics can have nothing to do with purporting, which is a property of name-types as well as acts of naming.[7]

It is quite clear that California pragmatics is not meant to have anything to do with the anatomy of reference. Barbara Partee (1979) has remarked that lexical semantics is a 'fundamentally different' kind of enterprise than 'structural semantics' (ibid.: 198) and offers an extremely 'rich avenue into the study of the mind . . .' (ibid.: 206). Lexical pragmatics (to coin an expression for space of one sentence) – inquiry into reference, application, meanings etc. entertained by users – is likewise entirely other than structural pragmatics and the study of reference schemes relative to index sets. Our pursuit is part of cognitive science, not of the abstract mathematics of possible worlds.

Others may of course pursue possible worlds semantics to their heart's content. However, I am not sure where it will end if reference itself is intentional, while it is not so recognized.

There are other paths to reference, meaning and the semantics of English. In the remainder of this book I will allude to real possible worlds only to enable my discussion of thinkers who see a use for them; or I shall otherwise think of them simply as things imagined.

CHAPTER 7

Steps Toward Naturalism

1. Philosophy – part of science

Despite its seminal treatment of truth for formal languages, Tarski's theory holds little for reference. His disquotational analysis of reference is *ad hoc*, does not mention purportedness and does not explain how reference links language to objects. Carnap seeks reference in logical truth (the analytic), but fails to find it there.

In ordinary language philosophy and in pure pragmatics we found emphasis on linguistic acts, but nothing to help us see how to explain reference and the linkage expressed in our familiar scheme ' "*a*" refers to *a*'.

Unfortunately, ushering the user into the picture and doing some empirically respectable testing on him seems to reveal only that there are no firm relations reference and application to theorize about. While persons successfully use language to represent the world and to represent themselves to each other, word–thing connections sought by the linguist in the context of actual human behavior are radically elusive – perhaps not accessible to science – there being no fixed relation of reference to explain. There is no relation R satisfying condition (R) to explain. This skeptical position is W. V. Quine's.

A radically different view, which does not deny there is a relation of reference, is Saul Kripke's causal theory of reference. Disquotation holds and, roughly, the explanation of reference is that an object *a* *causes* name '*a*'.

Although the two viewpoints seem opposed, I put them together as they plainly stand apart from the abstract word–thing tradition running from Frege through (with a detour) Russell to Tarski and beyond, and also from the use-theories of ordinary language philosophy. Quine and Kripke agree that language as a whole is an empirical phenomenon and should be understood as a characteristic of human linguistic behavior within societies. As we shall see, an attempt to reconcile them does not totally lack a certain interest.

Quine's writings, which occupy high territory in American philosophy, comprise the first steps toward naturalism. Naturalism amongst the pragmatists occurs earlier, but lacks (excepting Peirce in part) the analytic theme. Quine's classic *Word and Object* (1960) continues the tradition of British empiricism, reorganized so as to front mind on real objects, not sense data. It is an objective empiricism, not a subjective empiricism. Later volumes, notably *Ontological Relativity* (1969), are expressly naturalistic in the wide sense of John Dewey.

All of the varieties of reference I shall be discussing from here on follow Quine in his departure from the old Descartes–Locke dualism. Sense data, subjective images, inner pictures and Humean impressions both clear and dim, disappear in favor of stimulus patterns (inputs) at the surface of the body.

In Quine, philosophy of language has two parts, logical analysis much in the spirit of Russell's 'On denoting', and behavioral psychology of language. I am not one to attempt to boil this mixture down to a few paragraphs. But before trying a few pages I want to exhibit a 'Short Quine' to set the scene for my remarks on his view on reference and my criticism of it. The brevity follows from an assumption, not a part of Quine's naturalism, that 'reference' is an intensional term. I make no claim whatever that Short Quine is strictly accurate Quine.

'Reference' is a semantical,[1] even an intensional, predicate. If we drop the elliptical and ultimately misleading ' "Russell" refers to Russell' for ' "Russell" refers to Russell for *i*', where *i* knows English and might be either an individual or a community, its intensionality is clear according to the usual criteria (see Chapter 2, §5). Try substituting 'the junior author of *Principia*' for 'Russell', perhaps preserving the truth of the full sentence and perhaps not. It all depends on *i*'s attitude. Again, ' "Sagan" refers to the fourth moon of the outermost planet of Arcturus, for Schmid' is intensional. The description 'the fourth moon . . .' purports, but might not refer.

Now the language of exact science is ideally extensional; there is no place in it for intensional language. Therefore 'reference', short of the possibility of explaining it at a deeper level (e.g. in neuroscience) than is available today, is not a part of the vocabulary of science.

Meanwhile, awaiting developments, by examining the ontogeny and phylogeny of language we might undertake to learn how people manage to talk about things – how the child masters language and how society at various stages of developing science succeeds in reporting the world. Thus endeth Short Quine.

Turning now to a more literal exposition, the central idea is this: mathematics, empirical science, logic and philosophy all fall inside one boundary. Following John Dewey, Quine sees philosophy as a part of science, not as the science of science as it is for Carnap; philosophy has no privileged line to reality (nor does the philosopher deny that questions about the real are meaningful); and it means there are no first principles of logic or of methodology beyond the purview of science itself. The standards of philosophy in these matters are the very standards of science, not of an a priori science of science.

The closest thing to metaphysics in Quine's thought is his evolutionary theory of the development of language, including science as a network of illatively related sentences. Science is a self-correcting process, and Quine's account of it is close to Dewey's and Peirce's. Philosophy is self-correcting, too; for instance, as logic evolves it comes to have a therapeutic office in grooming language for good science; its goal,in logical analyis, is mainly reconditioning of referential apparatuses. Epistemology also emerges in studies of reference and meaning, and grows with linguistics and psychology. Using Quine's favorite metaphor (1960: 3), science is like a boat (philosophy is in it) being built while afloat, plank by plank.

Contrast this with Frege, Tarski and Carnap for whom daily language is a poor relative squeezed ill-fittingly into formal dress.

Quine's epistemology reduces to a branch of empirical psychology and linguistics, since the objects of knowledge are not Lockean ideas or Russellean sense data but, by his ontological principles, physical things in relationship to physical organisms. The knowing subject's representations of objects are not mental entities, but sentences. The old epistemology of perception gets replaced by a new enterprise that is developed hand-in-glove with empirical semantics. Philosophy, as prior to science in method and transcending science, disappears.

Returning to the two parts, Quine's psychology of language is discussed first and then we shall turn to his logical analysis. The latter depends on certain assumptions he makes in view of the doctrine of meaning and reference established in the former.

Semantics includes a theory of the interface between objects and sentences, and a theory of the development of linkage at that place. The basic organs of knowledge are nerve endings on which the external world impinges; the imposed patterns of stimulation are the proximal inputs to perception, cognition and action. A red ball seen by a subject is a light pattern spread over the surface of the eye, and a high middle C is a sound pattern diffused on inner surfaces of the ear. Our theories of the external world arise from the totality of input stimulations, and are proved successful or not by our ability to predict later stimulations that are partly the result of our actions on that world.

Quine is a dedicated behaviorist. Language is a disposition to respond (more accurately, a complex network of dispositions to respond) to stimuli.[2] Having 'knowledge' of a language is being disposed to respond to sounds from other speakers and environmental situations in ways appropriate to overt action. Experimental tools of the rat laboratory – stimulus–response, learning and reinforcement – suffice for semantics (Skinner 1953; 1957) and for research into all cognitive process.[3] The relation of stimulation patterns to sentences (the relation being the Quinean counterpart of the Cartesian abyss) is grasped by the subject through conditioning and reinforcement. Semantic linkage, therefore, is not anything like acquaintance of a person to a sense datum (or directly by perception to a thing). The linkage is of stimulus to sentence and is established inductively. And except for that external relation, epistemology and semantics bypass retinal, neural intervening processes; neural details fall outside the purview of behavioral method.

The test of the linkage of a red ball stimulation to a fluent speaker is that the stimulus object is present if and only if he or she responds by assenting or dissenting to a query 'is that a red ball?'. Linkage is individual, yet at the semantic level it is social. Each member of a community responds the same to the uttered question although there is a diversity in retinal and neural mechanism from person to person. 'The uniformity that unites us in communication and belief is a uniformity of resultant [language] patterns overlying a chaotic subjective diversity of connections between words and experience' (Quine 1960: 8).

To explain this more fully: in Quine's phylogeny of language, there is a grading of sentences from those bearing on immediate experience, *occasion sentences*, up to *eternal sentences* that are 'true for good' (ibid.: 12) and might be as abstract and general as the sentences of theoretical science. The distinction depends on notice of the roles played by stimulation.

Place yourself in the position of a third-person investigator observing a subject's stimulations and resulting responses. Occasion sentences are sentence tokens that 'command assent or dissent [on the part of the subject] only if queried [by the examiner] after appropriate stimulation' (ibid.: 35f). A response at one place–time by a subject might be the reverse of that on another occasion. 'It is raining' will call out different responses at different times depending on stimulations (in this case, rain or its impact or not).

However, eternal sentences like 'all men are animals' have no immediate connection to stimulations, and are sentence types (alternatively, each token has the same truth value as any other). Query a knowledgeable speaker and you will get the same response every time in every situation (allowing for obtuseness, bad livers, memory lapses, changed beliefs, insanity etc.).

Among the occasion sentences are *observation sentences* which are directly associated to external things; they may on an occasion of stimulation and querying elicit assent or dissent responses outright in relative independence of past memories, beliefs or other collateral stuff (Quine 1990: 3). 'The sun is rosy in the western sky' and 'It is raining' are both occasion sentences, but only the second is observational and is less likely to cause confusion or diversity of response.

There is a whole range of stimulations (think of pouring rain in many places and at different times affecting nerve endings) any one of which elicits assent to one and the same observation sentence type, 'it is raining', and there is a disjoint set of stimulations any one of which elicits dissent on dry occasions. These sets are the *stimulus meanings* of the sentence.

A sentence is observational (has a fixed stimulus meaning, as above) for an entire community when it is observational for each member (ibid.: 40). This notion is troublesome, for your stimulus set need not be mine; but for the moment we shall assume the ranges of stimulation are the same for all.

In Quine's epistemology it is the observation sentence that links language to the world.[4] This linkage, even as it arises in the pursuit of science, is *holistic*. There are one-word observation sentences like 'Rabbit!' which are observational paradigms at the time of seeing a rabbit. They are *holophrastic*. 'It is raining' and 'the pointer is at 10' also face the world holophrastically, as does 'Rabbit!': the separate lexical items in these sentences are analogous to syllables in a word, and have little self-contained meaning. It is only when such sentences are logically connected to higher level theoretical sentences that semantical articulation of sentence-parts emerges. In observation, 'raining' is part of the holophrastic 'it is raining' or 'see! it is raining'. But in the sentence 'raining in frequent, large doses is a condition for growing good corn' the word does have its own meaning which contributes to that of the sentence. To understand 'it is raining' in a live situation requires grasping the total sentence the way a baby grasps 'mama' on a live occasion. However, to understand the corn theory, one has to know a good deal about rain; in semantic terms this entails knowing the application of 'rain' and a large network of meaning-associations with farming, corn etc.

Observation sentences already display Quine's thesis of *meaning holism* as having roots in behavioristics of language. Truth and meaning pertain chiefly to sentences and whole theories, not to lexical particles, although of course individual words contribute.

Now contrasted with most modern empiricism, Quine's theory of knowledge is also holistic. In early twentieth-century thought new hypotheses are considered to be, or to tend to be, confirmed when they stand in deductive relation to observation sentences that square with immediate data; oppositely, they are disconfirmed when they entail false observation sentences – for Quine those sentences that elicit dissent when queried on the spot. The picture is this:

Established theory plus new hypothesis
implies
observation report

If the observation report is true it means the whole new theory, hypothesis adjoined, is confirmed; if false, the hypothesis is disconfirmed while the established theory stands.

However, as regards actual scientific practice, it is widely observed today, following the French physicist Pierre Duhem (1954), that in failed observation much more than the hypothesis is threatened. Quine's view, following Duhem, is that our statements 'about the external world face the tribunal of sense experience . . . as a corporate body' (1953: 41). The entire theory (established theory plus new hypothesis) is supported in confirmation. Also, significant portions of it, not just the hypothesis, are threatened in disconfirmation. Falsification of an observation sentence echoes throughout the total network of science. As a consequence, truth values apply to entire theories not to individual sentences, except derivatively. Construed as a truth condition, meaning also applies to entire theories, not to individual sentences or terms except as they participate in theory. Observation sentences, however, are the stably true (when true) points of contact of theory with the actual world.

2. Indeterminacy

The theory of indeterminacy of translation and reference, which is our main concern, both illuminates and is illuminated by this holistic picture of science. It sharpens that picture and at the same time seriously weakens hope for a theory of reference and meaning.

One can discern two theories of indeterminacy (cf. Hill 1984). The first (A) argues from considerations of identity and individuation. The principle of entity, which I borrow here from my later review of Quine's ontology (item (a), page 132) is at the heart of Quine's skepticism about reference. It says that if it is not possible to give conditions of the identity of a thing, the thing is not to count as an entity. This principle was already working more or less explicitly in Quine's criticism of Carnap on analyticity and abstract objects, and is reflected in our Commandments.

The second theory (B) stems from model theory and depends on the technical idea of proxy function which we shall consider in due course. First the relatively nontechnical part, which is a beautiful display of behaviorism at work.

(A) Imagine a field linguist intent on translating Jungle, the language of a remote tribe. Starting from scratch – knowing only how to tell when a tribesman by bodily action assents or dissents to test sentences fed to him by the linguist in the presence of stimuli – the linguist sets out to manufacture a manual of translation from Jungle to his home language.

To begin with, he has an initial collection of tribal expressions he guesses are associated with various situations; the thing is to test these by the method of querying the native and marking assent or dissent.

'Gavagai' is on his list, and the linguist believes it translates to 'Lo, a rabbit' or 'There's a rabbit'. To test his guess he prompts a native in the presence of a rabbit to reply one way or the other to 'Gavagai' – accompanied-by-pointing, and repeatedly gets assent from him and also from other natives. The linguist is then warranted in according 'Gavagai' the cautious translation 'Lo, a rabbit' or 'Lo, rabbithood' or 'There's a rabbit' (Quine 1969: 2). This translation counts 'Gavagai' as a rabbit-heralding sentence. Similarly for many other expressions; still others are scratched when natives dissent. In all experiments there is a putatively common stimulus meaning for all parties, including the linguist (but see Quine 1990: 41f).

Now the telling point: the tests and responses, definite as they are on the level of sentences, tell nothing about *terms*, e.g. about 'Gavagai' construed not as a one-word rabbit-announcing sentence but as a predicate.

> Given that a native sentence says that a so-and-so is present, and given that the sentence is true when and only when a rabbit is present, it by no means follows that the so-and-so are rabbits. They might be all the various temporal segments of rabbits. They might be all the integral or undetached parts of rabbits. In order to decide among these alternatives, we need to be able to ask more than whether a so-and-so is present. We need to be able to ask whether this is the same so-and-so, and whether one so-and-so is present or two. We need something like the apparatus of identity and quantification; hence far more than we are in a position to avail ourselves of in a language in which our high point as of even date is rabbit-announcing.
>
> (Quine 1969: 2)

In brief, holophrastic observation sentences can be translated with confidence while predicate translation is uncertain – there are many possibilities which are screened to the end of producing a usable manual.

To go on to construct a manual of Jungle, then, the linguist must read grammatical structure into the language, make decisions as to which terms refer and to what, and which do not refer. He 'has to decide how to accommodate English idioms of identity and quantification in native translation' (ibid.: 3). Because the meanings of 'Gavagai' and other expressions are uncertain he must make lexical guesses, checking himself by looking to contextual fit, consistency with the basic lists and so forth.

A central part of manual making is the introduction of 'analytical hypotheses', lists that equate English words and phrases with Jungle, lists constrained by the primal equation of observation sentences. Any list or lexicon is bound to be one among many possible ones, even in the presence of the observational constraints.

Proceeding in this way, the linguist fashions a manual of Jungle-to-English that correlates sentences compatible with the behavior of both linguist and native.

Now imagine another linguist out to construct a translation manual. His manual of Jungle might also be completely compatible with the behaviors of all parties, and yet not agree with the first. '[T]he English sentences prescribed as translation of a given Jungle sentence by two rival manuals might not be interchangeable in English contexts' (Quine 1990: 48). Another way to put it is that Jungle, English or any other natural language is not simply a group of concatenations of observational reports.

This is the principle of indeterminacy of translation.

The philosophical upshot is that predicate *meanings* are nonentities. By Quine's principles there is no way of deciding sameness of meaning – in effect of reducing all manuals to one on grounds of synonymy of entries one by one. And since there is no identity, there is no entity. The principle applies as well to propositions, except construed as the stimulus meanings of observation sentences.

The thesis also applies to our home language, not just Jungle. A child learning a language has to go on observation, induction, test and retest much as the native or the linguist does. And what is learned, although reinforced by phonetic agreement and a surrounding familial network of customs and attitudes not available to the linguist in facing Jungle, is subject to the same indeterminacy.

Furthermore, using rival manuals of translation between Jungle and English, you can translate English perversely into English by translating into Jungle by one manual and then back by the other (ibid.: 48). Our bet is that they will not read the same, and that 'rabbit' in one will not be synonymous with 'rabbit' in the other.

Returning to an earlier point on Carnap, p. 108, the looseness of manuals even at home scotches any proposal that 'synonymy' is a ground for 'analyticity' and might be 'clarified in terms relating to linguistic behavior'. Recall that Quine argued against Carnap that meanings have to be set behaviorally; now he has shown, as I suggested he must, that defining 'analytic' is out of the question altogether.

A similar indeterminacy infects extensions. The terms 'rabbit', 'undetached rabbit part' and 'rabbit stage' not only differ in meaning; they are true of different things. The *inscrutability of reference* in these examples hinges on the indeterminacy of translation of identity and other individuating apparatus (Quine 1969: 45). A query in Jungle with pointing, as a translation of 'is this the same as that', is as indeterminate as 'Gavagai' – there is no right way to understand it – and thus reference is indefinite.[5] So 'Gavagai' is variably translatable and has no fixed reference for us since there is no way to tell if two extensions or individuals are the same for the native. Translation of the apparatus of pronouns, pluralization and numerals (the tools of individuation) is as indeterminate as that of predicates and names (ibid.: 35). Both application and reference are indeterminate.

There is indeterminacy at home. A term can be used as singular or general, depending on the occasion. In 'grass is green' the term 'green' is general, while in 'green is a color' it is singular. 'Such ambiguity is encouraged by the fact there is nothing in ostension to distinguish the two uses. The pointing that would be done in teaching the concrete general term ... differs none from the pointing that would be done in teaching the abstract singular term' (ibid.: 38).

There is an analogy between the semantical role of terms in eternal sentences in science and in language translation. In both, meaning and reference are relative to the linguistic background of home language, consisting of all the predicates and auxiliary devices including identity and difference. The network of the devices is our 'coordinate system' (ibid.: 48), comparable to a coordinate system in relativistic mechanics, within which positions, elapsed times etc. are fixed. In the absence of such a system, meaning and reference are indeterminate. The guesses we had our linguist venture in aiding his translation of Jungle draw on just such a system, and if it be the same as that of his rival, then both would write approximately the same manual.

The theory of indeterminacy of meaning and reference thus supports Duhemian holism. Science is true or false as a corporate body, and our linguistic system has referential contact with reality only within the total coordinating background. However, the two holisms, Duhemian and meaning holism, are not the same, as we shall see in due course.

(B) Quine now asks us to suppose our own language is settled with respect to a stable system of individuated, identifiable objects. In this case reference and application remain inscrutable. They are indeterminate even when identity and the other devices of individuation are 'fixed and settled' and when we think only of the home language, not of translation into Jungle (ibid.: 41). Reference is elusive even within a single coordinate system. How can this be so?

The answer is related to Quine's ontological relativity, and draws on the idea of swapping objects in the domain of interpretation of a system of logic. The argument to follow, so far as I can see, applies only to extensional logics and therefore to the home language understood as susceptible to regimentation in canonical notation.

3. Regimentation

Since we have it available, let us use *L* (predicate calculus clothed in English) of the last chapter as our evolving, target regimented language, subject to some emendation as follows.

Quine proposes that the circumstances and context of utterance be expressed in the sentence itself, not in the metalinguistic conditions of statement, resulting in eternal sentences. This enables him to assign truth to types, skirting Strawson's insight (Chapter 4,

§5) that truth is often assigned to tokens of sentences, not types. (We avoided this issue in discussing Tarski; truth for tokens is a major question of research in pure semantics today.)

For instance, a sentence S uttered under circumstances C, S being a token with its truth dependent on C, is paraphrased 'S at C' in which truth no longer depends on spatial–temporal etc. features of context. For instance, 'It is snowing' is true in Chardon, Ohio, at 10 a.m. on 25 December 1989, while conceivably it is false in Chardon (or even Fairbanks) at 3 p.m. on 1 June 1990. However, 'It was snowing in Chardon at 10 a.m. on 25 December 1989' is true or false as the case may be at any time, and so is 'It was snowing in Chardon at 3 p.m. on 1 June 1993'. The verb 'was snowing' can even be used tenselessly, i.e. 'snows', in both, although the first is about a past space–time event and the second a future one.

Indexicals such as 'I', 'you' and 'that' can be given treatment allied to the one given to proper names, namely they can be treated as 'singular descriptions', joined with pointing, when circumstances of utterance are too shaky for communication to be served (Quine 1960: 103, 172ff).

Quine's ontology has a regulatory office in regimentation, and roots out spurious and superfluous objects – from unactual possibles and ideas to caloric and phlogiston – that attend the growth of ordinary language and science. For Quine this means dismissing all but physical objects and abstract sets.

Quine is no anti-metaphysician, as Carnap is, but he does not tolerate stuff on grounds of 'practical choices': the things our theories deal with are to be theoretically accountable, except in everyday discourse where community expression has other ends and uses.

There are three regulatory principles of ontology which collectively put limits on a strictly naturalistic empiricism. They had to await formulation until now as they are cogent only with respect to inquiries and their (regimented) languages employing firm logical devices.

(a) Do not admit inexplicable objects – typical examples are
abstract properties or other intensional items, and
mental states – unless they can be explained in ordinary
scientific terms. If you cannot deliver a criterion for
identity of two possible philosophers or of the Fregean

senses of 'rational animal' and 'human being', do not admit
them into theory – no entity without identity. We have
already used this idea heavily in criticizing Carnap and in
examining radical   Jungle to English translation.

(b) Occam's razor: do not introduce entities you do not need;
if you can explain reference, for instance, without appeal to
an intentional mind, do so. If you do not need both sets
and abstract properties to do mathematics, use one
category, preferably sets (since the criterion of identity of
sets is clear – (a)).

(c) Determine what entities you allow in your theorizing
(possibly in violation of (a) or (b)) by keeping track of
your use of names, pronouns, and quantifiers. If quantifiers
(recall that names and indexicals are eliminable in favor of
descriptions, he thinks) and pronomial devices range over
atoms and angels your ontology consists of atoms and
angels. To be is to be the value of a variable (Quine 1953:
15).

For a review exercise on these points, let us return to Titania whom
we left back with Russell and Strawson. 'Does Titania exist?' We
fleetingly entertain the thought that Titania is a possible but not
actual thing, but reject it since there are no criteria for identifying
possible things, certainly not whether a possible Titania yesterday is
the same as a possible Titania next week etc. (see (a)). We also reject
the notion that a thing can exist in one sense while not in another,
and so put aside a suggestion that Titania exist as a character in
fiction, but not actually. We make this rejection on grounds of
economy, of science's use of one, plain term 'existence' only and of
dislike of nonsense (see (b)) (cf. our rejection of relation (1) of
Chapter 1, §2).

Next consider 'there exists an x such that x = Titania' and assert
its falsehood. But this leaves us with the fairy in our thoughts, since
the position of the name in the last sentence is surely open to
substitution: the sentence is strictly extensional, and hence is
referential; see Chapter 2, §5. But this situation, consisting of an
empty name in a referential spot, is quite odd (Quine 1960: 176). So
we instead adopt the strategy of making a predicate of 'Titania' and
construing identity '=' as the predicate copula 'is'. Then we deny,
'there is an x such that x is a Titania (type of thing)'. This last

sentence does not tacitly refer to her, but falsely applies the predicate 'Titania'; so we deny it. If the verbalized name needs elaboration to insure the right reference it can be expanded to a definite description. All reference in such apparently contrary cases falls to the quantifier 'there is' (see (c)). The goodness of this strategy clearly depends on the assumption that there is always a description the name abbreviates.

Reference is thus no more than the ranging of variables in a language L with canonical notations, short of questions about verbalizing 'Titania' and the applicability of predicate expressions – all of which awaits our criticism in the following.

As we have adopted it, language L does not include intensional sentences. This is deliberate, for Quine accepts Brentano's thesis (Chapter 2, §3) in a kind of negative, semantical way. Brentano separates mind off from the physical and places it in its own realm. Quine follows in separating the intentional – but better to eliminate it altogether (1960: 220).[6] In the semantical mode this means, of course, no intensional sentences in regimented scientific language, and leads directly to the Short Quine argument in §1 above.

A good reason for keeping L pure and extensional in the present context is that inscrutability (B) presupposes many putatively scrutable (A) reference relations, but with indeterminate means of choice from among them. If a sentence has irreferential spots in it, even terms with otherwise fixed reference suffer an inscrutability more radical than that of fuzzy reference. Does Schmid's 'junior author of *Principia*' refer to Russell, the sense of 'Russell', Iris Murdoch or nothing at all? Any one of these might be a perfectly scrutable referent, but if we do not know which of them it is, the idea of permuting objects, now to be discussed, is simply undefined.

As in Chapter 5, §3, D is the domain of interpretation of L, and various perfectly clear (in virtue of the scrutability we just enforced above) assignments of its elements to variables and constants are possible; these assignments, focusing just on names now, are reference schemes as in Tarski's theory. In particular suppose that 'a' refers to a etc., and that the extension of a predicate 'F' is, as usual in logic, all of the objects 'F' applies to.

Let us permute the objects of D so that Perm(a) is swapped with a, Perm(b) with b, and so forth. This yields a new scheme in which 'a' refers to Perm(a), 'b' refers to Perm(b), and similarly for all other names. But now also let us construct the set of all the objects of D

which are the images under perm of the elements of the extension of 'F ': that is, if a is in the extension of F originally, Perm(a) is to be in the extension of a reconstituted F (Quine 1969). In terms of model theory, we have a new world or state description: same domain, but different distribution of predicates over it. Quine calls the permutation Perm a 'proxy function'.

Using relation (2) of Chapter 5, §2, suppose that 'a is F ' is true; then the object referred to by 'a' is in the class determined by 'F '. This is the same as saying a is F, as we saw. But under the proxy function, Perm(a) is in the new extension of 'F '. Consequently the object referred to by 'a', Perm(a), in the new regime is in the reconstituted extension of 'F '. Therefore Perm(a) is F is true.

Supposing we use a Tarskian definition of truth for L that recursively builds up from bases like 'a is F '; then all of the sentences of L are true or false independently of the reference scheme, either the initial one or any one of them under a proxy function. 'Perm(a) is F ' is true if and only if 'a is F ' is true.

All observation sentences 'remain associated to the same sensory stimulations as before. . . . Yet the objects of the theory have been supplanted as drastically as you please' by varying reference relations in ways depending on the proxy functions (Quine 1990: 32). In effect, each proxy function yields a different manual of translation from the home language into itself. The fact that choice of a manual is quite arbitrary marks the inscrutability of reference in sense (B). And the fact that truth of L is sustained no matter what the interpretation in D modulo proxy functions is approximately Quine's doctrine of ontological relativity.[7] What about disquotation? '[I]f we choose as our manual of translation the identity transformation [perm(a) = a] . . . the relativity is resolved' (ibid.: 52). Reference is then explicated in 'disquotational paradigms'. However, since the choice cannot depend on the facts of reference (inscrutability (A)), it must be essentially practical.

The holism of global science (Duhemian holism) is the doctrine that evidence does not 'clinch' the system. Science is underdetermined by the evidence. However, Quine is prepared to believe that 'reality exceeds the scope of the human apparatus in unspecifiable ways' (ibid.: 101). There is a reality we accept in our humanly relative ways. However, there is no reality of meaning of lexical particles.

Meaning holism follows in a clear sense of the expression if

135

meaning is the truth condition of global science. Sentences and terms take their meanings from roles in the total picture, within a coordinate system. We might holistically characterize 'singular term', 'general term' and 'sentence' as in Chapter 1; but there is no way to do so in terms of the isolated semantics of each as there is none, in principle, except for observation sentences, where meaning is just pattern of stimulation.

By way of summary so far: for Quine there is no reference to theorize about, hence no pre-analytic condition (*R*) to satisfy, and disquotation is a matter of practical acceptance, not of reality. If English is exact – its sentences true or false in a Tarskian sense and thus its sentences subject to recursive definition – we have the option of disquotation, that is all.

What about purported reference? Within a chosen scheme one could replace names with descriptions and, applying Russell's analysis, paraphrase over to first-order language. In such a case we have seen how the purportedly referring 'Titania' disappears into a false quantified sentence. Whether or not this analysis is adequate to purporting in general is moot. Even if it is adequate, the description theory of proper names has been threatened by Russell himself as well as Donnellan, Kripke and Putnam.

4. Identity and behavior

I question the inscrutability of reference, and accept disquotation as a hard empirical datum of natural linguistics, explainable in principle. However, disputing inscrutability is not the same as having a true theory of reference. I mean only that reference is possibly accessible to empirical address; and as is the case with other phenomena, any proposed theory is going to be under-determined by the data. What I mean to reject is the notion that there is something deep about reference, placing it outside the pale of ordinary science. The next step, in Partee's terms (Chapter 6, §3), then, is to explore the foundations of lexical semantics within a naturalistic setting featuring the psychology of the user.

To get around or through the inscrutability thesis we might shift to a stance wherein cognitive features of the speaker are taken into account. Rather than look at reference as a two-way relation (the logician's way) which is too open-ended for the field linguistic to define, move the native or other user in as part of the relation – not merely as a giver or withholder of assent – and probe the cognitive realm of which linguistic meaning is a part. Make semantics a part of cognitive theory. This is naturalistic enough; and the aims and methods of traditional pure logic and semantics can be recovered as normative idealizations.

Many writers have remarked that the indeterminacy of translation is a consequence of behaviorism. Quine agrees, and indeed thinks that in linguistics there is no choice (1990: 38). 'There is nothing in linguistic meaning beyond what is to be gleaned from overt behavior in observable circumstances.' The reader can check what counts as gleanable, using the foregoing account of how to construct a translation manual of Jungle and of its implications for meaning and translation in the home language. The tools are query, assent and dissent – input and output – and the rest is invoking of analytical hypotheses (rough translations of words to words) and grammatical guesswork.

There are two related arguments against behaviorism. They are addressed to psychological behaviorism as represented by B. F. Skinner and Quine, but apply as well, as I have shown (1969), to the views of the British (Ryle and Strawson, for instance – see Chapter 6, §2, and §1 of this chapter).

(a) Chomsky has argued at great length (1959, 1965, 1972, 1975, 1986) that language learning requires much more than simple induction from the observed behavior of others. As a case in point take the child (not the linguist who is out to learn Jungle, pretty much at ease, and working within a planned schedule of relatively clean assent and dissent to query) at home who learns an entire language in the course of two years or so from exposure to a remarkably small corpus of sentences, and having access to relatively uncontrolled, unsanitized input only. It is inconceivable that this feat be accounted for in behavioral terms. Stimulus input, for instance, is not even defined except with respect to the response psychology of the child (Chomsky 1959: 353).

(b) Moreover it can be shown (Nelson 1969) that even S–R – sanitized input–output – rat behavior cannot be explained, in principle, without appeal to inner states, that is to say, to cognitive process. Put as transparently as possible: there

are behavioral causes (say, of pushing a lever) that eventuate in more than one response type, even in a fixed
environment. Suppose, to use a Skinnerian paradigm, you
want to positively reinforce a subject's response R to a
stimulus type S, but as often as not you get a clear R', not
a clear R, even after following a neat schedule of reinforcements. There is nothing new in this, and the remedy is
usually to get a new animal. Unfortunately the phenomenon is not traceable to bad experimental conditions or
artifacts but to the nature of the organism.

Put to the present linguistic issue, it makes the indeterminacy
picture somewhat worse than Quine thinks. There is not only a
puzzle about scrutability – the extension of 'Gavagai' – but one
about the indisposition of the subject to respond unequivocally.
The experimental setting in Jungle is ill-defined.

A normal human being can in principle perform any programmable task. This is tantamount to saying he can, given time, pencil
and paper and training, find a proof, if asked, of any theorem of an
appropriately formalized system of logic. If he has trouble finding a
proof, there are software proof procedures to help him out.

No program, even for very simple proofs (in propositional
calculus, say) can be explained in input–output (also known as S–
R) terms. For instance, in a proof our subject might go from step A
(an input) to step B (an output) or instead to step C (a different
output). There is no hope whatever of explaining the two dissimilar
outputs short of knowing the rules of inference underlying the
program. The multiplicity of outputs (to stretch analogies slightly)
is no cause for saying that inference is not a genuine response to
premise input. Therefore, there are human behaviors, pre-emi-
nently linguistic behaviors, that cannot be adequately explained in
behavioristic terms.

As an addendum, observe that the recursive definition of English
(as recognized by Davidson, Montague and others) can be
expressed as a system of program-like rules for generating sentences
– put more picturesquely, as a computer churning out answers to a
programmed problem. Such a scheme for in part explaining natural
language, first proposed by Chomsky, by far escapes any
behavioral explanation.

Quine counters (a) by saying that a child learning his local tongue has perceptual and mental resources, including standards of quality comparison (1969: 123) for preprocessing input; and (b) by saying that the child has 'recursive habits of mind' (1974: 105) for organizing it grammatically.

(a) A youngster learning a language in a home social context has a native ability to match qualities – identify red with red say – and tacitly to process sensory data in habit-formed ways. Quine thinks consideration of these traits is consistent with behaviorism. They do answer Chomsky's criticism of the crude concept of stimulus typical of Skinnerian behaviorism, and of the equally crude concept of intervening variable (Nelson 1969). But I think he gives the game away.

In the past thirty years almost everyone except Quine and his followers (and of course psychologists in the wake of Skinner) have dropped behaviorism. This argument is not purely *ad populum* against behaviorism, since what characterizes the drop is precisely simultaneous adoption of the idea of 'recursive habit' in one guise or another.[8]

Quine's further response to this point defeats itself, it seems to me. He argues as follows.

(b) Yes, recursive definitions as proposed by Davidson (1967, 1977), for instance, might very well fit the corpus of English sentences and even exhibit their meanings. But this is no call for attributing knowledge of, or realization of, any particular set of generative recursive rules to the speaking or listening person as Chomsky does. The concept of fitting rules is not the same as the concept of guiding or real rules the child follows (Quine 1974); fitting is purely instrumental. Fitting recursive schemes to the data of a home language is no different in principle than fitting our idiolectical biases to Jungle.

The trouble with this line is that it represents a paradigm shift in philosophical attitude. Quine certainly does not mean that the behavioral tools of theory building he allows in field linguistics lead him to a strictly instrumentalist hypothesis about translation. He means that translation is *really indeterminate* period. He certainly does NOT mean we should opt for the stingy methods of behaviorism and hence for indeterminacy on merely practical grounds of convenience, economy, fitting the facts, theoretical coherence etc. He does not mean anything of the kind. In linguistics, *behaviorism is true*; it is forced on us; it is no option.

In my opinion this is a radical shift from the naturalistic doctrine that philosophy – including doctrine on method – is a part of science and evolves with it. I am saying Quine cannot coherently keep both his dogma of behaviorism and his more tolerant philosophy of philosophy.

I conclude that either behaviorism has to admit a richer approach to psychology, linguistics and theories of reference and meaning; or that it should be accorded no more scientific status than other instrumentalist theories. In either case it does not support a dogma of inscrutability.[9]

We are by no means done as the indeterminacy thesis might be true and behaviorism false, in which case the former has to be faced on its own terms.[10]

Inscrutability is established by showing there are no grounds for choice between this or that object as the real bearer of a term. There are no grounds, so the argument goes, for individuating the referent of 'Rover' (I am sticking to home language) in direct experience. It might be a part of, or a stage of, a dog, or a wolf. Hence there is no relation in extension to be explained in field inquiry. Viewed in a slightly different way, 'Rover' has a bearer or, if it is a general term, things it applies to; but we do not know from the experiment which object or objects it is; the same holds for all names. Hence we cannot identify the extension of 'refers (x, y)'; hence by the principle no entity without identity (§3) there is no relation of reference; it is inscrutable.

A definition or explication of a term is one thing, and evidence for its application is quite another. There is no entity reference without identity. It seems to me this is beyond dispute. However, 'identity' can mean one of two things (at least), which for the sake of discussion we might call 'theoretical identity' and 'criteriological identity'. We could conceivably explicate reference (establish its scientific identity) without having within reach a surefire means of sporting cases (criteriological identity) – say, of testing effectively for pairs 'Abel', Abel, . . . 'Rover', Rover. We might explicate reference without having an effective criterion for deciding cases, or (more weakly) of inductively forming its extension.[11]

Good examples come from logic, which is home territory. To keep to purely physical examples, the syntactical definition of 'theorem' in predicate calculus is one thing. But effectively establishing whether a given sentence is a theorem or not is impossible. The reader is no doubt familiar with this result as Church's Theorem (1936). Identifying the concept theoremhood by the usual definition is one thing; identifying a theorem by testing is another. The definition of 'theorem' is not a generalization from observation of formulas, although of course it is an explication of a pretheoretical notion of theorem. Similarly for reference.

Viewed historically, mathematical logic is a theory of the logical reasonings of the working mathematician and scientist.[12] The data are sentences of science and the reasonings of the scientist establish them as true or false. Logical theory explains the activity, not by attempting to compile the extension of 'valid inference' by some inductive criteria, but by the well-known methods of reconstruction and formalization of axioms and rules of inference. This does not exclude checking of real cases (in terms of an adequacy condition of some sort); but it does not start with them either. Logical theory, I am claiming, stands to scientific inference as semantical theory does to reference and meaning. Formalization, proof theory and model are later steps which perhaps find no parallel in natural language semantics. But on Quine's own philosophical grounds, living inferences are evolutionary outgrowths of a society's primitive knowings of the world just as references are. Tellng what is a valid inference and what not in Jungle or at home is as possible or impossible as telling what reference is.[13]

Parts of Quine's semantics already entail noncriteriological individuation. The individuation of stimulation patterns (stimulus meaning) is direct. If the linguist could assume only by an effective check of stimulation patterns that he and a native assent the same he would never get his tests off the ground. Rather, he latches onto the same stimulus meaning of an observation sentence by empathizing with the native (Quine 1990: 42f).

The same is true of standards of quality comparison already mentioned. The issue reminds one of Plato's versus Mill's views of mathematical objects: do we grasp the idea of a straight line prior to cases or do we get the idea of the straight line by induction? The child has a native similarity standard of redness and other qualities, Quine says. Of course this is nominalist Quine, not realistic Russell (Chapter 4, §3); but my point is that the concept of *similarity standard* does not rest on checking cases.

Again, the 'knack' of divided reference – being able to tell one individual dog or tree from another – although acquired by the child, is taken for granted by the linguist in his theory. Quine is not one, despite his teaching of the learned (rather than native) character of divided reference, to argue there is no such semantic phenomenon on grounds that the linguist cannot tell it when he sees it. Divided reference is not inscrutable although reference is?

Equally, the subject of divided reference – at the level of telling one individual, not just one sort, from another – already contains the seeds of a realistic causal notion of reference in Kripke's sense, which is to be considered here soon. The point shows up in a disagreement with Geach, of which Quine makes some issue. According to Geach, one can say that two things x and y are the same only if 'we understand [by "the same"] some general term – "the same F"' (Geach 1962: 39). He calls this a 'criterion' of identity. But Quine holds 'they are the same F if and only if x and y are the same outright, and Fx' (1981: 125n). Ability to pick out the individual x is learned by the child, but certainly is not inscrutable to the enquirer.

My further point is that identifying the individual does not depend on understanding that a property F applies (hence a description applies). Hence it does not depend on an understood meaning or criterion in Geach's sense. So, it seems to me, either the learned trick is ineffable or *explainable in direct causal terms*.

These considerations combined with the challenge to behaviorism show, I think, that inscrutability of reference is not an ultimate truth impervious to scientific advance, and even show that it is not unreasonable to dispute 'there is no fact of the matter'. Of course what the facts are is open at this point.

How about inscrutability (B)? The utility of the proxy function in Quine's ontological relativity depends on a rather fine distinction between there being a reference relation and there being a specification of it. Inscrutability (A) says there is no relation: there is no fact of the matter. A proxy function, however, cannot even be defined unless there is a firm domain D of distinct objects. There is no sense in the idea of swapping vague bearers of a name ('Gavagai' is a good one) around with vague bearers of another name. Saying there are a lot of possible reference maps – but we cannot specify the correct one – is not the same as saying there are no maps. Every proxy function is a definite set of pairs of objects. And if (B)'s support from (A) is undercut, there is no reason not to settle hypothetically on a proxy much as one settles on other hypotheses in science.

So rather than foreclose, on behaviorist grounds, any conceptual scheme for reference and other parts of semantics, why not accept naturalism and the basic realistic point of view Quine already espouses, adopt a 'coordinate system' and see where it gets us? In particular, adopt disquotation, as we ourselves have, as a social given. Develop semantics *within* a scheme, but not rule out from *outside* the possibility of semantics, from a dogmatic behaviorist stance. Hilary Putnam, airing this view (1981: 46, 52), claims that Saul Kripke and himself adopt a conceptual scheme *within which* they advance a causal theory of reference.

Another approach, roughly under the same ground rules, is *cognitivism*. Cognitivism is basically a theory of mind, not of reference and meaning, but it has developed in such a way as to tend to absorb causal reference. Kripke's work hits reference head on; cognitivism, championed by Jerry Fodor, approaches from within a cognitive theory that replaces behaviorism at all points. Both may be thought of as alternatives to the indeterminacy thesis.

CHAPTER 8

Cause and Function

1. Rigid designation

Suppose, then, we switch Quine's theory around, pursuing semantics in accordance with a chosen proxy function that fits disquotation and home language practice. The relation of observation sentence to object and stimulus meaning in this fixed scheme is of course causal as before. Holophrastic reference is therefore causal; outer events, stimulations, not inner senses or beliefs, except revealed in overt behavior, are the determiners of reference. Similarly now that we have fixed objects for names to name it might be reasonable to ask for a causal account of reference of names within the working conceptual scheme.

The idea of causal reference represents a paradigm shift away from theories that say reference is determined by, or guided by, subjective meanings in the mind or by Platonic senses. Most often its champions attack the theory of descriptions, descriptions as expressing subjective or internal Lockean representations or ideas.

According to Saul Kripke (1972), names refer directly to objects as do logically proper names in Russell's theory; names have no intension – meaning is just reference. Kripke initially allies himself with John Stuart Mill (1843: Ch. I, §5), who denies proper names have connotation or sense; and it is not too far-fetched to associate him with Peirce, for whom proper names are indexical (3.363).

Thus Kripke rejects Russell's theory of meaning of names. Names and descriptions like 'Abel' and 'the second son of Adam' are logically proper names for Kripke, on a par with 'that' and 'she'. There is no dividing off of denoting from referring terms and no such epistemic rift as that between immediate (acquaintance) and mediate (knowledge by description) reference. However, ordinary names do not shift from object to object in use as indexical terms do. As Kripke puts it, they are 'rigid designators' or, in our terminology, rigidly *referring* names. All tokens of a name refer the same in all circumstances.

Kripke's explanation of rigidity is causal. 'Russell' refers to Russell in virtue of a causal connection, not one between stimulus and a yes or no response to a queried sentence, but one between a direct naming situation or an indirect surrogate situation (through a kind of social passage). No inscrutability, in principle.

Definite descriptions also refer owing to their epistemic ties to names. But description-tokens might refer to different things at different times and places. Hence, to say that descriptions are not rigid is not to say they are irreferential. According to Kripke, all singular terms refer unless they are empty.

Kripke's is not the only causal theory. Many writers classify him with Donnellan (1966), who, we recall, thinks definite descriptions can be used to refer to things ('refuting' Russell) or to attribute qualities to objects. For instance, Schwartz (1977) and Devitt (1981) classify Kripke and Donnellan together in a rough way. I think this enclouds both, one in the other.

One could consistently accept Donnellan and reject Kripke, or the other way around. One could use*, Donnellan-style, the description 'the man in the corner drinking beer' in a speech act, making reference to a plain woman drinking ale, and yet deny that reference is causal. In fact Donnellan suggests there is a historical relation of an object to a name used* for it on occasion, although I do not care to attempt to explain the difference beyond remarking that a historical relation could be intentional, not causal (see Chapter 6, §2). Kripke (1977) is careful to separate 'semantic reference', his concern, from 'speaker's reference', Donnellan's concern. Kripke's semantic reference is basically my reference; and his speaker's reference is my reference*. The basic contrast is just ours of user to user*. A quick way of marking the difference is this: Donnellan's reference* is (if not intentional) causal, but not rigid, while Kripke's is both. It seems impossible to have a doctrine of rigidity squared with one that makes reference depend on use*. This is not to say that Donnellan is wrong; he is different. And conflating the two without a far deeper understanding of the uses of 'use' is a conceptual disservice. Both theories are perhaps causal in some sense or other, but not easily compared, as Kripke shows. For this reason and others already discussed at some length in Chapter 7 I shall leave Donnellan alone.

A rigid designator is defined to be a name that refers the same in every possible world in which the object exists. As examples think of the grammatically proper names on our preliminary list summarized in (1), Chapter 1, §2. 'Russell', for instance, refers to one and the same person in this world, in a world in which he is both bald and an Earl, in another in which he is not bald and not an Earl etc. Our intuitions seem to tell us ordinary names are rigid while definite descriptions are not. Thus although Nixon was the President of the USA in 1970, Hubert Humphrey could have been. But no one other than Nixon could have been Nixon. 'Nixon' refers only to Nixon in any conceivable state of affairs; and so the name is rigid.

Against Kripke, it might be argued that the identity of Nixon from world to world ('crossworld identification') certainly must rest on *some* essential qualities of Nixon no matter what affairs obtain. Nixon is essentially an animal; and therefore 'Nixon' could not refer to some nonanimal, since the term carries with it a tacit restriction to animality. Names, at least in part, are connotative (against Mill) and not strictly indexical. This comment does not end the matter.

The question of identity across worlds seems to presuppose an understanding of 'possible world' as a real but nonactual world of possible affairs, a realm of entities bearing many of the qualities that subsist in our own actual world in our space–time. These worlds might be thought of as variations of the actual world. Call these 'O(ntological)-worlds'.

Kripke often dismisses real possible worlds, O-worlds, including metaphysically essential attributes, in favor of *conceived* worlds or contrary-to-fact conditions. In such a mood he urges thinking of possible worlds as imagined states of affairs. For instance, you can imagine a bald-headed Russell, or a Walter Scott who writes only his money accounts. A case like ' "Russell" refers to Russell in any possible world in which he is bald' simply means 'if Russell were bald (if a bald Russell is imagined), he'd still be the man referred to by "Russell" '. Or 'In a possible world in which green things are red, Schmid is not confused' can be read 'If green were (imagined to be) red, Schmid would not be confused'. Call these 'I(magined)-worlds'.

Now given that states of affairs are just contrary-to-fact conditions, anyone who understands 'If Russell were a robot, he could not have written *Marriage and Morals*' knows it is about Russell. If what is possible is just what is expressed subjunctively, there is no constraint on what can be said about Russell so long as he stays put as Russell.

Of course this raises the question whether Russell imagined as a robot is really staying put as Russell. It seems he must have some essential attributes after all, Kripke thinks. But these are to be found in our experience of actual things. Possible worlds are *stipulated* not found: 'we do not begin with worlds (which are somehow supposed to be real, and whose qualities, but not whose objects, are perceptible to us) and then ask about criteria of . . . [identifying objects from one world to another]; on the contrary we begin with the objects, which we *have* and can identify in the actual world. We can then ask whether certain things might have been true of the objects' (Kripke 1972: 273).

This simple argument is possibly the best Kripke has to offer for the I-world interpretation of 'worlds' and it directly supports the notion of rigidity of names. However, it does not obviate need for a notion of individual essence, which I shall return to in due course.[1]

Coming next is Kripke's response to an objection that if names are said to be rigid we violate some very sophisticated opinion about identities in science. For example, we know (Frege reminded us) 'Phosphorus' and 'Hesperus' both refer to Venus, so

(1) Phosphorus = Hesperus

is true. But (1) must be true in all possible worlds if it is assumed the names are rigid, that is to say, if 'Phosphorus' and 'Hesperus' refer the same in all worlds. Hence (1) is necessary – it holds no matter what is the nature of things. (Note that here Kripke is appealing to O-worlds; a concept of all possible I-worlds is unintelligible: would 'all worlds' mean the total of your imaginings? Mine? Schmid's? All the above?)

In the literature, however, it is generally agreed that the identity (1) is an astronomical *discovery* and hence is a contingent, not a necessary, truth. Therefore the assumption of rigidity is false, it might be claimed.

This common view is wrong, Kripke says. The empirical discovery that (1) is true is of course a case of knowledge a posteriori. However, the tradition should not have inferred (1)'s contingency from its being known after the fact. Contingency and necessity are metaphysical categories – the contingent obtaining in some worlds and the necessary in all. Matters of epistemic primacy – what is a priori or not – however, are not questions of worlds but of knowledge. Metaphysical necessity is one thing, epistemic aprioricity another.[2] The objection to rigidity from (1)'s supposed contingency is traceable to deep philosophical confusion (provided we think of O-worlds).

Let us now assume proper names like 'Russell' have been shown to be rigid. Names, being rigid, are not abbreviations of or substitutes for definite descriptions or clusters of them. Names are rigid, definite descriptions are not. 'Russell' is not an abbreviation for 'the junior author of *Principia*', for the junior author could be Hegel in some possible world, while Russell could not be Hegel anywhere. Likewise, 'Sir Walter Scott' is not an abbreviation of 'the author of *Waverly*' since some other person might have written *Waverly*; or Scott might not have written anything. Russell's theory is false.

Kripke has two main arguments against the description theory besides this bare statement. They hinge on a couple of familiar interpretations of Fregean 'sense': (a) 'meaning' or 'way of understanding'; and (b) 'mode of presentation' (Chapter 3, §§3 and 5). Description theories divide into those taking descriptions to be synonymous with names and those that fix the reference.[3]

(a) Russell must have meant in his theory of denoting for names not to fix reference but for them to mean the same as the descriptions they stand for. For consider

(2) Aristotle was the greatest man who studied under Plato.

Suppose Aristotle did not exist. Then if Russell meant the description merely to fix the reference, there is no reason to suppose also that the greatest man did not exist (Kripke 1972: 276–7). He might have indeed existed and been Eudoxus. But for the logical analysis of descriptions to be adequate to Russell's problem of empty names, it must be that the one and only greatest man etc. did not exist. So descriptions have to be synonymous with names in Russell's theory. They are not merely reference-fixers.

But this same-meaning theory cannot be true. For assuming it is, (2) is necessarily true. However, its necessity gets denied by the fact that 'the greatest man who studied under Plato' is not rigid while

'Aristotle' is. So Russell's theory that names are abbreviated descriptions is false.

(b) Kripke's next argument says we can have definitions which are only contingent, yet are a priori and analytic. If so, descriptions might as modes of presentation (second interpretation of Fregean 'sense') fix reference, without the description being synonymous with the name. Consider

(3) The meter is the length of a certain stick S at time t_0

where S is the standard meter in Paris. (3) is a *stipulative* definition, which in some quarters (Quine 1953) provides the clearest (or perhaps only) case of pure analyticity. Now 'the meter' is a proper name of an 'impure' number, and as such is rigid. However, S, being a physical stick, could have been any length, within limits, at t_0. So 'the length . . .' is not rigid. Nevertheless at that time it was used to define the meter. It fixes the reference; but no one would use that very stick in Baku to measure off a meter. (3) is an example of an analytic, a priori, but *contingent* sentence. The lesson Kripke wants to teach is that descriptions often fix reference (1972: 276); and at the time of the fixing certainly refer the same as the name being fixed. But they are not rigid. The description 'the bright morning star in the eastern sky' fixes the reference of 'Phosphorus'. It has an epistemic moment, bringing the planet into awareness; but in another world it could be about a genuine star, say, not about Venus. So the main thing in general is that definite descriptions do not fix reference in the sense that knowing the description enables identification of the object in all worlds, nor are they synonymous with names (Kripke 1972).

Furthermore, if a description is to provide knowledge of the object, it must not contain occurrences of other proper names or otherwise must contain only occurrences of names replaceable by descriptions, and so on. For example, consider

Cicero is the Roman who denounced Catiline.

'The denouncer of Catiline' does not fix Cicero unless 'Catiline' is independently describable. Devitt (1981), a causal theorist, examines various responses to the requirement (for instance, that 'Catiline' be eliminated) and reaches the plausible result that in general it cannot be met. Even if you were to borrow the referential knowledge of a classicist to fix 'Catiline', you (and he) might run (in circles) into other names and have to draw on information such as that Catiline is the man denounced by Cicero.

Again to fix reference, a description or cluster of descriptions should be true and should pick out a real object. But this requirement fails to hold more often than not (Devitt 1981). For instance 'the first person to think the Earth is round' no doubt fixes the reference of 'Columbus' for many people; but it does not determine true reference.

Add these criticisms to Donnellan's observation that descriptions in use* might be attributively false, and the case against the Russellian theory of names is compelling.

Let us turn now to the question of the rigidity of application.

Both Kripke (1972) and Putnam (1975: 215–71) think of certain general terms such as 'man', 'oak' and 'water' as rigid. These are often called 'natural kind' terms as they reflect a distinction between species and natural groupings of things on the one hand and 'accidental' assemblages such as blotched red things, bald-headed men, scarred oaks and polluted water on the other.[4] A natural kind thing such as an oak is what it is essentially, and not another thing. A fire-scarred oak, however, would be an oak even if unscarred, but could not be an oak without being an oak.

Natural kind terms refer to objects independently of imagined circumstances (being scarred), much as rigid names do. Proper names are connotationless and refer independently of descriptions; likewise natural kind predicates apply independently of meanings (picked up in learning language) housed in our minds. One way Putnam puts it is this: application of natural kind terms like 'water' or 'oak' depends on objective chemical or botanical traits and laws, not on criteria laid down in advance of inquiry (1986: 71). A catchy slogan of his is, ' "meanings" just ain't in the head' (1975: 227). They are not a priori.

It may help to remember that some philosophers often talk of properties as meanings: the meaning of 'red' is the property *red*; others talk of psychological objects – like Frege's senses psychologized (or 'subjective' intension) as meanings: the meaning of 'red' is its sense. Putnam seems to be advancing the first view as regards natural kind terms – meaning is objective and public.

Parallel to definite descriptions fixing reference, there are stereotypes we appeal to to fix application of natural kind terms. Just as one might fix the reference of 'Russell' by 'the junior author . . .', so one might fix the application of 'water' by the stereotype 'colorless; transparent; tasteless; thirst quenching; etc.' (ibid.: 269). But, pushing the analogy, 'the junior author . . .' might have named other than Russell in some possible world; and similarly the stereotype might have applied to some totally other compound having a molecular composition XYZ in some imagined world. Neither descriptions nor stereotypes determine reference although they can be used to fix (in Kripke's sense of the word) reference in daily speech, and might express the meanings learned in various situations by most people.

I come now to the causal theory as such. Rigidity and fixing of reference could all be explained in terms of intentional mind. Names might express rigid intentions to refer and descriptions might express intentions to guide or fix reference. However, Kripke's view is that reference is caused, not intended. Of course the two are not necessarily exclusive as it might turn out – contrary to Brentano – there are intentional elements in some causal, physical complex.

A name is established in a naming event or baptism (Kripke 1972: 298f) and is passed on up through society. 'Abel', 'Russell', 'QE2' and the rest get their bearers in direct confrontation in naming ceremonies and baptisms, and thus are immediately linked to things much as demonstratives are. 'I hereby name *this* child "Abel" '; or 'we hereby name *this* ship "QE2" '. Although Kripke does not go into it, you can think of the causal relation in baptism as one between the object (a child, say) and some sort of brain event in the speaker's head which is conventionally associated to the name.

However, in indirect situations names are causally connected to their bearers by a kind of socio-psychological linkage, traceable back to the naming. Naming ceremonies are not descriptional or (perhaps) linguistic, but brute causal events. A speaker 'who is on the far end of this chain, who has heard about . . . Richard Feynman, in the marketplace or wherever, may be referring to Richard Feynman even though he can't remember from whom he first heard of Feynman . . .' (ibid.: 299) or remember a single thing about him.

Reference is thus communicated via a 'chain' from person to person, and it is echoed in eternal sentences that could be expressed in remote places and times. Chaining is of course a metaphor; and Kripke claims no more.

However, being handed a name and a referent from a speaker is not reference borrowing, briefly alluded to above. Reference borrowing is getting to know a name via description from an expert in classics (say) – 'Catiline is the man denounced by Cicero' – while a link is just a stage in the handing on of the pristine name–thing disquote 'Catiline' – Catiline itself.

The theory of causal reference brings us back face-to-face with the question of individual essence. Our conception of cause seems to involve a notion of *similarity*, at least in the sense that there is something about Russell that causally determines 'Russell' but never 'Ottoline' or 'Bush'. This is again to say that Russell must be Russell; and in the I-worlds' interpretation, as noted at the head of this section, the essence of Russell is grasped in actual experience.

Study of this matter leads Kripke to the view that an individual is singled out biologically, in the parents' giving of their very tissues to form the Russellian zygote (ibid.: 313). Russell might have been bald, a bricklayer, a rabid Tory or whatever, but never anything but the offspring of Lord and Lady Amberly. It is this Russell that is Russell in all possible worlds and is causally connected to 'Russell'. A similar tack would identify the essence of the QE2 with its original parts and construction.

Application of natural kind terms is also supposed to be causal, although it seems to me the analogy to reference is mightily strained. Predicates, as well as proper names, Putnam says (1986: 73), apply to 'things which are given *existentially* and not by [verbal?] criteria. . .'. A term applies if 'it stands in the relation of "sameness of nature" to . . . existentially given things'. What this might mean is that the mind grasps the essence directly (shades of Russell on universals) in objective things. General term tokens have indexical ingredients in them, as do 'I' and 'now'. 'I', as we observed back in Chapter 1, has the same meaning for you as for me; but its reference depends on who is speaking. Similarly 'oak' could have different subjective meanings for the two of us, but only one application depending on the stuff that the object really is (Putnam 1975: 229ff).

What makes this view more problematic than it already is, is that true application (within a working conceptual scheme) of predicates is established by science, according to Putnam. The discovery that water is H$_2$O is possible only for a highly advanced science. But this is not the same as establishing its reference existentially, if that concept entails 'immediate causal connection' as in a baptism. In science water is and always was sensibly colorless and tasteless H$_2$O. Subjective meanings, however, change and are parochial, which suggests a division of labor between the common person carrying his subjective meanings-in-the-head and the scientist and his objective essences. If the stereotype theory is true, the two groups share use of stereotypes as well as of indeterminate predicates, but not essences. Of course this is reminiscent of primary and secondary qualities in Locke.

In summary, reference of names is rigid and causal. One named individual is distinguished by his individual essence from another, and essence is basically genetic. A baptism establishes reference, which is passed in a social chain through the language-speaking society. Definite descriptions often aid, epistemically, in fixing reference but do not determine it. Reference by speakers originates in naming ceremonies and passes up through a social chain.

Application of natural kind predicates is also rigid. One kind is distinguished from another by its essence, which is established objectively by science. But the nonscientific meanings of predicates are holistic and indeterminate. True application of a term like 'water' passes from scientific to popular use in direct indexical situations by instruction – 'That, my friend, is water' – aided by sensible stereotypes which are necessary ingredients of objective meaning. Application (for Putnam) is determined by science and is passed down (if at all) to ordinary speakers.

There are two theories in Kripke: O-worlds used when he is anxious to distinguish metaphysical necessity from the a priori, and the I-worlds when he is anxious to make essence a question of science. The first is most relevant to concerns of modal logic, which are not ours. The notion of rigid-designator seems to go pretty well with either.

What reason do we have to think this theory is true? Well, it satisfies a kind of disquotation requirement. 'Russell' refers to Russell if and only if the reference is fixed in a baptism by agents. So the theory, as regards proper names, meets parts of our condition (*R*), although there is no hint of interest in purporting or empty names. 'Russell' does not refer the same as 'the junior author . . .' as the latter might fix reference in some worlds, but not in all.

Indirect disquotations, as I called them in Chapter 1, are false, in general. 'Russell' does refer, however, to the son of Lord and Lady Amberly, since being the son of them makes him what he is.

Similarly a general term 'oak' applies to *a* if and only if *a* is an instance of the kind oak, as determined by science.

Some of our posed puzzles about reference deriving from Frege and Russell are still puzzling here. '*a* = *a*' and '*a* = *b*' are both necessarily true, and neither '*a*' nor '*b*' has a sense. Devitt (1981: 122) has suggested that the difference in cognitive significance or meaning might be explained in the causal theory as a difference between the fixing of '*a*' and '*b*'; in perception, for instance, 'Hesperus' and 'Phosphorus' are fixed differently. Devitt also discusses empty terms, making some interesting suggestions; but like the question of cognitive significance this awaits more detail on 'cause' itself.

The notion of rigid designator does not get us very far in meeting the puzzles of substitutivity in belief sentences. 'Hesperus' and 'Phosphorus' are rigid as can be; but there is no substituting in sentences reporting Schmid's beliefs. He believes Hesperus is Venus, but not that Phosphorus is. We still lack any criterion whatever for substitution in all such cases (cf. Quine 1981) except in primary (*de re*) occurrences; and a *de re* reading of an intensional sentence is as of this date a matter of intuition and membership on the right team in philosophy of logic (Chapter 4, §5).

The causal theory claims reference and essential meaning are objective; it rejects the subjective, and in this respect is similar to Russell's atomism and knowledge by acquaintance. For causalists, inner beliefs and meanings are basically irrelevant to reference and application of natural kind terms.

The attribution of a Millean theory of names by Kripke to himself has to be qualified. Kripke has no liking for Fregean senses or Carnapian individual concepts. But he needs individual essences or otherwise does not seem to be able to account for rigidity. These are objective traits of the bearer which are grasped meanings in reference. In effect, essence reinstates definite descriptions as expressing objective meanings while discrediting them as expressing meanings in the head.

Cause and Function

2. Folk psychology

Supposing reference survives Quine's inscrutability arguments, we next have to reckon with the intentionality of it. According to Short Quine (Chapter 7, §1) scientific psychology has no place for intentions (read 'intensional vocabulary'). Reference, if causal, might have its place; but purported and empty reference are intentional, and if insisted on might contaminate pure science.

A broad alternative, now that we have shed any vestigal loyalty to behaviorism, is to explore naturalism as a philosophy of psychology that gets inside mind and takes intentionality into account, one way or another; that includes a theory of language and meaning; and that recognizes causal reference. If it could be pulled off, such a thing would be a theory of reference far removed from the 'pernicious practice' of separating semantics from psychology.

There are several approaches. The first two, flying under the banner of 'cognitivism' strive for a comprehensive philosophical framework for cognitive science. Intentional attitude, which is perhaps the most problematic feature of mind, is conceived of as a property or state of a person; otherwise, as a relation between a person and an object believed or desired. According to one it is a state, and to the second it is a relation to thought.

Cognitivism, in all its guises, is intuitive, programmatic philosophy that strives to be a theory of mind, semantics and a foundation for cognitive science all at once, and at the same time to accommodate Brentano or refute him. Unfortunately, reference tends to get lost as a tail-end nuisance tacked on to belief-psychology.

Beginning with the most conservative view, 'folkism' as I shall call it, is not far from Brentano, and accepts the thesis that psychological concepts are not reducible to physical or biological science. It promotes a two-level holism: following Brentano and Quine (Chapter 2, §5), mental concepts cannot be expressed extensionally. Furthermore, it is skeptical of analyzing intensional concepts in terms of any collection of primitives. In this camp you can find a theory of reference of sorts. However, its salient feature is its denial of all attempts to understand reference as a word-to-thing intentional link, as we should like.

This avatar of holism accepts the everyday language people use in talk about each other, predicting behavior and attributing motives to each other. The corpus of daily talk supplies data for a loose

155

discipline called 'folk psychology' consisting of principles underlying the psychology used in everyday life (Hill 1988: 169). These are approximations to the tacit principles people in the street are guided by in dealing with each other. The principles are, of course, precisely the kind Quine means to eliminate from science.

Folkism, however, is no mere compilation and generalization of folk psychology. It defends basic philosophical premises. To provide substance to our coming review, here are a few typical laws of folk thought (Hill 1987, 1988). These are empirical, socio-psychological propositions, but of course not reducible to physical science.

(a) If i believes that p, then i is disposed to act in ways that would tend to satisfy i's desires if p and the other propositions he believed were true.

(b) If t exists, then 't' refers to an object only when the object is identical with t.

(c) If p is saliently instantiated in i's immediate environment, i is attending to information from the part of the environment in which p is instantiated, i has concepts that pick out the various individuals, properties, and relations that are involved in p, and p is compatible with i's prior beliefs, then i comes to believe that p.

These generalizations are meant to explain our informal folk talk in the following way. Your and my concept of belief, for instance, is derived from acquaintance of laws like (a) (Hill 1988). The laws have a dual role: they aid in explaining human behavior to ordinary people; and they are also the ground of concepts of the intentional we use in building a scientific psychology.

The main principles of folkism are, first, that laws such as (a)–(c) derive from actual folklore. The laws are empirical, predictive and general, and have the same epistemological standing (but of course not the precision) as those of hard science.

Second, they are largely true. Law (a) expresses the holistic interaction of belief, desire and act as they occur in intelligent behavior. Law (b) expresses a disquotational fact about reference as it actually figures in folk psychology. Law (c) expresses the basic conditions underlying perceptual belief.

Third, following Brentano and Quine's semantical version of

him, the predicates 'believes', 'act', 'desires', 'refers', and 'attending' occurring in the laws are not analyzable in extensional terms. The laws are expressed in intensional sentences, while yet being empirically verifiable.

Fourth, following the very influential thought of David Lewis (1972b) and Paul Grice (1974), the predicates in question are implicitly definable only. There is no intensional dictionary, so to say, and no primitive intensional terms like 'act', 'expect' or 'pain', in terms of which other terms 'belief', 'desire' etc. can be defined. That people do not believe *p* without reliance on other beliefs *q* or in fulfillment of expectations, and do not act or desire without believing, is hard empirical fact. 'Belief' and 'desire' accrue meaning in contexts like (a)–(c). The meaning of an intentional concept is the role it plays. For suppose, following the behaviorists, we try to analyze 'belief' in terms of 'disposition to act' (cf. Chapter 6, §1, and Chapter 7, §1), and in fact obtain the definition '*i* believes that *p* when she is disposed to act as if *p* were true' (Grice 1974: 24). But what about 'act', which is also intensional? What do we mean by 'act as if *p* were true'? Grice suggests its meaning reciprocates with those of 'desire' and 'belief' itself: it means 'act in ways that would tend to satisfy *S*'s desires if *p* and the other propositions he believed were true'. Believing *p* depends not only on act and desire but on other belief.

Meanings in folk psychology are embedded in indefinitely large, complex, sentential contexts of intensional terms. Grice concludes from his observation that laws like (a) are in effect *implicit definitions* of the terms.[5] There are no *explicit definitions* and this apparently means that there are no primitive, undefined intensional concepts.

This doctrine of *intensional holism* carries us significantly beyond Brentano (third point above) to a teaching of holism *within* psychology. It differs from Quine's meaning holism in several ways. Implicit definability is not a sign of indeterminacy; meanings of 'belief' etc. are determinate enough, but only within socially established linguistic contexts.[6]

Fifth, principles like (a)–(c) constrain our use of intentional concepts in philosophy. We do not, and in writing theories should not, attempt analysis of an intentional concept by wrenching it out of context. In isolation, there is no meaning of 'belief' to explain. Theoretical questions about reference, too, can be properly answered only by heeding basic folk principles and inquiring into their logical and semantical properties (Hill 1988: 169).

So then what does folk theory say about reference? We find a dual theory. The first part of it is just (1) and (2) of Chapter 1, §2, which we now know are summaries of our lists early on, of Tarski's enumerations in Chapter 5, §3, and of the basis clauses of his definition of 'satisfaction' in Chapter 5, §2. Hill holds that particular disquotations are 'partially constitutive of the concept of reference' (1987: 2). The variables in these earlier summaries are quantifiable, so the laws of both reference and application relations are general. For folkism this is the ultimate explanation of reference, including that of absolute assignment schemes in Tarski-type theories of truth.

The second part of the theory of reference is a collection of folk principles about reference construed as in our original definition. Familiar principles of reference we are all inclined to accept find explanation in folk law. One principle, for instance, says that terms in natural science refer. It is a fact of folklore that 'water' refers to water, if there is such stuff, and 'quark' to quark. Thus the warrant of disquotation in linguistic science goes back to social use. Another says that proper names are normally introduced in baptisms, which is a folk principle used by Kripke. And yet another, that if i knows 'water' refers to water, then others can use the word to enlist i's aid in preventing someone from dying of thirst or drowning. Each of these principles is grounded in everyday folk use of 'reference'.

Hill claims that our (his) analysis of 'N refers to o' in, Chapter 1, §2, is *epistemically prior* to laws of baptism and the others exemplified in the previous paragraph. A ceremony naming Russell 'Russell' is an instance of the a priori law (b).

For reasons we have been belaboring for many a page, folkism is completely inadequate as a theory of reference. The mix of quantifiers in (1) of Chapter 1, §2, is not coherent, as argued back in Chapter 1, §4. Moreover neither (1) nor the a posteriori part of the theory (the second part) say anything about linkage or about the intentional nature of reference.

Of course according to folk-theory we are not entitled to expect further elucidation as disquotational lists are methodologically a priori and thus closed to the kind of empirical enquiry folkism countenances. Moreover intentional holism allows only principles of reference, beyond basic definition, that characterize it implicitly in terms of other intentions. Explicit analysis is out.

Allied to these objections is another of long standing: there is nothing in the theory relevant to names without bearers or to the speculative; (1) of Chapter 1, §2, expressly states that bearers must exist. This compromises the note of purportedness in reference that it seems to me folkism means to sound. Either the intentionality of reference is accepted as a datum or it has to be explained. Folkism short-stops the question, both ways.

At any rate, folk theory makes clear what we, even after having answered Quine's skepticism, have to face in seeking to understand the anatomy of reference. If intentional holism is true, it seems the impenetrability, if not the inscrutability, of reference must follow.

3. Mind as functional

Could folk theory accept holism of the mental attitudes without slipping into Brentano's mind–matter dualism? A devotee might answer: while reference and belief are holistic, there is no tacit commitment to nonphysical mind. Although folk laws are largely true of persons, their beliefs and other states of mind, the laws do not entail any particular ontology. Folk theory is about the nature of psychology, not of mind.

However, without compromising the doctrine of folk laws, one might suggest that mental states picked out by the concept of belief, for example, are brain states in the head. Furthermore one might cling to the holist view, suggesting that the logic of belief, desire, act etc. is reflected in an ontology of causally interacting brain events. Belief and the other attitudes are what they are owing to causal role in the brain/mind life of a person. Thus conceived, cognitivism not only reinstates our plain picture of people with minds and thoughts, thinking and doing things and expressing some of what they think in words, but offers an ontology of mind and a putative reduction of intentionality to causal interaction.

The fundamental, essentially materialistic idea behind functionalism is that two different physical things can be used for the same purpose. A stone or a book can function as a paper weight; and a bird's wing or an airplane wing, either one, can function as an airfoil. Similarly, different material states (perhaps as different as

159

states of wires in a robot's head and states of neurons in a person's) can play the same role in thought.

What makes a physical state mental is its function.[7] Belief plays the role of mediating between desire and action (cf. (a) in §2): if you desire *D* and believe condition *B* for getting *D* obtains, then you act in a way *A* depending on belief *B* so as to get *D*. Exactly the same might be reported of me in the same situation. The functional claim is this: the same folk descriptions fit both of us. We have the same belief *B* despite our being physically distinct right down to the working nerve cells.

Thus functionalism declares that psychological facts about beliefs and desires are *realized* in material brains, meaning that mental terms and descriptions can be interpreted in a domain of brain states and processes, in principle, and under this interpretation the facts are true (Field 1978). Brentano is answered by our heeding holistic interaction: the intentionality of belief is accounted for in its role-playing with desire and other attitudes, which come down to material states.

Thinking of a psychological attitude thus as some kind of inner state, functionalism is a *token identity* theory of mind. What this means is that a mental (functional) state *B* is (contingently) identical to a physical state in one physical system *P*, while the same state *B* might be identical to a dissimilar physical complex *P ′*. While the states qua physical are individuated by physical properties (as are stones and books), states qua mental are individuated by role (being weights). Two beliefs can be type-identical by function (same role in mediating desire and act, say), non-type-identical by stuff (the belief realized in your head in a system of neurons totally unlike a complex in my head or in a robot) and token-identical to one stuff in one system and to another in another.

As a philosophy of mind, functionalism holds that mental states are not type–type reducible to brain states as they might be individuated differently, as just explained; so psychology is autonomous with respect to biology, as Brentano claimed. However owing to the contingent identity of mental and physical all around, the picture is not dualistic. Everything mental is material. Moreover the idea of intentional holism is preserved. The folk laws of §3 are true; they are true under the interpretation of 'belief' etc. as causal, physical process.

Thus this version of cognitivism also offers a kind of semantics.

Once again, consider (a) in section 2. 'Belief' in '*i* believes that *p*' and elsewhere in the law has meaning in context. On the functionalist account, the content of the belief is determined in causal role of belief interacting with desire and act. The idea of causal role presumably catches the purposive aspect of the intentional, and then arrogates sentential meaning (of '*p*' in the example) to that. So we might suspect that functionalism does not contribute to reference theory or to other concerns of directedness and inexistence posed by Brentano. We would be right. Here is more detail why.

Throughout the foregoing account, attitudes are seen as states. However, they are understood by logicians and semanticists to be *relations*. '*i* believes that *p*' is a dyadic predicate analogous to '*x* is a brother of *y*'. *p* is a *propositional object* or *thought*. The relation, psychologically speaking, is just Brentano's directedness from person to inexistent object. What does this have to do with states?

The answer is far from clear, except in the received scientific meaning of 'state', which I shall invoke later. Right now, belief qua state is a physical thing having psychological properties owing to its interactions with other states. That is the core of the doctrine. However, as a relation, belief is semantical, person to object.

The functionalist (in my somewhat unelaborated version) in his love of holism fuses attitude with object,[8] combining intentionality with semantics. Here is how he does it.

Make belief-that-*p* (alternatively, state-of-belief-that-*p*) a property of *i*; and then explain that belief in terms of its holistic commerce with desire-that-*q* and act-on-knowledge-*r*. . . . In other words, collapse the object of belief into the belief, and explain intention and meaningful content by cognitive role. The idea is captured by rephrasing '*i* believes that *p*' so as to be read 'believes-that-*p* (*i*)' or 'in-state-believing-that-*p* (*x*)'. The latter are clearly monadic predicates over a domain of persons. Object *p* is fused with belief as its 'content'; and there is no separate, meaningful object to be believed. '*p*' is not a quantifiable variable.

The state interpretation is nice, as by using it you might think of attitudes qua states as interacting, roughly like physical state-to-state transitions in mechanics, but of course according to folk law. But it is not so nice as an answer to Brentano. It smothers the semantical issues. The meaning of 'belief', on the relational account, is not exhausted in its intentional connections with desires and acts.

The point is best appreciated when we are reminded that

'believes-that-p' can be true of x independently of the truth of p. For instance, 'believes-that-there-is-no-train-just-down-the-track-from-the-crossing' is true of Schmid at time t. Now according to fusion functionalism, we explain a section of Schmid's life at t by alluding to the interaction of his belief states, including this one, his desires, hopes, other beliefs etc. Moreover the explanation runs the same way whether there is a train down the track or not. Schmid wants to get across. Believing there is no train and that his car will not stall, he starts across. All that counts is the belief, true or false. Or so it is said.

But this is not so. True beliefs support survival better than false ones. If Schmid's belief at t were false his beliefs and desires would be drastically changed forever, even if the train did not hit him full on. Truth or falsity of an attitude certainly plays a part in *change* of attitude over and above the holistic interactions.[9]

Again, truth and falsity of belief influence other persons. Schmid's belief that p, might influence Jones to believe that Schmid's belief is true. That is to say, Jones might come to believe not only that Schmid believes there is no train, but that there is no train. Or, since Schmid is notoriously unreliable, that there is a train (Field 1978: 48; Grover 1990).

4. Mental representation

The foregoing criticisms presuppose that belief is a relation. If it is, we are not going to get a semantics of belief by examining the commerce of belief, desire and act. What is wanted is an explication of it in terms of persons and objects. But there is the rub: if folkism is right, an explicit analysis of the relation itself is out of the question.

According to the folkist incarnation of holism (§2) the only possible definition of 'belief' is implicit, in terms of desire, action, other belief and so on without end. Indeed, Hill has no doubts. Efforts at explicit definition – which would be of the form 'i believes that p if and only if S' where S contains no occurrence of 'belief' and is preferably extensional – are literally false (Hill 1988: 178). This out-Quine's Quine's Brentano for whom the attempt would be merely senseless.

I see no way of countering the holist position short of a very long argument, in some respects appealing to points similar to those against inscrutability in Chapter 7, §4. It would say that folkism confounds analysis of belief with contextual conditions of belief; and that use of the belief, desire, act (as (a)–(c) of §2) principle in anything that resembles scientific inference presupposes assertability (hence meaningfulness) of the separate belief, desire etc. reports. For instance, using '*i* believes there is a tree and desires to get under it to avoid the rain' cannot be used to predict that *i* goes under the tree without separate assertion of '*i* believes there is a tree' – which obviously has its own meaning independently of the belief–desire–act whole.

But the best response, I think, is to grab the bull by the horns and go straight toward an extensional analysis of intention and, especially for us, of reference. Furthermore, if all functionalism has to offer is a folkist theory of reference as above, it falls short of goodness; its treatment totally misses crucial issues about empty terms and purportedness. I shall assume as a methodological principle that intentional holism is false (cf. Dummett 1975: 121) and give defense of the assumption later.

A semantical theory of belief requires persons and objects, at least. So we hereby introduce objects, reclaiming a domain of interpretation for the two-place predicate '*i* believes that *p*'.

Think of the object of an attitude as being an unuttered sentence: in the report 'Schmid believes Russell is an Hegelian', imagine the object believed is a tacit sentence, probably unvoiced Bavarian. Thus, as a first approximation: '*i* believes *p*' is rendered '*i* is in a belief relation to an unuttered sentence that means *p*'. And similarly for desire and other attitudes.

What is being posited is an inner language of thought consisting of *mental representations* (MRs) – a medium for planning, conniving, speculating and worrying – typical of all minded beings. The inner language of MRs has its own syntax and semantics. 'Snow is white' means snow is white since a corresponding MR in the head means snow is white. But the character of the relation of spoken to internal language of thought is ahead of us, and I will set it aside for the moment.

A reason for positing MRs is that many of the things people hold true (like 10^{10} is greater than 10^9-23) are never overtly expressed; however, they are eminently things believed. Another is, if animals have intentions (contrary to Descartes), they must have objects to intend, say some cognitivists; but these cannot be expressly linguistic as animals do not have language (whether they do or not is a distraction we are not going to deal with yet).

The MR language might have little orthographic resemblance to English. If you want, picture sentences of the language as inscribable on a chalkboard or cathode-ray tube (Stich 1983), or as a kind of 'brain writing' (Fodor, 1975; Dennett 1978). However, you might do well to skip the pictures and think of the internal language for speakers of English as consisting in large part of tokens of English sentence types we think about but do not utter (Field 1978; Harman 1973). We might suppose that there is a syntactical-type-preserving map of spoken English to MRs, and leave the question of shape and quality open.

The particles of inner language are physical, of course; they are brain occurrences. Sentences of the language of thought stand to sentence types of English as neural things do to belief qua functional, token to type. Thus the theory says that if the sentence 'it is snowing' is instanced in our heads, your token of the sentence need not be any more like mine than your brain states be qualitatively like mine, while they are of the same type. So the notion of MR squares well with functionalism.

It has been argued often recently that spoken sentences cannot be the objects of belief. The argument is plain. If you attribute to Schmid, who understands German only, belief that it is snowing, then you can hardly endorse a theory that says the object of his belief is the English sentence, 'it is snowing'. The argument means trouble for internal tokens as well, if the MR theory as just sketched is true. Schmid has tokens of German sentences only in his head.

Representationalism, whatever its difficulties, is thus a variety of cognitivism which, in any of its versions, pictures the causal network of beliefs, desires, acts and so forth typical of folkism and functionalism as relations instantiated in the brain where the relata are symbols (not to be confused with stimuli, which are *not* symbols!). Roughly the semantics of the system is to be sought in the relation of individuals to MRs, and the intentionality of the beliefs etc. in causal role.

Field's (1978) seminal idea for the analysis of belief is to exploit an ambiguity in the word 'representation': an MR is both a concrete, formal object (a representation of a sentence is a *token* of it, a representation as an agent) and also a symbol or *carrier of meaning* (a representation as a sign of an object). To believe something is to entertain a relation to a *tangible object that has a meaning*.

Hence Field's prescription is just this: to say that Jones believes it is snowing is to just say that she has a relation to an inner token of 'it is snowing' whose meaning is the proposition that it is snowing. Field calls the inner relation to a token, 'belief*'. In Field's words (roughly):

(1) i believes that p if and only if there is an MR S such that i believes* S and S means that p.

Now provided that 'i believes* S' can be explained in physical terms and that 'means that p' can be explained in a semantically neutral way, we seem to have gained meaningful objects for thoughts to be about.

As to belief* of a sentence token, a suitable analysis is attainable, he thinks, in materialistic terms (ibid.: 13); and to get on we shall suppose this can be done.

Let us turn briefly to some old problems. For one who is attentive, as the reader is, to the problems of substitutivity of names in belief sentences, the MR idea provides explanation. Once again, consider Jones' belief (not Schmid's, as at the moment he speaks German only) that Russell is an Hegelian. Even though it be true that Russell is the junior author of *Principia* it does not follow that Jones believes that the junior author is a Hegelian. We now see why. 'Russell is an Hegelian' is not the same syntactical type as 'the junior author is an Hegelian', so the physical belief* relation to MR need not hold for both MRs although they are equivalent in truth value. Therefore, 'Jones believes* S' can be true in one case and not the other (cf. Stich 1983: 39).

The question of the meaning that p of the token S arouses some sympathy for functionalists who fuse belief and object in their narrow semantics. But being determined to get objects, we might follow Carnap and the pure semantists and consider the propositional meaning of an MR to be the set of possible worlds in which the sentence is true (Chapter 6, §3). For the benefit of skeptics and materialists (followers of Commandment II) who think the notion of possible worlds abuses good sense, Field reduces the meaning of an MR to the reference of names and designation of predicates in the actual world as follows.

From Tarski we infer what it means for a token in English to be true in our actual world. His semantical theory has to be extended to English and to sentence tokens rather than types (Chapter 4, §5). For the present exercise, the domain of objects of other possible worlds is the same as the actual world; '*a*' refers to the same object in each world, i.e. names are rigid. What about the predicate '*P*'? Its application is different from world to world; in fact it is easy to see (think of Carnapian state descriptions) that different worlds on a common domain are generated precisely by assigning different extensions to predicates.

On the other hand, the property the predicate refers to (cf. Chapter 1, §3, on predicate reference) is the same in all. 'Russell is a philosopher' is true in this world, but undoubtedly false in a world in which the Amberlys are ditch-diggers. Different world, different extension. However, 'philosopher' has the same objective meaning, i.e. refers to the *same property* in both.

Given these assumptions the truth condition of our sentence with respect to any world is given by just the reference scheme for names and predicates used in the actual world. This fixes reference schemes for all possible worlds; and consequently the truth condition of '*a* is *P*' in any possible world is the same as it is in ours.

If we suppose that these notions are without fault, (1) may be rewritten:

(2) *i* believes that *a* is *P* if and only if *i* believes* an MR *S* of the type '*a* is *P*', '*a*' refers to *a*, and '*P*' refers to the property *P*.
(Field 1978: 39f)

If intentionality of mental attitude is to be accounted for in causal interaction, we read '*i* believes* *S*' in (2) to include the notion of state: '*i* is in some belief state *B* that relates to *S*' (cf. Schiffer 1986). Then belief analyzes out as both an unfused relation to an object and a functionally interactive state. We seem to have caught both the semantics and the intentionality of belief, thus conquering Brentano, although Field does not seem to insist on the second.

Relation (2) is a most plausible step in explicating belief as a relation. Nice as it is, however, it leaves a lot undone; we seek more light on the following.

(a) the putative physical relation of belief* from person or state to mental representation.
(b) intentionality. Is the semantics of belief (2) all there is to it,

or is the content fixed by role-playing a separate ingredient? A negative answer to this point is a main theme of Jerry Fodor's theory, coming up.

(c) The type-token relation of MR *S* to '*a* is *P*', which we have so far taken for granted. What is it for a brain configuration to be of the same syntactical type as a natural language sentence?

(d) Predicate reference and indeed plain reference of name '*a*' which is simply assumed in (2).

If reference is intentional, as I insist it is – even though causal – then Brentano survives Field's analysis. However, if it is explained in terms of attitude, we shall have got into a circle. Of course this might please the holist for whom all intentional schemes are circles, but it worries us.

5. Machines and representation

Let us turn to the question (a) of the relation of belief* to mental *representation*. The key idea for many cognitivists is that believing* is a computation of some sort in the brain (Fodor 1987: 17). You might leave it at that, claiming belief* of a sentence as a disposition 'to employ that sentence in a certain way in reasoning, deliberating, and so on' (Field 1978: 13) is just a description of a computable relation.

A good analysis of 'belief*' might also elucidate causal role (b) if the functionalist view of mind is still in the running. Despite doubts, just expressed, that the meaning of 'belief' is implicit we might rescue role in terms of belief computationally interacting with desire etc. This move would gain, together with Field's analysis, a holistic-type theory of intentionality in addition to a semantics of attitudes.

From a broad point of view common in cognitive science, all cognition, including belief, perception, concept formation and conscious states such as images and pains can best be explained in computational terms. Mental activities that are usually thought to require human intelligence are programmable. These include, besides technical and business computations, learning skills, mathematical theorem-proving, composing music, drawing pictures, parsing sentences, chess-playing and much else which I will assume all who read this are aware of.

For the cognitive scientist there is therefore an inviting parallel between computer and data on the one hand and mind and mental representation on the other. By adopting a computer framework for explaining cognitive activity he hopes to replace appeal to talents, drives, habits, dispositions and suspect psychic powers and spirits by genuine explanation. For example, off-hand remarks might ascribe Jones' success at chess to his unusual talent or Jane's obsession for Picasso's paintings to her having 'a thing' about Picasso. These have the ring of explanation but of course are not – or at best are merely dull, inductive summaries of Jones' winning chess behavior and Jane's frequenting of museums. The proposal is that genuine explanations can be made in terms of computations with MRs in Jones' and Jane's minds.

A retrospective criticism of plain functionalism points at its poorness in explaining Jones' talent or Jane's obsession. It does not explain much about anything to say talent is token identical to some nerves and Jones' intentional using of it is causal role. The computationalist thinks a genuine explanation of the particulars can be supplied.

In describing computer processes the situation is analogous. You say, 'the computer intends to checkmate at Qa5', 'it is hunting for the last name in the file', 'it does not understand English, only APL' or 'it is too stupid to look in the corner of the graph'. Such talk ascribes intentions and mental powers or shortcomings to machines. However, none but the most naive and hype-stricken thinks these comments are anything but suggestive summaries of explanations in terms of algorithms. This is common knowledge in our society and requires no deep, special information.

The computationalist hypothesis is that our folk ascriptions of belief to persons are likewise short, predictively convenient ways of talking, and are replaceable in principle by computer explanations (cf. Dennett 1978: 1986).

Neither the folk nor the computer explanations are physical. If you were to explain a computer's chess move in terms of its working program, you would quite obviously not be explaining it at the level of wires, chips, miscellaneous electronics and printing mechanics. You would be explaining it in terms of the logical game strategy it was programmed for. More tellingly, as the writer of a chess-playing routine, you need know next to nothing about hardware; in fact, the less the better.

Put another way, in the realm of computers we have a new version of functionalism. A computer program, in respect of its role in processing data, might be run on various machines, all quite different. In running, it could be token identical to a sequence of hardware events in computer 1, yet token identical to a totally different sequence in 2.

Similarly a computer or program as replacement for part of a folk theory might have many different realizations in different brains. The program underlying Schmid's speech, for instance, might be token identical to a brain complex quite other than the complex underlying Jones' speech for the same program.

In both the 'psychic' world of real computers and the psychic world of persons, we thus locate three levels of description: basic folk ascriptions of belief etc.; explanation of belief and other attitudes and actions in terms of programs; and finally engineering or neurobiological explanations of how programs work in hardware or nerves (Dennett 1978).

I shall say that folk ascriptions are *replaced* in cognitive science by program accounts; and the latter are *reduced* to brain or hardware terms. By contrast, fusion functionalists teach the token identity of belief state to brain state, with beliefs as such identified by causal role. Computer cognitivism, on the other hand, replaces 'belief' by 'computation' and goes on to claim that the latter is token identical to the physical complex. The role of belief rendered as a type of computation is now not a causal role at the physical level, but a computational role realized in the brain.

So in all you can imagine a kind of 'transitivity' of belief to program and program to hardware whereby belief comes out to be token identical to a physical thing as in basic functionalism.

None of this is quite intelligible without having in mind *one* programming language and some enlightenment on the matter of replacement. Let us consider the latter first.

Replacement is akin to Russell's handling of definite descriptions. Recall (Chapter 4, §4) that Russell rephrases entire sentences such as 'the present King of France is bald' in predicate calculus. Replacement as we contemplate it is also close to Quine's policy of couching logically troublesome locutions of ordinary speech in regimented language. These exchanges are not reductions, as there is no term-by-term translation, and no attempt to show the replacing theory entails the replaced, as is demanded in reduction (Nagel 1961). The guide for both Russell and Quine, and now for computer cognitivism, is aptness and intuitively sensed equivalence.

What is the replacing target language to be? For the Russell–Quine exercise there is in essence but one, predicate calculus. There had better be but one here, too, for else cognitive psychology including its philosophical part might find itself in the same fix as the information age: dozens of programming languages and software packages but a very thin population of customers who understand any of them or each other.

A fortunate thing about computer science is that all computers and programs, from BASIC to graphics software, are equivalent to certain abstract models of computists, human and metal, known as *Turing machines*. The language of these idealized machines is the one Fodor (1981) and others recommend as a canonical language for mind and semantics.[10] Fortunately for us, at this stage, there is no need to do more than assume such a medium exists. We may cover central points here in an informal style and turn to the Turing machine and its language when we really need it. Meanwhile, when we speak of computer language, think of any familiar programming language and of the ordinary distinction between symbols or data and program. For the reader who is reluctant to wait, see the appendix on Turing machines.

The notions that belief is a computation and that there is a canonical language of MRs desirable for use in cognitive theory are all traits of Jerry Fodor's representational theory of mind (RTM). The way I am presenting things, Fodor's theory is a culmination of cognitivism, along the same line as Field's in many respects.[11]

The language of MRs, which Fodor (1975) calls 'Mentalese', is for the most part common to speakers of all languages, since strings of symbols are common to all speaking human beings. This does not imply that Mentalese is literally Turing machine language. Although Fodor does not explain this (so far as I know), the situation is that there could be varieties of Mentalese. But any one version is translatable by a computer program to any other, preserving syntax and meaning. In this sense they are of the same type.

However, none of them is necessarily of the same syntactical type as any natural language, contrary to Field's view. This presents

170

problems for RTM, as we shall see. The best thing is to avoid the issues for the time being as they threaten the very idea of RTM before we can even get it down on paper.

We opened this section with the suggestion that belief* as relation of individual to MR is a computation. Now that we do have an approximate notion of what a computation is, we obtain the revised version (Fodor 1987: 17) of Field's relation (1), §4, using 'computation' as a replacement for 'belief*':

(1) *i* believes that *a* is *P* if and only if *i* is computationally related to an MR *S*, and *S* means a is *P*.

This relation follows Field in making the object of belief a meaningful MR. Being computationally related is a rough concept; but our computer model suggests symbol *S* is related to belief much as data is to program. And since engagement of this kind works everyday in hardware, it seems plausible for RTM to claim it is explainable in physical terms in the brain.

Another point: since the MR *S* is no longer a token of '*a* is *P*' as it is in Field's theory, there is a question about *S* having the meaning that *a* is *P*. The meaning of *S* (in (2), §4) for Field is just that of the corresponding English sentence type; but for Fodor it has to be the other way. The meaning *a* is *P* of *S* is basic; and the meaning of the sentence '*a* is *P*' is parasitical on that of *S*. We shall return to this semantical situation in §6 and Chapter 11, §2. All attitudes are relations to semantically interpreted MRs.

Desire, expectation, seeking and other attitudes are also computational, and supposedly can be characterized much as in (1). The lazy practice, which we ourselves have indulged in, of using belief as an exemplar of all attitudes now has to be paid for. If we repeat (1) for desire, for instance, in the state version, we must enlist 'desire state'; for seeking, 'seeking state; for regretting, 'regretting state'; and so on. And what are these in Turing terms? There are no parallel Turing state distinctions,[12] although there are Turing *systems* that match up with the different attitudes (see Nelson (1989a: Ch. VIII) and §4); it turns out that the attitudes differ as computations.

This brings us to belief–desire–act interaction and the question of content mentioned in (b) at the end of the last section. The idea is very foggy in straight functionalism, to say the least, and depends on physical interpretations of intensional terms in folk law. The question might be put in the following way: is there intentional content in role-playing independently of the semantical interpretations of MRs just dealt with in (1)? This is a stronger question than our earlier one of whether to append semantical relatedness to functional role: now we want to see if there is such a thing as intentionality without any semantical connections to MRs.

Let us try to clear the fog, or at least condense it. A computationalist might try to catch the companion ideas of role and intentional content in programming terms, not in the fusion functionalists causal role-playing. Perhaps propositional attitudes, the question then goes, have meaningful content generated in computational interplay of computer states? The answer to this surmise is going to be no: from RTM's standpoint computer working is not the source of any content. The old functionalist idea remains as vague as it seems, or if trimmed to precise canonical terms is quite empty. Content depends on *relational semantics*. Here is how the argument goes.

For Fodor, intentionality derives from computational interplay of meaningful symbols (1987: especially Ch. I). If we think about folk psychology generalizations (like Hill's (a)–(c) in §2), 'what's striking is that . . . all of them are generalizations that apply to propositional attitudes in virtue of the [semantical] content of the . . . attitudes' (Fodor 1981: 25). Arguing from analogy, computer processes, he insists, are purely syntactical; machine programs govern data manipulations mechanically much as the formal rules in an uninterpreted logic govern formal proofs. These moves are not genuinely informational processes unless the data involved are semantically interpreted; no interpretation, no true computation, only physical combinatorics. In the realm of actual computers, symbols must be interpretable in order that one construe a list of computer strings as a program and a machine sequence as a computation. To be computational a process must be of interpretable data (see also Chapter 9, note 2).

It is interesting to note, on RTM's behalf, that in the computer world the semantics of symbols directly affects *design*. For instance, using truth functional logic, a formal, syntactical string '1 ○ 0' (meaningless to us and to a machine) leads by a truth-table-based algorithm to design of a HALF-ADDER if '○' is interpreted as binary addition and '1' and '0' are interpreted as binary numerals; and leads to an AND switch if '○' is interpreted as multiplication.

Meanings determine computer hardware logic and/or program structure (cf. Pylyshyn 1984; Nelson 1987), and a fortiori determine process. Fodor puts it so: 'computers . . . just are environments in which the syntax of a symbol determines its causal role in a way that *respects its [semantical content]* (my italics) (Foder 1987: 19).

Completing the analogy, the conclusion for psychology is that cognition, here replaced by computer process, is belief only if the MRs related to the cognitions are meaningful. A not inappropriately pious hypothesis might be that God or Nature's design determines attitudinal structure and performance in persons by installing meaningful MRs.

So Fodor's stance is that MRs must be interpreted in order that cognitions be intentional. No intentionality without semantics. Put otherwise, psychological entities that interact as input, inner states and output (i.e. belief, desire, act) are attitudinal because they have semantically endowed objects. Or better, turning the sentiment around, intentionality cannot be accounted for by role-playing or cause alone. No intentionality without semantics.

I think this means to settle item (b) in §4 from the point of view of RTM. Role determines content, but only for semantically meaningful MRs. This doctrine reduces the functionalist component of RTM to just the notion that mental events are ontologically neutral or functional, and discharges the idea that intentionality of the mental arises in causal (or computational) interaction – input, state, output business without interpreted symbols.

6. Nativism and causal reference

Mental representations bear a very heavy load in RTM. Interpreted MRs are the objects believed and desired. But they are of course the meanings of sentences of natural language in extensional semantics. The meanings of 'snow is white', of 'der Schnee ist weiss' and of 'la neige est blanche' are given by an MR which all of these sentences express. And the truth conditions of natural language sentences derive from those of Mentalese.

From the professional linguist's point of view, RTM offers one way of locating the semantics of natural language with respect to grammatical theory. The semantics of English might be enabled by translating English into Mentalese (Lakeoff 1987: 227). However, whether semantics done in this way would be technically fruitful (Lakeoff does not claim so) or even possible from the point of view of the working linguist is debatable.

Fodor often compares RTM with (causal) Locke (see especially Fodor 1981: 257–316 *passism*). The MR is essentially the Lockean idea bereft of phenomenal qualities (the quale of the idea is regarded indifferently, pretty much), and the object–idea relation, where there is one, is understood as a physical connection, not a cartesian enigma. Meaningful MR's may be imagined to lie in a combinatorial hierarchy, lexical items like DOG, MAN, WEAR, HAT, UNMARRIED etc. on the bottom, and phrasal items like UNMARRIED MAN or DOG WEAR HAT on top. Thus Mentalese consists of interpreted terms and sentences generated by a recursive scheme of some sort, a kind of combinatorial semantics.

One may also sort MRs psycho-epistemologically. Amongst the lexical items are *primitive* MRs, corresponding to Lockean simple ideas; the primitive representations are interpreted open MR sentences or, following Frege fairly closely, *concepts*. Primitive concepts are innate (at least 'not learned' (Fodor 1975: 96)), while complex concepts, which include both complex lexical items such as UNMARRIED or MAN and phrasal MRs like DOG WEAR HAT are learned according to the empiricist, but not according to the rationalist (Fodor 1981: Ch. 10). And Fodor is a rationalist.

Learning should be understood as a process of fixing a thing in a category, of finding the route from objects to correct application of phrasal concepts; in Tarski style, of learning satisfaction conditions of open sentences. To say primitive concepts are unlearned means correct application is built in. You do not have to learn to classify a thing as a LINE or RED (cf. Quine's 'similarity standards'). The primitive components of complex concepts are thus native in the sense of being not learned; but the concept as a unit may be learned, although every constituent is innate. Mentalese is innate in the sense that the categorical scheme of it is generated recursively from an innate basis all they way up through sentences. Some of them are true, some false, and some are the objects of attitudes. 'True' and 'false' (I am glossing, lightly) are Tarskian (ibid.: 328). Sentences have truth conditions that are satisfied or not in the actual world. Of course no one has much of an idea of the rationale of a truth definition, as no one knows the structure of Mentalese.

The idea of a universal, internal language of semantically interpreted MRs is fundamental to RTM, and leads to a philosophy of nativism that comports well with Noam Chomsky's theories of grammar and mind (Fodor 1984). The topics just discussed are thus extremely significant for current linguistic theory; and Chomsky's underlying philosophy of language might well stand or fall with RTM. We shall turn to the issues in Chapter 11.

The upshot and, it is to be hoped, payoff of RTM is its word on semantics and reference. Fodor has no explicit theory of the latter, but he does have interesting suggestions as to application (Fodor 1987). The key issue is to reconcile a causal view of application of predicates such as 'horse' with the RTM position that the MR 'horse' is associated to a belief that is individuated functionally.[13] In order to understand what Fodor is about, I want to firm up some needed vocabulary and call attention to an important distinction.

As to vocabulary, the content of a belief as determined by its native semantics is 'narrow content'; and including the truth conditions for the belief is 'broad content' (ibid.). I will get to the difference in a moment.

Narrow content can be the same for two individuals, and yet the belief be true for one and false for the other. Roughly two individuals i and i' can entertain one and the same concept, while it applies in one context for i, but not in another for i'; so a fixed narrow content belief can be true in one context and not true in another. Let us see how the distinction works out relative to Putnam's arguments for rigid application of natural kind terms.

Adverting to a popular example (Chapter 8, §1) of his, the meaning of 'water' is H_2O independently of any believed descriptions in person's heads. Suppose there are two individuals i and i', i a denizen of Earth and i' of Twin Earth. i and i' are identical down to the last molecule save for residency. In particular their beliefs about water are the same: water in both cases is tasteless, odorless, has low viscosity, quenches thirst etc. Likewise Earth and Twin Earth are the very same, except for water.[14] On Earth water is H_2O and on Twin Earth water – stuff having the same subjective properties – is XYZ. 'Water' is a natural kind term that means different things on the two Earths.

Putnam, we recall, concludes from this that meaning (at least for natural kind terms) is an objective kind in the world; and application of natural kind terms is strictly causal. So meaning is not generated solely by functional role and the semantics of belief.

Functionalism does not and on its grounds cannot, tell the whole story of mind and meaning.

Fodor meets this issue by making the objective meaning qua truth condition of a general term (MR) like 'water' or 'horse' depend on both, that is, both on MRs as thoughts and on the causal relation to the object.

The idea seems to be as follows: Tokens of the MR type 'water' have a different context of interpretation on Earth than on Twin Earth. This means that a truth condition of an MR is a function of both causal context and thought (ibid.: 47). For you, a token of 'water' denotes the property H_2O while for twin-you a token of 'water' expressing the same thought – colorless, tasteless, low viscosity liquid – denotes the property XYZ. This violates the classical prejudice that same intensions (thoughts) determine same extension (objects satisfying the relevant property). But as Putnam insists this is an ineluctable consequence of a properly causal conception of natural kind terms.

Fodor proposes a theory of denotation as cause.[15] The source of (extensional) meaningfulness throughout mind, Fodor says, is causal denotation. Denotation of English predicates comes through association to Mentalese concepts which are subjects for a causal theory (ibid.: 100).

Keeping in mind the double distinction (drawn above) of lexical-phrasal and primitive–complex MRs, we find Fodor asking us to suppose a context is fixed for tokenings of a Mentalese sentence, e.g. one corresponding to 'this is water'. Granting an interpretation of primitive lexicals, the interpretation of phrasals is given by truth conditions along Tarskian lines.

> Given a truth condition, the content of mental representations is determined by the interpretation of their primitive nonlogical [lexical] vocabulary. So it's the interpretation of the primitive . . . vocabulary of Mentalese that's at the bottom of the pile. . . .
>
> (ibid.: 98)

The needed interpretation of primitives at the bottom is determined by causal context and the thought a primitive MR expresses. For instance, going back to (1), in the last section, the denotation of an MR which is computationally related to an individual believer is *causal* and yet the MR expresses the native thought.

The basic idea is that symbol (concept or MR predicate) tokens *denote their causes,* and the (Mentalese) symbol types 'express the property whose instantiations reliably cause their tokenings' (ibid.: 99). Assuming the predicate type 'horse' is primitive and letting a token be HORSE, then

(1) HORSE denotes an object *a* if and only if *a* reliably causes HORSE

By convention, 'my utterance of 'horse' says of a horse that it is one' (ibid.). That is, 'horse' applies to *a* in virtue of HORSE denoting it – of HORSE being caused by *a*.

Reliable causation depends on a law about properties and symbol types: a relation between 'the property of being an instance of the property **horse** and the property of being a tokening of the [Mentalese] symbol "horse" ' (ibid.). This relation is *lawful,* and it is expressed counterfactually: if an instance of a property were to occur it would cause the occurrence of a token of the symbol type.

A symbol expresses a property 'if it's nomologically necessary that . . . instances of the property cause tokenings of the symbol' (ibid.: 100).[16] We might try the following, attempting to line up (1) and the commentary following with our explication of application ((2) in Chapter 1, §3), wherein we invoked an agent:

(2) *P* applies to *y* (or Tarski-style, *y* satisfies *P*) if and only if *P* is some primitive predicate on our English list, *u* is a corresponding Mentalese symbol type and *y* is an instance of the property expressed by *u*, then *y* would cause the occurrence of a token *U* of *u* – alternatively, *U* denotes *y*.

I am not sure Fodor quite explicitly means (2), but it indicates how a truth condition could develop in RTM from basis clauses of a truth definition (cf. Chapter 5, §2). Note that application entails predicate disquotation: 'horse' applies to horses and 'water' to water etc. On the other hand, the intentionality of denotation gets no billing. The sense of the MR HORSE, such as it is, comes from the native MR type, not the caused token. So denotation as such is not intentional.

Note as well that (1) – in the light of the comment on reliable causation – has little in common with causal reference in Kripke's sense. Kripke never says 'Russell' would refer even under the circumstance that Russell did not ever occur, either as subject of a baptism or as end of a social chain. In causal reference, as we have understood it heretofore, a baptism causes a reference to be set up, to be *constituted*. 'Cause' is ambiguous. In a non-Aristotelian world, events can *cause the formation of a type or a relation*. A good example is the evolution of species, and another is the Kripkean fixing of reference. On the other hand, given a species or kind and a relation a priori an event is said to cause another under that relation. An example is Fodor's denotation. This distinction will figure in Chapter 9, §4 and on.

In Fodor's theory of denotation, occurrence of an instance of a kind 'triggers' a token of the type that expresses the kind necessarily. A triggering cause is by no means constitutive. The requirement that there be a nomological relation of symbol type to property is in fact simply acknowledgment of the antecedent meaningfulness of the symbol type. See note 16 above and the comment following (2).

From the position of the true causalist, RTM seems still open to Twin Earth arguments as well (see §4 and Putnam 1988), which of course are not outside the pale of human criticism. But supposing they are accepted: symbols express properties, which in Putnam's reckoning are objective meanings, to be sure; but Putnam's causal theory includes more than that. Reference of English 'water' to H_2O is established by science, and is not (based on) a nomological relation a priori of Mentalese symbol types to properties. However, I am not absolutely certain that Fodor's treatment is meant to exclude the possibility that the law is acquired (cf. Putnam 1986: 148).

Note also that the theory does not apply to proper names. Offering a rather conservative exegesis: an MR corresponding to a proper name obviously cannot be a primitive of Mentalese; consequently it must be a complex, lexical item of the form ABCD. . . . 'Russell', for example, would have a bearer determined by the constitutive primitives A etc. at 'the bottom of the pile'. A proper name so construed does not even have the semantical status of 'water'; that is to say, it does not directly denote an object or a natural kind. The reference (denotation?) of 'Russell' would come down to a Mentalese description ABCD believed by the individual, which in principle could be disassembled to caused parts that severally denote (shades of Russell on reducibility of descriptions to acquaintance – see Chapter 4). But this is open to all of the usual objections to description theories of names. Of course Fodor does not advocate such a theory, as he does not advocate any.

Assuming RTM enjoyed a full theory of names and satisfied condition (*R*) there would remain some substantial puzzles of a rather deep sort, which there is good reason to think Fodor is aware of but which I note explicitly here. Unless one is unsalvageably enmired in intentional holism – in which case there is no hope of individuating the intentions – cognitive science needs some help in distinguishing beliefs from desires from seekings etc. other than box-labeling (see note 12). Beliefs, given the category, are individuated by contents; the category of belief qua computation itself is not so far satisfactorily determinate within RTM.

The relationship of English to Mentalese is quite problematic. In Field's theory there is some small hope of clarifying how a mental representation of the thought that *a* is *P* could be a token of '*a* is *P*'. It has to be syntactically the same up to within some modulus that could conceivably be set in neurobiological inquiry.

But the nature of the sought correspondence between Mentalese and between Mentalese and English or German or . . . is less transparent than that. There must be a *good* translation (or, in general, some kind of mapping) of English, German, Russian etc. to Mentalese (cf. Stich 1983: 42ff). One can, of course, *posit* a translation; but it is difficult to see how to remove the promissory note without assuming a good deal of semantics in order to get the translation. We shall return to this issue in Chapter 11, §2.

If the reader is of the opinion that the theory of Mentalese and its semantics mainly shifts into a subliminal, unconscious realm all of the problems of intentionality and meaning as occur in folk psychology and surface-analytic philosophy of language, he is not alone. In spite of Fodor's heroic efforts at founding a conceptual basis for cognitive science, nominal reference is simply presupposed as work for later analysis.

CHAPTER 9

Mechanism

1. Top-down semantics

A basic aim of semantical theory is to explain reference of word to thing. Therefore, if cognitive science is to be broad enough to include semantics it must face up to reference. Unfortunately a causal theory of reference, which we now require, does not seem to be in sight within the precincts of cognitivism.

The source of the trouble is not a principled antithesis of cause to purpose (if purpose is connoted by 'role') but is the notion that reference could be reckoned an intentional attitude only within a holistic network of belief and desire. If reference is contextual, the theory is open to the standard objections to Russell's theory of descriptions. For, 'Ottoline' would refer only if some beliefs about Ottoline were true, i.e., in virtue of a description; and reference by description violates the thesis of rigidity and hence the causal theory.

If reference is a relation, we run into about the same trouble. For instance, as intimated at the end of Chapter 8, §6, in suggesting a theory of reference for RTM: if Schmid refers to Russell by way of a mediating phrasal MR, say the complex representation AUTH PRIN MATH or whatever, he is in effect referring by description, this time in Mentalese, but still by description.

The underlying disturbance is holism, which forecloses analysis of reference and meaning. Consider the crude idea that belief in p cannot be differentiated from desire that p except by boxing them differently (Chapter 8, note 12). If there are no explicit marks of attitude, including reference, there are none at all save by arbitrary indexing.

Holism nurtures a preference for 'top-down' philosophy. You

begin with the big picture: in cognitive science, taking folk psychology as given, then establishing a broad theoretical framework and within that fitting the conceptual parts. At the top comes belief described folkishly and functionally as an ingredient of a network of attitudes; then it is construed as relational and analyzed in terms of mental states and representations to which are attributed a causal semantics (in RTM; see also Loar 1981; Stich, 1983). Reference, if it enters the picture in any way at all, is fitted into a theory of belief, and not belief into a theory of reference.

This is the top-down history reported in Chapter 8. At the very bottom causal reference emerges, still enclothed in its full semantical mystery. If an adequate theory is sought, we must either start with a different mind-belief scheme at the top, or start at the bottom with lexical semantics and work up.

The second approach is already in the wings in Fodor's semantical theory. Following his lead, let us try the idea that reference, like his denotation, is causal; and following our own lead, let us also try the idea that it is computational. If reference is computational, it is surely causal. Again, let us look for intentionality in reference itself and not in its commerce with holistic, belief, desire and act.

Now this exploratory step has both good and bad features. The good one is its locating of intentionality in the reference relation, generally within the computation itself, and not in holistic intercourse with other attitudes, a notion we have rejected. This much at least in part meets ordinary as well as Brentanoan intuitions that cognitions are purportedly directed to objects, and also meets Fregean demands that the content of belief depend functionally on naming, and not naming on belief.

The next step is to disencumber ourselves of the debilitating notion that computation must have semantically interpreted input. According to RTM, to be a computation reference must have interpreted input. However, if we stick to our causal guns, *there can be no such input.* Here is why.

The name in ' "*a*" refers to *a*' cannot be the input to a causal computation involving an object as that would perforce make the name the cause of the thing named, which puts things the wrong way around. The MR, if there is any in the situation, is surely the effect of the occurrence of an object, not the cause. Hence, if the relation is truly a computation *à la* Fodor's cognitivism, either the object of reference itself must be semantically interpretable, or there must be an intervening MR through which the protagonistic MR refers. However, the idea of a nonlinguistic, external object having the properties of a mental representation is suspect, to say the least; and the very being of an intervening MR leads to regress. Ergo, reference cannot be a semantically interpreted computation (Nelson 1989a: 160).

If this is right, reference is a *syntactical* computation if it is to be a computation at all; intentionality cannot be traced to the meaning fulness of inputs. On the other hand it is hard to see how this theory could be right as it runs in the face of extremely deep prejudice: no intentions without semantics. And, we are still insisting, no notion of reference is adequate that does not explain its intentionality.

2. Up from reference

I now want to project a bottom-up theory of reference based on the thesis that reference is direct.[1] In this theory, reference is a causal relation of objects *directly to names* in spoken languages, not to inner mental representations. An object causes a name in natural language, not a Mentalese mental representation.

Meaning and reference, like belief and other attitudes, are computational: the direct theory I am limning rests on a computational-functional theory of mind. However, the theory differs from intentional holism in repudiating the idea that belief and desire are intentional, owing to the holistic role.[2] I claim the opposite: the interacting system is intentional and purposive because the separate attitudes are.

What remains of functionalism here is therefore just the idea that physical brain complexes realize computational descriptions. As such, mind/brain process is uninterpreted ('syntactical') and is subject to worry as to how intentional attitude is possible.

Anxiety over this is dispelled, I shall suggest, by a theory that is extensional – in computational terms – and yet expresses all of the intensional properties of belief, desire, reference etc. sentences. Specifically, *taking* a thing to be such and such (basically, Peirce's interpretant or conclusion to an abductive inference) can be explained in Turing machine terms;[3] and other intensional terms including 'reference' can be explained extensionally in terms of it.

The semantics of all linguistic entities and the intentionality of cognition arises bottom-up from purported reference of names and application of predicates directly to objects.

The direct theory makes no wide assumptions about the warrantedness of folk psychology. I doubt folk thought is true as a whole not even in the key Gricean–Hill generalizations (Chapter 8, §2). But I am not going to insist on this point one way or the other.[4] However, key concepts such as belief, perception, naming, concept formation etc. establish the subject of our present considerations. They provide fuel for analysis, bottom up. We are not out to eliminate 'belief' or 'reference' but to explain them, even though most folks' belief about belief, desire and act is false or poorly warranted.

Much as cognitivism, in my view mental representations figure in semantics and a theory of belief; but if they are singular, their reference derives from that of proper names, not the other way around. *MRs are tokens of spoken types.*

Singular mental representations are grounded in namings past, in baptisms. Sentences of thought are tokens of spoken language sentences, and the semantics of thought derives from that of utterance types of English, not from an imagined universal language.

One can divide semantics in this theory into two sections: 'front-end semantics', which deals with immediate reference and application, the semantics of observation sentences, compounds of them and a 'core' language, which is roughly Quinean; and 'back-end semantics', which is essentially the same subject, but might not turn out to have the same method, as semantics of natural language as thought of in modern transformational grammar.

In the front theory, immediate reference is (tacit) computation from object directly to name: Jones to 'Jones', on occasion when you see or hear her down the street. The computation is virtually abductive inference (Chapter 2, §4) within a syntactical, sub-symbolic system of production rules (as explained later, and in detail in the appendix).

Reference is causal in both senses of the word 'causal' adumbrated in Chapter 8, §6. A naming ceremony establishes a computational path in the brain; and given the path, future occurrences of Jones in perception yield tokens of 'Jones' by abductive computation.

Application of sensible (or observational) predicates to objects is causal as well. Thus 'red spot' computationally applies to red spots either through an innate path (if we are all built to see **red**) or through a constructed conceptual path induced by the findings and communications of established science, in conformity with Putnam's theory of natural kind terms. These constructions are the main topic of Chapter 11, §3.

In all cases of direct experience, taking-to-be and expectation are explicable, I shall endeavor to show, in extensional, computational terms. Taking thus accounts for purported reference, on concrete occasions; and the disquotation condition (R) on the theory is to that extent satisfied.

Reference and application, hence singular and general terms, are distinguished by inferential role in a logic of atomic sentences wherein indexical terms play a key part in binding subject to predicate. In part, the theory says that in direct perceptual experience, 'atomic' sentence 'a is F' is tacitly inferred from 'that is a' and 'that is F'.

Atomic observation sentences combine truth-functionally to yield an interpreted *core language* where lexical items are those arising in direct confrontation with the world. Truth conditions for core language are founded in the Tarkian idea of satisfaction; but satisfaction is a type of computation, a theory reminiscent of Dummett (Chapter 5, §3).

This much, as just reviewed, is the bottom of the theory and comprises front-end semantics. Going up, mental representations appear as memory marks, are vehicles of thought, planning, oathing, urging etc. and are tacit tokens of English, essentially 'post-language' symbols having their roots in the observational core of English. The objects of belief and thought in nonobservational cognition are indeed mental representations; but they are tokens of natural language sentence types and trace natural language after that language is learned. Mental 'states' are not functionally individuated by role, but by abstract machine structure, intrinsically embodying intentional ingredients (e.g. the ability to take things to be other than they are).

The interdependence of belief, desire and act, which the holist makes so much of, is explained in the direct theory by the interconnecting of belief and desire computationally, and the intentionality of the context arises from that of the component attitudes. Intentionality is a property of certain computations underlying belief and other attitudes.

A consequence of the direct theory wherein the language of thought is just tacit English accrued in direct learning experience is that semantics is in a sense primary, and syntax is a higher-order structure of rules constrained by the meanings of lexical items. Linguistic competence in syntax and semantics are learned hand-in-hand. Acquisition of syntactical competence goes with development from a semantically rich core up to the full vernacular. Put otherwise: meanings are not somehow affixed to syntactically well-formed entities (roughly 'interpretative semantics') by way of mappings of native Mentalese, but are intrinsic to primitive lexicals as developed in referential experience, and are the stuff of syntactical growth. 'Dog' or 'red' or 'Jones' have sense as learned and enter into syntactical structures both as components and as meaning-bearing constraints on the sense of the generated sentences. The idea is, of course, Fregean, not holistic.

The issues in semantics at this level are extraordinarily complex, and I cannot hope to do more than sketch out tentative suggestions of what would seem to be the implications of direct reference for a larger theory. More of this, but not much more, in Chapter 11, §2.

The theory of direct reference rests on three subtheories, the first philosophical, the second computational and the third semiotical. These have to do, respectively, with the concept of cause, algorithm and the proper analysis of 'syntax' and 'semantics' in general philosophical discourse.

3. Algorithms: free and embodied

Computationalism is the doctrine that brains are computers of some sort, and that having a computer in it makes a brain a mind. There is widespread acceptance of this notion in cognitive science where it usually takes the form of an image of programs running in a neural substrate. The mind is a collection of programs; there are stored 'packages', such as *Word Perfect* or *APL*, residing in the head. When you solve a problem or desire something because you believe the facts are right, or the reverse, you (or more likely the executive system in your head) recover a program and run it through the brain.

This crude but pervasive notion is inimical to a direct, computational theory of reference. If computation means program-running over interpreted data, it appears from previous argument that reference is no computation – a consequence contrary to my purpose. What are we to make of this?

The trouble stems from an ambiguity of 'program', which can be resolved only by doing some basic computer theory.

Cognitivism in just about all of its forms views the mind as a programmed processor of symbolic data. According to Pylyshyn (1984), following Newell (1980), the points of agreement – the properties common to mind qua cognitive and machine – which make RTM and other computer theories of mind attractive, are the folowing five:

(A) Digital computers share an enormous body of cognitive capabilities with human beings; we already enumerated a variety of specimens in Chapter 8, §5.

(B) Of all possible cognitive processes, only those that are finitely describable can be carried out by finite minds. These finite mental processes are programmable or algorithmic; for if one can describe them in finite terms they can be described step by step, and this just means they are algorithmic. Such processes are, in turn, precisely those that can be carried out by some Turing machine.

The last statement is a form of Turing's thesis (Turing 1936), which is of inestimable significance in our subject and is worth framing:

(1) All effectively computable functions (processes) are Turing computable.[5]

The expression 'effectively computable' means 'computable by specificable algorithm' (Shapiro 1981). From the fact that digital computers are run by programmed algorithms, it follows (under certain idealizations that need not concern us) that they are (equivalent to) Turing machines.

From the empirical fact (if it is one) that cognitive activities in the brain are algorithmic – or as Newell equivalently expresses it, 'finitely describable' – it follows by Turing's thesis that they too are Turing computable, which means there is a Turing machine for computing any such process.

Mechanism is the theory that brains do realize Turing machines, or the equivalent – in which case Turing machines are 'models' –

which accounts for perception, conception, the attitudes, under-standing, language, reference, problem-solving ability and in general all forms of intelligence. This is a somewhat stronger commitment to machines than RTM's use of them as providing 'canonical language' for cognitive psychology (Chapter 8, §5). Mechanism is an explicitly *realistic* thesis.

(C) Turing machine computations, hence both cognitive and computer processes, involve symbols, including the sensing of them, identifying tokens as types, varying occurrences of symbol tokens and permuting them. Formulas in such processes have transportable parts, i.e. symbols with integrity. For instance in lexicographically ordering formulas, symbols are transportable as wholes (Fodor 1987: 193). I shall give an example of the difference between trans-portable and nontransportable symbols below.

(D) There are two categories of input symbol in both mind and machine: program and data. Data input must be separated from program input (although of course in memory they are indistinguishable, except by address). The clearest example of this separation is found in the action of commercial computers; but the same holds for Turing machines.

A standard computer chip houses a random access memory, a central arithmetic unit, a program control and input–output hardware. When operated, computers per-form one function at a time, one after the other, as directed by a program. The typical running sequence is as follows: fetch a program instruction; obtain from the memory the data addressed in the instruction; execute the operation on the data specified in the instruction; fetch the next instruction; and so on. A chip or central processing unit designed to work this way is a 'von Neumann machine', so named after the principal inventor of the stored-program computer (von Neumann 1961).

(E) Human cognition and computer computation as well, pre-supposes semantically interpreted symbols, just as Fodor maintains (Chapter 8, §5).

Collectively, items (A) to (E) constitute an argument for the doctrine that mind is a computing machine and at the same time they are meant to establish benchmarks for the development of cognitive science and its top-down methods.

Items (C), (D) and (E), which are of central concern at the moment, might be elevated to the status of a cognitivist principle (Pylyshyn 1984):

(2) If a process is algorithmic, equivalently turing computable,
    (C) it must operate on transportable, interpretable symbols;
    (D) the data and program must be separable;
    (E) the data must be semantically interpretable.

We are now ready for the punchiest punch line to be found in this book: Only the Turing thesis (B) ((1) above) is essential for a computational theory of the mind; put more plainly, none of (C), (D) or (E), all of which appear to be basic to RTM and other forms of cognitivism, is essential to a process being algorithhmic, and hence to being Turing computable. So (2) is false.

Most philosophers of mind and cognitive psychologists who are inclined toward computers (or away from them) think of a computation as running a program, say BASIC or word-processing software, and of a computer as a paradigmatic symbol processor. However, (C) and (D) are in fact properties of only *some* mental and/or computer operations, not all.

Contrary to Newell and Pylyshyn, *none* of (C), (D) or (E) fit well with much of the work in artificial intelligence (AI) of the present day, with many current theories of brain biology (e.g. Edelman 1987) or with some newer psychological theories.

More momentously (for us) the three propositions conflict with the theory of reference I am proposing. Direct reference is computational but it does not compute from symbols in the sense of (C), as I have already argued, and the computation is not executed by a program that is separable from the data in a way anything like that of a sequentially operating computer chip, as described in (D).

In a way, our discussions since Chapter 8, §4, with the introduction of belief as a relation and the assumption, in Field's treatment, that we may read reference causally, have been building up to this stance. For causal reference, though intentional, does not appear to be wrapped into belief–desire cognitive wholes, but is another sort of phenomenon, recognized even by the folkist as different (Chapter 8, §2). Now we are removing it further from the environment of intrinsically semantical, interpretable symbols – erstwhile mental representations – and to do so are working to rescue the idea of computation from total dedication to the programming and sequential computer bias toward mind.

The situation here is fairly complex. As further introduction to the issues and their development, let me break them down into two sections: (a) the importance of Turing's thesis for a theory of direct reference; (b) mustering of evidence to the effect that (2) is false, i.e. that for a computer theory to comport with Turing does not demand interpretable mental representations, driven by executive, data-separable programs.

(a) Fodor is committed to the thesis (1) in his choice of the Turing machine paradigm for functional descriptions in cognitivism; and his notion of belief as a computation is given some substance with Turing backing. However, *mechanism*, which I am now introducing, depends on Turing's thesis essentially. The computationalist finds the Turing idea to be handy; the mechanist necessarily depends on it.

The basic idea – in enough detail now to explain my fondness of (1) and rejection of (2) – is as follows. The purportedness of reference is explained in my theory in terms of *expectation* and *taking*, which I regard as fundamental among intentions – a stance just sketched in a preliminary way in §2. The required analysis uses Turing (recursion) concepts essentially; so far as I know, there is no other way of replacing the intensional idiom within sight. If mechanism were not a plausible theory for the mind, the thing could not be done.

(b) The items processed, inputs and outputs, in a standard personal computer are dealt with as complete symbols by the programmer. But in the machine interior, on the level of hardware process, they are not. For instance, as I edit this very sentence, if I want to move 'For instance' from its present location to a place after 'sentence' I can take it from where it is, put it in temporary 'clip board' memory and then read it out to obtain '. . . sentence, For instance . . .'. Then I change 'F' to 'f' etc. and go on with my business. From the software programming point of view, *I move the word intact*, tacitly following a program for manipulating 'For instance'.

However, what happens within the computer on the hardware level is another thing. 'For instance' is broken up into a dozen bytes, each consisting of eight bits which are moved serially-by-bit (in slow machines) into a swap memory from main memory, then out to a new main memory location; and as a block are trickled byte-by-byte to a register that feeds the monitor.

The bits and pieces are embodied in electrical pulses and are parts of whole symbols of the software computation. They are certainly 'symbols' in the sense of inner circuit logic, but from the point of view of outer word processing they are underlying 'subsymbols' (Smolensky 1988; Harnad 1990), syntactical particles from which symbols are formed. They are processed by an algorithm built in the hardware of which the programmer is not aware.

These inner events are *not* under the total guidance of a fetch, exectute, fetch program, but are automatically channeled by the immanent logic of the hardware once a fetch instruction is decoded. Symbols in 'for instance' lose their integrity in the decoding and processing of independent bits; and the process is not programmed but is guided and constrained by the logic of circuitry. The machine operation in this example (and any other you care to imagine) is a clear violation of (C) and (D), yet the internal process is certainly a computation as it is finitely describable, hence Turing computable, by (1). Moreover the logic of the circuitry is describable in Turing language as is that of the software program, in principle.

Examples of the distinction between a programmed and an automatic hardware procedure are easy to find as the distinction exactly characterizes the programmed digital computer. Program that governs is one thing; hardware that self-governs is another. In a more general setting, there are two sorts of algorithm in this world, *embodied* and *free* (Nelson 1987). *Reference is an embodied algorithmic process with the hardware being the brain. It does not process symbols (MRs) and is not directed by an algorithm programmed by a homunculus.*

Free versus embodied can be made exact in terms of universal Turing machines, and I do so in the appendix. For the reader who can program, a better example is addition.

It is possible to build a useful computer – we are talking hardware – that can (i) store numerals and shift them from register to register; (ii) add 1 (one) to the contents of an addressed random access location; (iii) branch on 0 (zero) or, if the contents are equal to zero, subtract 1 from the addressed location. The machine has all of the other computational properties – of analyzing instructions, displaying stuff on a monitor, printing and so forth – fabricated from the two primitive operations; and there is a machine language programming system available for it. Your favorite interpreter or compiler can be run on it, in principle.

Any process that can be performed on a full machine including a supercomputer can be performed on this bereft one. You can program it to add, multiply, find numerical solutions to partial differential equations, play chess and do graphics.[6]

Now let us return to more familiar and wieldy machines which have, in hardware, circuits for addition, multiplication and much more. On this familiar machine you do not have to program routines using only ADD 1 and BRANCH, as there is available an ADD, MULT, SHIFT, BOOLEAN OR etc. instruction and so forth for other operations. All of these apply to symbols (contents of symbolic addresses) in programs in which the symbols are moved about as atomic units.

The point of the story is that the algorithm for addition can either be *programmed* on the simple machine, or *built into the hardware* in the more complex, standard machine. In either case there is an *algorithm* (otherwise addition would not be computable); but in the simple machine the algorithm is *free*, independent of the computer, and can be transported, thrown away – i.e. given to Schmid – all without compromising the hardware. In the other, 'friendly' machine, the addition algorithm is built into the hardware; the algorithm is *embodied*, and the only way of altering it or getting rid of it is to wreck the hardware. The one processes interpretable, transportable symbols; the other processes parts of symbols, bits or ternary or quaternary subsymbols, that have no independent semantical meaning.

Similarly, systems of neurons have been modeled as embodied algorithm logic devices for years, from McCulloch and Pitts (1943) up to Waltz and Feldman (1988), for instance.[7] The models might be inadequate, but that does not mean they are outside of the Turing machine category.

The point of the above exercise is not new instruction for the reader (although I hope it might dissuade him or her from referring to everything under the sun as a 'program'), but emphasis on a distinction, which is as old as the hills in computer engineering circles and is a part of your sophomore engineer's lore. But what happened to Schmid?

What I am claiming is that reference is a computation governed by an embodied algorithm realized in the brain, e.g. Schmid's. Indeed, as a first approximation, we have

(3) '*a*' refers to *a* for an individual *i* if and only if *i* realizes (embodies in his head) a set of Turing rules that compute the name '*a*' from the object *a*.

There is no separable, free program and no free-floating symbol involved, and, in particular, no mental representations. The set of rules is a piece of brain hardware. As we shall see soon, the inputs to reference (the causal objects referred to) are basically Quinean stimulation patterns ('subsymbols') or, distally, the objects that cause proximal patterns at the surface of the body. They are not mental representations. The output of reference is the name 'Jones', say. Whence ariseth the symbol and the instruments of higher cognition.

Reference is of course not all there is to mind and language. The hardware of a standard computer, to which I have drawn analogy, is a species of *connectionist* computational system. Reference as an embodied algorithm phenomenon is another. Connectionist systems are highly parallel, distributed memory affairs, which we shall see exemplified in lexical semantics in the next chapter.

My point, which I have been driving quite hard, is not that all of language and mind can be explained in such terms. Speech and thought most likely cannot be, as they seem to depend on processing of semantically interpreted symbols, much as is claimed by cognitivism. There is recent evidence that even refined grammatical detail cannot be explained solely in terms of either the free algorithm or the connectionist paradigm. Pinker (1991) has concluded that regular verbs (*walk, walked*) are computed by a 'rule-and-representation' (free algorithm) system, while irregular verbs (*run, ran*) are retrieved from associative memory – i.e. from a connection system. More generally Marvin Minsky (1988), one of the central figures in the history of AI, has remarked that our understanding of the mind and language from a broadly computational point of view will ultimately use both bottom-up (connectionist) and the traditional (since the late 1950s) top-down (free algorithm, cognitivist) methods.

I have located reference and association as embodied or connectionist territories. The Pylyshyn–Newell view that all mind is symbolic processing is therefore not true to all the facts; but that does not mean their paradigm (A)–(D) does not fit some, perhaps the most important and interesting.

4. Cause, computation and reference

The concept of cause in physical science has three ingredients: the causal *event*; the *law* covering the event; and, in biology anyway, the higher-order *lawful evolution* of the law. In causal semantics an event *a* causes '*a*' and thus '*a*' refers to *a*, as Fodor says. A temporal reference is an instance of an underlying law or *disposition* to refer. And in a full causal theory such as Kripke's, the law is *acquired* at the instance of a naming. ' "a" refers to *a*' is clear as far as it goes; so let us consider disposition now, and put off the question of how a disposition is acquired until a later section (Chapter 11, §3).

Reliable causation, Fodor says, depends on a counterfactual relation between the property of being an instance of a natural kind (horse) and the property of being an instance of the MR ('horse'). When I say in the previous paragraph 'there is a disposition to refer to *a* by "*a*" ' I mean just what is meant by the subjunctive sentence: if the instance *a* were to occur, so would the tokening of '*a*'. Hence, the subjunctive conditional affords an analysis of the expression 'disposition'.

This way, which is the right way, of viewing 'reference' makes it a *dispositional relation*. A short review of the situation is this: a name (person knowing the name) dispositionally refers even when not uttered on some occasion. The distinction between disposition and event is a bit like Strawson's and Searle's (in Chapter 4, §5) – entertaining versus asserting a sentence – and largely motivates our Chapter 6. Donnellan (for whom all reference is found in use*, Chapter 6, §2) seems to overlook it. It appears in Tarski-like theories of truth for natural languages. There, asserted sentences, sentence tokens, are true or false (its particles refer*) while types are only 'thought' or 'entertained' and as such are in a sense dispositional.

Similarly, tokens of '*a*' refer, while the type '*a*' is associated with a disposition of a speaker who would refer to *a* under this or that circumstance. Again, for Quine, English is a disposition to behavior (Chapter 7, §1) shared by speakers (instantiators) of English.[8]

Now a subjunctive sentence expressing a dispositional relation is not truth functional, and for this reason should (if we do not lose too much) be kept out of our theory – for much the same reason as extensionalists ban belief sentences or somehow replace or reduce them. I need only remind the reader that a sentence 'if *a* were *P*, then it would be *Q*' is not always regarded as true when the antecedent and consequent are both true; nor is it true when the antecedent is false. The joint truth of 'snow is white' and 'Bush is a Republican' does not imply 'if snow were white, Bush would be a Republican'. Again, the falsity of 'Bush is not President' does not render 'if Bush were not President, the country would be better off than it is' true. These sentences are thus intensional.

Now the causal law covering reference is intensional; and for this reason extensionalist semanticists might prefer to use 'disposition' itself instead of the analysis of it as a subjunctive conditional. But an alternative to the intension-style analysis of 'disposition' is the *place-holder* account of dispositional predicates (Quine 1973: 12–13; Levi and Morgenbesser 1964).

According to this theory, dispositional terms like 'soluble' stand for, or hold a place for, some mechanism that might eventually be revealed in scientific inquiry. The theory advocates straight use of disposition-terms like 'soluble', 'malleable' 'referring' etc. until chemistry, metallurgy or semantics develop sufficiently to supply an extensional explanation of the underlying physical mechanism. To say a thing has a disposition is therefore to say there is a mechanism there, yet to be described. And to say 'there is a mechanism' is short for the subjunctive 'if such and such were, then such and such would be . . .'.

The most evident, most compelling and most germane examples of the place-holder theory come from engineering, where inner mechanisms are known and indeed designed to be and to do just as they are. Consider an adding circuit in a computer. To say the machine houses such a circuit is the same as saying it would add two numbers together if it were given the right input. Indeed, the following statements are equivalent ('*x*' and '*y*' are current levels of a transistor switch, etched in a chip, token identical to strings of binary or ternary (or whatever) numerals; and '$x + y$' is the coded binary sum):

(a) If x and y were input (on the right leads) to this chip (placed in the relevant control setting) you would get $x + y$ out;

(b) This chip has a disposition to add.

(c) This chip has an addition circuit etched in it.

Item (c) is the transparently adequate place-holder version of (b).

Now the theory of direct reference I am proposing suggests the hypothesis that the purported reference relation of 'Jones' to Jones is an algorithm embodied in neural circuitry, analogous to (c). For short, Schmid, or other, has a Jones reference circuit in him which incorporates his disposition to refer to Jones.

On an actual occasion of an object a appearing to Schmid, if Schmid refers to a, uttering a token of 'Jones' (a causes 'Jones' just as Fodor would have it), what we have is a computation on that occasion via the embodied (in the circuit in Schmid's head) algorithm from a to 'Jones'.

This catches, I believe, the distinction between the causing of reference on an occasion and dispositional reference, the latter of which might be expressed in one of the two obvious ways analogous to (a) and (b) above: (a) 'If individual i had an experience of an instance of x, then (*ceteris paribus*) i would refer by a token of "x" '; (b) 'Individual i has a disposition to refer to x by "x" '. The mechanist version, then, is (c): 'Individual i has an "x" ' reference algorithm (Turing machine) embodied in him.

It is interesting to see, somewhat prematurely, that purportedness is both *dispositional* and *manifest*. Dispositional reference – the having of the right built-in computational rules – already catches some of the Brentanoan spirit: it is conceivable that Schmid could enjoy an embodiment of a Pegasus referring algorithm even though there be no Pegasus. The type 'Pegasus' p-refers for Schmid to Pegasus; he realizes a Pegasus algorithm.

On an actual occasion, however, a person might purportedly refer to Pegasus owing to real-time computation from input. How this can be done without Pegasus actually entering the scene is one of the heavy burdens of Chapter 11.[9]

Finally, let us look at the third part of the notion of cause. According to Kripke, a causal relation is literally *established* at a baptism. As Devitt fittingly puts it, at the naming of his cat, Nana, those in attendance gained 'an ability' to refer to Nana by 'Nana' (Devitt 1981: 20). Where there was no disposition before, one appears. Fodor's theory, if he had one, would not be able to cope with this component of 'cause', i.e. with the concept of *the constituting* of a causal law. The concept of causal reference (or denotation) of natural kind terms for which he does have a theory entails the existence of an innate disposition; Fodor's counterfactual statement about horse and 'horse' is true of the individual speaker of English owing to dispositional endowment, the etiology of which remains very obscure.

I am not going to attempt to explain how this demand of a causal theory might be met in logical mechanism until I can get around to the details. Suffice it to say, there is a better chance of accounting for new reference in terms of a new physical system emerging than in terms of a new causal law (which might be said to be immanent) emerging. In Chapter 11 I shall argue that emergence of reference in a baptism is very nicely accounted for in recent theories of the post-natal evolutionary development of the brain (Edelman 1987). In a nutshell, the suggestion is simply that formation of a mechanism for using a name is of the same logical ilk as formation of a category or species in a population under natural selection.

Looking back over the present section and the previous one, it is now more evident than it was in our review of RTM why a friend of Pylyshyn's principle (2), §3, is bound to have trouble with reference, if it is causal. Starting pretty much from scratch: calling a person by name on an immediate occasion, once the baptism has taken place, is essentially perceptual (Devitt 1981: 25ff). There is a process involving an object that causes a stimulus pattern, and a subsequent identification of that pattern.

Now perception of the thing (as named) is, as Arthur Burks has compellingly argued, a finitely describable process (Burks 1972). By Turing's thesis it follows that the process is Turing computable. A computation for 'Jane' has to be distinct from one for 'Nana', under ideal circumstances of a clear view, no confusion, honesty etc. If our speaker knows n names of people (by a baptism or Kripke chain) he must have access to n algorithms that guide n computations simultaneously. I take it as empirical fact that if you see a and correctly name him 'a' – in a matter of a few milliseconds at most – you do not run n computations serially in your head to pick the right label. The process is parallel, not 'programmed' or serial.

The very fact that we seek an analysis without sneaking in semantical ideas (of the sort I meant to banish in §1) rules out any idea that the input to the reference relation on immediate occasions is symbolic, certainly not of interpreted symbols. A pattern stimulation consisting of subsymbolic elements is *not* a symbol, and processing thereof does not presuppose principles incorporated in C, D and E of §3.

5. Syntax and intention

A name refers owing to causality and intentionality of the relation (cf. Devitt 1981: 28f). In my theory of direct reference the presence of embodied machines explains cause, intention, and reference and meaning as well in one swoop.

But according to popular perception this is not possible because machines are syntactical devices and naming is *semantical*. A little man translating Chinese by following a perfect program and using a perfect dictionary need not have the slightest understanding of what he is doing in order to produce a correct output. He need merely follow rules blindly; he is only a computist. So computationalism as a theory of mind and language is wrong (Searle 1980).

Searle's trouble is poor understanding of symbols, computers and syntax. In formal logic, a syntactical system consists of an object language O and a metalanguage M having no provision in it for expressing interpretations or meanings of the purely formal vocabulary of O. Presumably, in the Chinese picture, the object language O Searle has in mind is machine language of a computer or Turing machine. In Searle's view on the topic (1990: 24), the machine language is one associated with a free algorithm, since he sees no sense in the idea of embodied logics or rules. O is symbolic and is interpretable (by humans), but in itself has no meaning or sense. Consequently the machine that does the manipulating knows or understands nothing about what it is doing. It certainly cannot refer. I think this is certainly correct.

It does seem reasonable that O (or a higher-level language) is graced with meaning only through human agency, unless assumed to be realized in a human head and innately meaningful, or left as a semiotical puzzle to be explained in a later stage of biological science.

But there is nothing in this view precluding explanation of meaning and intentionality within an embodied algorithm-based theory involving no language O, syntactical or not. What we are up to is *not* how to paste meanings onto the symbols of some machine or compiler language O, or onto MRs, but how to generate lexical symbols, meaning and all, from scratch.

Look at it this way: In Frege's thought the sense of a name, in one of the senses of 'sense', is an attribute of, or is associated to, a name; in another reading sense is a mode of presentation (computation?) and hence might be seen as attaching to the relation of word to thing, not to the word (see Chapter 3, §5, and Kripke's distinction in Chapter 8, §1). What I am saying is, roughly, that meaning might be algorithmically explainable as a relation, if not as an absolute adornment of a name itself.

The remainder of this book is devoted to reference in terms of embodied algorithms that are meant to satisfy definite intentionality adequacy conditions, including of course condition (R). For instance, reference involves taking (or 'interpretation') in something like Peirce's abduction (Chapter 2, §4); taking is shown to be intentional, although subject to extensional analysis; and other intentions involved in semantics reduce to it. We shall show how, among other things, 'a' p-refers to a even if there be no bearer a, and how Schmid might refer to Russell by 'Lady Ottoline', and mean it. In a word, we shall get semantics out of intentional syntactical systems.

CHAPTER 10

Direct Reference

1. Words, states and rules

Any semantical theory of lexical terms of a natural language must allow that conventional names are associated to mental entities. Thus an assumption in the direct theory is that a name refers owing to its conventional association to an inner state. Specifically, if a state is causally correlated to an object and a name is fixed to the state, then we say the name refers to the object.

Reference as it subsists full-blown in an English-speaking person's repertoire is the central topic of the next two sections; how it develops is indeed speculative; and in the present chapter I remain neutral as regards acquisition of language and of referential dispositions. Acquisition of language by a child occurs in confrontation with the world in a society that speaks that language. In the process, learning of lexical terms and acquisition of the underlying dispositions contributes to formation of the the whole language, grammar, semantics, phonology and all.

In the next sections I abstract from this complexity and pick out reference itself as a relatively isolable topic. In the final chapter I shall suggest that the springs of reference – baptisms, namings, teaching of words – are to be found in the postnatal evolution of the brain.

I finally assume that reference in immediate experience is perceptual (cf. Devitt 1981; Fodor 1984). Suppose a disposition to refer to Rover has been acquired. If you see Rover and say something about him on the spot, the saying involves a perceptual process in which Rover is recognized to be or taken to be Rover and subsequently named.

In the following sections I begin with perception and reference as computable relations and then, in §4, introduce p-reference and intentionality. This means I shall first discuss reference as causal event and then add the ingredient of intention, although the adding will prove to be more of a weaving than a pasting.

Parts of the study are technical, and I have relegated them to the appendix. The reader who insists on precision might find more there. For others I believe the more easily paced text itself conveys the essential ideas.

2. Observational semantics

The first step is to discuss reference and application for a core language. That language consists of observation sentences, truth functions and quantification, much as Quine's (1960: Ch. II), the fundamental difference being that our reference is scrutable in the modest sense that there is something to be studied.[1]

The core language is the English counterpart of the observational part of Jungle that Quine's linguist sets out to translate. The domain of the core consists of all of the 'middle sized' objects of ordinary experience, things we see, hear and smell. I shall call these things 'sensible objects', and the predicates and relations that apply to them, 'sensible predicates'. In basic respects they are just Russell's atomic particulars of knowledge by acquaintance.

We should snuff out such illusions we might have as to the reality of core. There is but a dim resemblance of a predicate-calculus type core language to the first stages in a child's learning or the socially evolving language. Core is a model for enabling exploration of wild terrain, and that is all.

Recall that in his schedule of behavioral tests Quine seeks to establish philosophical points about reference by having his imaginary linguist prompt a native's assent or dissent to objects observationally open to both: show the native a rabbit and get him to assent or dissent to 'rabbit' (or 'Gavagai', or 'Lo! a rabbit' etc.).

By contrast, our direct report of Rover on the site is not lumped, as in 'Rover' or 'Lo! Rover', but is expressed in a sentence articulated as to grammatical subject–predicate structure: 'There's Rover', 'Rover is a dog' or 'Rover is hunting for Fanny'. We want explanation of empirical givens: a competent speaker of English in a Rover situation applies 'dog' to dog and he or she refers with 'Rover' to Rover when he or she sees him. Predication or identification are given but are not exempt from explanation. We assume, making some adjustment here and there for miscueing and bad intention, that the evidence is in, and we are not totally in the dark as to what refers or applies to what. Our mission is to explain what everyone knows, beginning in midstream with disquotation understood for all proper names and predicates (cf. Chapter 7, §4)

The story goes like this. Jones observes Rover; and introducing him to you she says, 'this is Rover'. By hypothesis her reference is causal, and hence it is an effective process; and therefore by Turing's thesis is a Turing computation from the pattern Rover to 'Rover'. Jones' statement is of an event, and the computation underlying it is likewise an event. We say that Jones *realizes* a Turing system of production rules embodied in her brain that guides the event of computing the reference. See the appendix section on Turing machines.

But her realization of a Rover-rule system is not a further event; it is a disposition, i.e. as we discussed previously, an abiding structure, a mechanism in the brain. And because of it, Jones has a disposition to refer to Rover whenever she sees him.

Similarly, Jones reports 'that is a dog'. The partial explanation of her application of 'dog' is that she computes from object to 'dog'. The computation is done by an underlying, dog-computing machine. Embodying the machine is just having a disposition to respond to the dog by uttering 'dog'.

Mathematically speaking, there is a function whose domain is sensible objects of all kinds and whose range is {yes, no}. Corresponding to dogs is a *characteristic function* f_{dog}, say, whose output is yes if its argument value is a dog, Rover say. There are characteristic functions, from this mathematical point of view, of all named objects and sensible predicates to yes and no: one for Rover that says yes if Rover is argument and no otherwise; and so on for Jack, Schmid, chairs, ferns etc. See the appendix section on the characteristic function.

The embodied Turing machines for recognizing objects or properties and assigning names or predicates (more precisely, for computing characteristic functions) are called *acceptors* or recognizers. Even though acceptors recognize by signaling (figuratively speaking) yes or no it is better to think of them as having more elaborate output which we simply discount in discussing reference itself. In physiological terms, an acceptor is a *neuronal group* whose output

201

processes (axons) spread out every which way in the brain. However, for the moment we are interested only in the assemblage firing a yes or no signifying recognition of an input or not.

Inputs to acceptors for all sense modalities are *parts of stimulus patterns*. For example, Jones' inner acceptor computes from a stimulus pattern to the name 'Rover' or not according to whether it has a Rover-pattern part. If it is Rover, the output of the computation, whatever it is – it might be input to other cognitions – is labeled yes, Rover; and if not, no. See the appendix section on acceptors.

Similarly for 'dog'. If her Rover-acceptor spots Rover as a dog, its output is labeled yes, otherwise no. And so forth.

Thus, an acceptor puts particulars under universals or 'assigns' universal to particular, as is sometimes said, which, again, is just computation of a characteristic function. The Aristotelian medievalist (and Bertrand Russell, too) would say an acceptor perceives the universals in things. Cognitive scientists would say Jones *categorizes* dogs as dogs, cats as cats and so forth. We say acceptors compute characteristic functions for dogs, cats etc.

When I speak of characteristic functions and acceptors I mean a unity of many systems working in parallel. Mary spots Rover the dog. But the spotting involves all the senses, visual, olfactory, auditory etc. Input stimulus patterns cover her body and excite all senses. So when she spots him a parallel, interacting array works in concert, although we think of the process as sensitive to a single individual or property type.

Most of the examples I use as aids to our collective intuitions have a serial character. Thus, although the total impingement of the world on the body yields rich stimulus patterns with component parts processed in parallel, simultaneously, they march along step by step in a line.

If a pattern is represented in our descriptions as a string $x = \ldots$, each element is a parallel structure. For instance $x = abcadeb \ldots$ is processed by an algorithm beginning at the left scanning a, computing, then scanning b, and so on. Each input is actually a column vector,

$$
\begin{array}{ccccccc}
a & b & c & a & d & e & b \\
\cdot & \cdot & \cdot & \cdot & \cdot & \cdot & \cdot \\
\cdot & \cdot & \cdot & \cdot & \cdot & \cdot & \cdot \\
\cdot & \cdot & \cdot & \cdot & \cdot & \cdot & \cdot \\
\end{array}
$$

but a, b, ... need be thought of only as simple entities.

Selection of the individual Rover is a filtering process reflecting Mary's current business, her interest (moments later she listens for Bach in a room full of chatter and noise) and attention. We assume the selection has taken place and give attention a central place in perception.

Acceptors are labeled as follows: '$A_{=a}$' for acceptors that recognize particulars a like Rover; and 'A_F' for properties F like dog. Acceptors are labeled decision automata that algorithmically decide whether a given thing has or does not have a certain identity or a certain property, by computing functions. If you are worried that 'accepts' might be intensional, stop. In this realm, accepting is computing, as shown in the the appendix section on decision and decidability

All inputs are *sets* of parts of stimulus patterns. In the case of acceptors for properties this is the way it should be. Predicates apply to sets of things, their extensions. However, acceptors for individual objects also apply to sets, which is hardly a standard idea in logic. A name 'a', for instance, refers only if an acceptor $A_{=a}$ computes yes for any one of a collection of individual things. For instance 'Rover' refers to the pattern Rover lying under a tree as well as to Rover standing by a fire plug. The patterns are not the same, but both are Rover. This situation already exhibits the rigidity of reference, but temporarily should be kept out of mind. From a logical (not a physical, stimulus pattern) point of view, names refer to distinct individuals only.

The outputs of acceptor computations labeled 'yes' and 'no' are Turing machine outputs token identical to brain configurations of some neuroanatomical description. An output state yes caused by Rover is tacitly associated in the speaker's head to the English name 'Rover', and similarly for 'dog', other proper names and all sensible property types. All human beings incorporate similar but nonidentical acceptors for reference and other cognitive tasks. See the appendix section on equivalence and physical identity. Processes might be radically different in physical aspect and yet enjoy equivalence in what they accept or reject. Therefore, as in functionalism, accepting is token identical to brain process, and accepting in one brain is equivalence-type identical to that in another.[2] Furthermore, we need not suppose distinct acceptors are anatomically separate. One and the same neural complex might embody different functions, singled out by the individual's attention (neural biasing). For instance one and the same neuronal group might detect (accept!) straight edges up-to-the-left given one biasing input, and curved arcs convex-up-to-the-right under another. Again, acceptors feed into belief and desire systems – they function pretty much as inputs to the folkist's belief–desire–act contexts, as we shall see in §4. For the time being, however, just consider that they compute to values yes or no.

We are now ready for our first, simplified, version of basic lexical semantics. First come 'refer' and 'applies' as dispositional terms. In relation (1) below, '*a*' is a proper name from the original list of Chapter 1, *x* is a particular, *i* is a speaker of English, and $A_{=a}$ is an acceptor that decides whether input *x* is or is not *a*:

(1) '*a*' *refers to* *x* for *i* if and only if *i* realizes an acceptor $A_{=a}$ for which *x* is acceptable, and name '*a*' is associated for *i* to the yes state of $A_{=a}$.

The dispositional rendering of (1) reads subjunctively as follows:

(1a) '*a*' refers to *x* if and only if, if *x* were input to $A_{=a}$, its output would be the symbol token '*a*'.

Thus in (1), to say '*x* is acceptable' is dispositional.

Our explication of 'refer' suffers the same disadvantage as Field's Tarski in Chapter 5, §3: we are not allowing quantification over quoted names '*a*'; there has to be a separate definitional clause for each name in core English.[3] Relation (1) stands for a long list, and exactly the same remark holds for application.

The companion treatment for application is the following, where '*F*' is a sensible predicate:

(2) '*F*' *applies to* *x* for *i* if and only if *i* realizes an acceptor A_F for which *x* is acceptable, and predicate '*F*' is associated for *i* to the yes state.

Notice that (2) is about the same as (2') in Chapter 1, §3, but explains the vague notion of 'determining' *x* is *F* by a precise notion of computation.

Relation (2) may be read in a manner similar to (1a) to express dispositional predication. Simply replace 'refers' by 'applies', '*a*' by '*F*' and '$A_{=a}$' by 'A_F' throughout.

The next thing is reference and application as *events*. For reference,

(3) '*a*' *refers to* x for i at time t if and only if i realizes $A_{=a}$ which accepts x at t, and '*a*' is associated for i to the yes state.

(4) '*F*' *applies to* x for i at time t if and only if i realizes A_F accepts x at t, and '*F*' is associated for i to the yes state.

The contrast between (1) and (2) as expressing disposition and (3) and (4) as expressing event is worth emphasis. In (1) and (2), *acceptability* is expressed, while in (3) and (4) *accepting at time t* is expressed. The first pair explains the nontemporal relation, the second the event. This corresponds to Fodor's distinction between causal law and an event of a causing '*a*' (Chapter 8, §6), except here we think of law as embodied in a mechanism. In (1) and (2) an input is required to be decidable even though no decision is made; while in (3) and (4) a decision is made one way or the other at time t.

The logical distinction between accepting at t and acceptability is typically made to fall on one between indicative and subjunctive conditional. However, in our theory the contrast can be made pretty well by separating mathematical description from description of events, as we have just done.[4] One can imagine a neural description of Jones' acceptors, written in terms of acceptor anatomy. But one can also imagine a description of computation, given input, presented as a time-dependent physiological process. The two are basically just descriptions of a Turing machine as a mathematical, embodied system on the one hand, and of a real-time computation on it on the other – disposition verses event. See the appendix section on decision and decidability. With few exceptions, we may pass from an event mode to a mathematical mode of expression by dropping references to time and replacing 'acceptability' by 'accepting'.

Most often expressions of core English are used on actual occasions in social circumstances, and the referential, declarative use is of course only one among many, including questions, commands and so forth. The direct theory abstracts from these rich contexts except for attention and temporal spread.

No embodied acceptor computes unless the normal individual's attention is triggered 'on'. I suppose a basic datum of psychology of perception is that you perceive only when your attention is up – focused on events indicated or prompted. Peripheral images are normally present in receptual preprocessing (you see the whole room, not just the chair), see note 10 below; but they are *perceived* as this or that only when attention is appropriately directed.

I mean for the concept of attention to comprehend that of particulars or individual objects. Attention not only passively *attends*, but it *selects* individuals from a pattern array. Thus when I speak of a stimulus pattern input x, I mean an individual thing that is part of a total pattern. For instance the pen on my desk now is an individual selected by my attention (which led to my predicating 'pen'). Individuals x in our computer model have constituent parts represented in strings of s's; and now we are specifying that each string is a pattern part selectable in attention.

Objects are observed and verbally indicated over a small spread of time, the 'specious present'. An occasion, therefore, is not an event of a tick of a clock. When I say an individual refers at time t, I mean he or she refers during an interval as long as his or her attention span around t. I have little idea what that span is; but it has to be long enough for him or her to believe that Rover is a dog at time t, and/or that the drinks are ready at t, and to desire to hear Bach at t, and so on. Likewise I assume that certain intentional computations – in particular taking things to be as they are or other than they are – occur within the specious present.

Continuing on to a part of simplified cognitive psychology, we come to the concept belief^, which is a precursor to the concept of belief. What is simple about it, mainly, is the absence of intentionality. You might here imagine belief^ as being a disposition of a machine-like thing that knows only our small, sensible, fragment of English and causally reacts to input. Alternatively, you might think of him as an idealized believer who never gets things wrong (the exemplar of truth in §6).

Belief^ basically comes down to a matter of applying 'F' to a, as we might expect:

(5) *i believes*^ a is F at t if and only if there is an x such that 'a' refers to x for i at t and 'F' applies to x for i at t and i knows (in the sense of generating the sentence) 'a is F'.

Relation (5) should be understood to mean both (as the explication expresses) that i's belief^ is an event at t, and that 'a is F' is a *token* of the indicated sentence type. Thus the theory of truth forthcoming in §6 is about sentence tokens, in conformity with Strawson–Dummett strictures.

Belief^ is like belief, except for intentionality, and can be compared with Field's and Fodor's treatments. Here, however, belief^ is direct; there is no mental representation S ((2) in Chapter 8, §4). Belief^ is meaningful – a function of input and computations on it – but there is no proposition or thought in it since there is no MR object to be thought. The object of belief is just the set of patterns or 'states of affairs' that satisfy the acceptance conditions (see Chapter 11, §1). Meaning is engendered in computation; there is no idea here that computation is meaningful only for interpreted MRs, as Fodor requires it be. Things are the other way around. Computation is meaningful in itself and lends sense to causal reference.

3. Perception and meaning

Intentionality is a matter of degree and intrudes itself into our account gradually. For consider perception. Accepting x to be an F or x to be identical to a in the environment of a sensible experience is a first approximation to perceiving. In fact, decision by realized acceptors has several properties of perception. Acceptance is 'object directed' and is by nature dedicated to assigning types to tokens.

From the perspective of the cognitive scientist, stimulus patterns are complex physical occurrences at the surface of a person's body. For the logician and ontologist, too, they are physical objects. But they are remarkable only as instances of universals. Chair patterns come with four or more legs, with or without rockers, cushion or back, and in assorted colors. Assuming (momentarily) the class is well defined and speakers of English apply 'chair' to any one of them, the semanticist's task is to explain the application: how come 'chair' applies equally to Grandma's rocker, a doll's chair and a bishop's throne?

Our question is the classical one of the epistemology of universals (see Chapter 1, §3):[5] how does the mind assign types to tokens? In the present semantical environment the question is how to explain application of predicates – of the one to the many.

The answer has two parts which, though not directly of interest to semanticists or cognitive psychologists, I recommend to meta-physicians. The first part is that acceptors compute *characteristic functions*, such functions being mathematical counterparts of the relation of particular universals (or of token to type – see Nelson 1987). Acceptance of a pattern as a chair-pattern no matter whether cushioned, small or large etc. is precisely computation from a domain of patterns including *chair-tokens* to a range of {yes, no} standing for the *type* (*chair*, *nonchair*) respectively. See the appendix section on characteristic functions.[6]

The second concerns *discrimination*. A perceiver accepts books, trees and dogs as well as chairs, which means he or she is able to tell a book is a book as well as tell it from a dog etc. Perception involves both *universality* and *discrimination*.

In our theory, discrimination of one type from another (typal individuation) is secured by having many acceptors deciding input simultaneously. Take a stimulus pattern and feed it into two acceptors at once; or, better yet, build a robot with several acceptors in it – a book acceptor A_{book} and a tree acceptor A_{tree}. Now assuming for the moment that instances of pattern types do not overlap, and the only things in the phenomenal world are trees and books, the input pattern will produce a yes output of one acceptor and no of the other at the same time, approximately. Thus given the appropriate simultaneous transductions, the construction fits the empirical condition that our minds house parallel-function organs that are operative at one and the same time.

Suppose, then, the mind embodies an acceptor for every perceivable type, all acceptors hooked up in parallel in such a way that a stimulus input goes to all at once for processing when attention is on for all. The situation can be pictured as shown in Figure 10.1. A pattern input at IN will, under our assumptions, eventuate in an output yes at exactly one of the lines at OUT, and no at all others. This construction plausibly explains, I submit, how it is a person or thing endowed with an embodied acceptor system can both discriminate and type input data. In real minds perceptions do overlap: a thing can be taken to be both a red square cloth and a red square tile or the first bar of Beethoven's *Fifth* and the first bar of Pete Johnson's *Rocket Boogie*. Overlap may be undone by expecting and taking in pattern contexts; both can be accounted for in strictly mechanist terms (Nelson 1989a: Chs VI and VII). Expecting and taking are the main topics of the next section.

The parallel composition of embodied acceptors is an example of

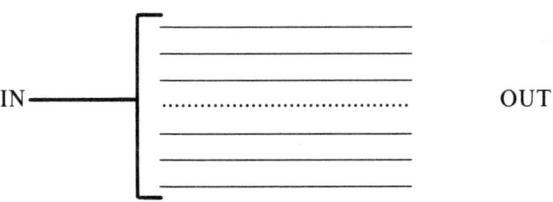

Figure 10.1 Acceptors in parallel

a parallel, distributed processing system (Rumelhart and McClelland 1986). If the diagram is interpreted as a model of a supercomputer capable of running with many free algorithms at once, it is an example of a multiple instruction, single data-stream (MISD) computer (Hwang and Briggs 1984).

Human beings often perceive pattern tokens as instances of *two* or more types. The celebrated phenomena of gestalt perception comprehend an array of ambiguous patterns that can be typed several ways. Good examples are the familiar duck/rabbit and the Necker cube. The latter, which we can consider without the aid of art, is a (set) of two-dimensional projections of cubes having vertices and/or edges accented in such a way as to determine to the eye two distinct types of figure. If you look at the cube in Figure 10.2 in one way you see it with the square of vertices a, b, c and d well to the fore, while in the other way you see square e, f, g and h to the fore. I shall call the cube seen in the first way 'pattern type I' and in the second 'pattern type II'.

The phenomenon of two or more pattern types tokened in one scene exemplifies another feature of perception I claim for acceptors. There are acceptor systems for either pattern type I or pattern type II or both.

Discussions of gestalten in the literature are not always marked by clarity. For one thing, notice the problem is not to explain how the cube in the figure, for instance, can be recognized as a token of type I or of type II. Obviously, anything can be classified in any number of ways, in general, and the point is not worth much exercise except for a follower of Wittgenstein.

The issue here, by contrast, is one of a *set* being taken as token of two types. The collection of all Necker cubes could be thought of as

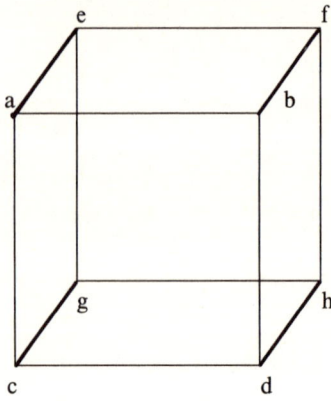

Figure 10.2 Necker cube

type I or as type II. Then the semantical issue is, how might there be two acceptors deciding the two predicates 'type I' and 'type II' differently? In terms of our sought-after analysis of application, the issue is, how is it that two intensionally distinct predicates might apply to one extension?

This is the oldest question in philosophical logic. Every student of 'Logic I' or 'How to Think?' is aware that 'human' and 'featherless biped' have the same extension and different intensions; and now we are asking how, in the realm of sensible objects, intensions can be explained extensionally in algorithmic terms.

The answer I have in mind calls for some elementary mathematics (cf. Nelson (1976, 1987) and see the appendix section on partial functions and base machines) but happily can be packaged in fairly digestible form without it as follows. Acceptors as forms of simple Turing machines are truncated computers and, as stipulated in §2, we ignore their outputs except for yes and no. But now suppose we go back to full machines with output and consider functions over a domain of two-dimensional projections of cubes, prisms, spheres, pyramids, cylinders and others. The values of these functions are shaded graphic figures that enhance certain surfaces of the input entities in contrast to others left untouched. In particular one such function f, given a cube (all sizes, attitudes, drawing styles) as input, paints the dominant surfaces for a Type I perspective of the cube; this is f's value output. It also paints other input objects in certain specific ways. Another function g, has the same inputs, but paints the dominant surface for a Type II perspective of a rule. Let M_f and M_g be Turing machines for these tasks. Functions f and g are hereby called *base functions* and the corresponding automata, *base machines*.

Now what we are going to do is convert both machines to acceptors, M_f to A_f and M_g to A_g, by cutting off the outputs – shaded graphics – and replacing said outputs for *cubes* everywhere by putting yes for both machines. On the other hand, for all input other than cubes, the output of both acceptors is to be no.

What are left over after surgery are two embodied algorithms having exactly the same input domain and deciding yes or no equally to tendered cubes or noncubes respectively, yet differing in respect of the two functions their parent machines M_f and M_g compute.

A_f and A_g are as different in point of computation as they can be, yet decide exactly the same set, showing that in principle the Necker cube, duck/rabbit etc. perceptual distinctions can be explained in terms of algorithms. The claim of course assumes that what is seen subjectively depends on *how* it is seen, and that relevant differences in algorithm (which capture the howness) are rooted in diversity of functions computed by base machines.

A bonus of this treatment of gestalten is that the technique also accounts for intensionality of observational predicates in a principled way. 'Type I' and 'Type II' are associated to acceptors that decide the same things to be cubes, but perceive them differently as they compute differently to different types. Both apply to projected cubes but have different meanings. If it is proposed (as I propose) that 'difference in meaning' be explicated as 'difference in computable function', we have succeeded in naturalizing Fregean sense qua mode of presentation, and have got, it seems to me, a purchase on 'predicate meaning' at the level of observation pinned down extensionally. 'Type I' and 'Type II' have the same extension but different intension, the latter construed in a completely extensional way.

Using the idea of base machine as parent of acceptor for perception of identities, we might run through essentially the same argument to an explanation of how 'a' and 'b' refer the same while having different individual intensions. What has to be shown, by analogy to predicates, is that there are base machines computing different functions over a common domain. Using this device we can manage Frege's puzzle about the informativeness of '$a = b$' verses the emptiness of '$a = a$'; we can do this despite the fact that 'a' and 'b' refer causally and have the same referent. We will discuss this more fully in Chapter 11, §1.

This is the first result on the thesis that meaning arises in the reference relation, not from (gratuitously!) pinning a semantical interpretation on a mental representation.

For the time being we may also explain difference in sentence meaning in these terms. *Two atomic sentences of core mean the same for i* if the computations underlying reference and application, respectively, operate on the same base functions. Further, *two beliefs^* (see (5) above), *are the same if their sentences mean the same.* This criterion does not quite give anything corresponding to a Fregean thought, but it is enough for now.

There is abundant work in philosophy affirming the identity of intensions and intentions. Some philosophers who are sympathetic to modern phenomenology have expressly linked Fregean senses with intentional acts of mind. In Edmund Husserl's phenomenology (see, for example, Kockelmans 1967) the directedness of mind toward objects is explained by appealing to abstract entities Husserl calls 'noema'. To each intentional act of mind there belongs a noema, whether there is an object of that act or not.[7] Noemata are thus supposed to explain directedness without our having to fall back on Brentano's suspect inexistent objects (Chapter 2, §3) or Meinong's unactualized possibles (Chapter 1, §2).

Now according to Føllesdahl (1969) the assimilation of the concept of sense to that of noema is complete: 'noema' is a generalization of Frege's 'sense'; and indeed Smith and McIntyre (1971: 543) declare that noemata are intensional in 'exactly the same sense' that intensions are the meanings of words.

With this encouraging support, if intensions – limited to senses of names and predicates in the Fregean mode of presentation – can be analyzed away in our way, we shall have already achieved a grasp on the intentional to boot.

Intension, however, is not the whole story. 'Intentional' connotes something more than intension of words, since animals, in my view, have expectations and desires and beliefs, but lack speech.

4. Intentionality

The intentional quality of p-reference or indeed of any of the attitudes is not exhausted in its intensionality; 'Russell' does not purport because of its sense but because of the cognitive attitude of its speaker.

Consider a crowd in the street waiting for the President. A certain Republican, Schmid, expects to see Bush emerge in a parade. A tall figure surrounded by plain clothes men strides onto the scene. However, it is not Bush. In the excitement of the moment, Schmid takes the advance man for Bush and hollers 'Bush'. This is no uncontrolled outcry: he *purports* Bush, but semiotically misses.

It is not the intension of 'Bush' that accounts for Schmid's cry and for his misreference; it is Schmid's attitude of expectation. p-reference on occasions is accounted for by expectation. *i* expects to see or hear an object named '*a*'. If the object is there, *i* refers, whereas if it is not there, or if there is a different object there, he takes something to be *a*; p-reference of '*a*' is either reference or empty or misdirected, depending on how expectations turn out.[8]

These rough remarks already suggest a next step in the characterization of p-reference for core. I shall restrict remarks as I go along to proper names, with comments later on indexical names.

(0) '*a*' p-*refers* to *x* for *i* at *t* when *i* takes *x* to be *a* in order to fulfill his expectations to sense *a* at *t*, and *i* knows '*a*'.

There is a similar description for application:

(0′) '*F* ' p-*applies* to *x* for *i* at *t* when *i* takes *x* to be *F* in in order to fulfill his expectations at *t*, and *i* knows '*F* '.

Schmid could take someone else to be Bush and also, unpredictable as he is, mistake Bush, whom he expects, for someone else: he might take the President to be the Chairman of the Grand Old Party, but probably not Saddam Hussein. Within limits persons mistake as well as take.

I think (0) and (0′) are part of folklore: I think that speakers of English do use proper names on occasions in misdirected ways to satisfy expectations of certain occurrent events and that spectators do attribute expectations to those speakers in such situations. The job of capturing 'p-reference' for the core thus specializes to one of extensionalizing 'taking', 'fulfilling' and 'expecting'.

As before, we assume all individuals realize the same acceptors. See the appendix section on equivalence and physical identity. Acceptors, in the present discussion, are the same from one person to another up to within equivalence. Further, there may be many extensionally equivalent acceptors, one to each pattern type, accounting in principle for gestalt patterns, as already said. Of two acceptors, such as for the two pattern types of the Necker cube, only one is operative 'on' in actual occurrence. The acceptor that actually computes on an occasion depends on the attention of the organism.

An occurrence that fulfills need not be the kind of event expected. Jones could be fulfilled by the arrival of something other than the dog she expects – by a large cat, say. Similarly an event that disrupts Jones' expectation could be a cat. Or, what arrives could be an instance of the very kind of thing she expects: Jones might *take* a starved, mangy dog to be a large cat, thus disrupting her own expectation to see a dog.

In general, fulfilling and disrupting of expectations can be summarized in the following terms:

(1)   A person expects x at t if and only if he is in a bodily state such that x fulfills or is *taken* to fulfill that state at t; or x disrupts or is *taken* to disrupt the state at t.

(Chisholm 1957: 102ff)

As Chisholm remarks, the fulfilled bodily state could hardly be a behavioral, reinforced state (i.e. reinforcing the expectation or the behavior prompted by an expectation). For a behavioral explanation of expectation would not account for the intentionality of it. The reason of course is that reinforcement is either positively effective or not. If an organism *took* reinforcement to hold or not as is its wont, the whole theory and practice of behavior modification would go by the board. However, for a state of expectation to be fulfilled, taking is sufficient, as our examples and many others we might cite show.

Before doing anything else we should note that (1) forces a distinction, until now optional, between a proximal stimulus pattern on the body surface and a detached distal object. The reason for this is found in the nature of disruption.

Suppose the pattern type in question in (1) is F. A pattern (token) x either fulfills the state of expecting F or is so taken to fulfill; but if it disrupts, then either x is not F, or it is F (remember the mangy dog!) but is not taken to be F. If x is an instance of F but is taken to be otherwise, then what replaces x cannot replace x itself, but some surrogate of x. This funny situation, which I suspect is often at the heart of epistemological quandries about objects and sense data, is twisted but can be made clear.

In the machine model, if x is a clear instance of F, it must be in the set of inputs acceptable to A_F. Then by our analysis of 'take' (below), x has to be taken as x and nothing else. So if there is to be a taking it must be of some surrogate object y.[9] For this reason, we distinguish the particular x in the outer world from the directly replaced entity y, which we consider to be the immediate stimulus. Therefore we must have two types of entity that figure in p-reference and elsewhere, the *distal* and the *proximal*.

Henceforth in our deliberations we shall let 'x' range over distal patterns (sensible physical things) and 'y' over proximal patterns at the body surface. The relation between the two is frequently referred to as 'reception' (cf. Pylyshyn 1984; Quine 1973: 16ff). I shall use 'Re' for this relation and write '$Re(x, y)$'. To illustrate: if we had taken distal objects into account in our sketch of p-reference, (0) would have read

'a' p-refers to x for i at t when there is a y such that $Re\ (x, y)$ at t and i takes y for x to fulfill his expectations to see a at t, and i knows 'a'.

Re is a component of the causality of reference, application and all other attitudes. 'Re' expresses that if x were to occur y would also occur, other things being equal. If a dog were to appear on the scene, then a proximal dog stimulus would occur at Jones' sense organs, other things being equal (she being there at time t, the light being right etc.).[10]

The possibility of lapses between x and y (a circle is patterned as an ellipse in vision) in reference brings up the old epistemological problem of veridical perception. The correct reference of 'a' at t depends in part on the receptional relation of stimulus object to stimulus plus much more that is still in the offing in my theory.

Picking up now on 'taking'. I will abstract from persons in order to make the exposition less cluttered than it otherwise might be. The treatment is essentially mathematics without the formality – which goes into the appendix. I shall write freely of acceptors expecting individuals or types of properties to occur, and of acceptors taking objects and patterns to be of such types.

My writing is not 'metaphorical' (Churchland 1986: 252); when I ascribe intentions to machines, not persons, the ascribing is abstract, and abstraction is not metaphor. Later on, the algorithmic systems in question will turn up realized by persons.

Now let us consider Chisholm's notion of bodily state and of taking.

> (2) A state of an acceptor A is a *winner* if and only if there is an input x which A starting in that state accepts.

(See the appendix section on winner.) In dispositional phrasing, this says a state is a winner when some input x starting from that state would be accepted by A.

The intuitive idea caught in (2) is that acceptors, imagined in the middle of a computation, can ultimately decide yes for some continuing input string and no for others. To be a winning state, the first section of input leading up to the state must be such that there is a further section leading to yes. This is what (2) says. If there is no such continuation the state is not a winner. But even if the state in question is a winner, the next section of input need not lead to yes.

The situation here is straightforward but not simple, and it is best to study a very easy example. Suppose A_{alt} is an acceptor for patterns consisting of alternating 0s and 1s. The acceptable patterns are like the following:

0 1 01 10 010 101 0101 1010 . . .

Consider string 010. If it is input, it leads to a winning state q of A_{alt}. q is a winner because there is another section of input, 10 or 101 or . . . (leading to 01010 or 010101 or . . .) that would yield an alternator and cause A_{alt} to accept.

However, a further section of input might *not* lead to yes. For instance, 0101 concatenated to 010 would lead to no since 010010 is not an alternator.

The moral is that winners do not always win, for some continuing input could lead to decide yes, accept, and some to decide no.

Now consider 0110. This leads to a *nonwinning* state. The explanation for this is that 0110 is already a nonalternator. There is no continuing input, therefore, that might lead to yes, alternator.

So there are three cases that might arise in a computation of an acceptor A from an initial stretch of input x.

- (a) A goes to a winning state from x and the next input leads to yes;
- (b) A goes to a winning state from x and the next input leads to no;
- (c) A goes to a nonwinning state from x.

- (3) An acceptor A_α *expects* α if and only if it is in a winning state,

where α is either a particular or a property. For instance if 010 is input to A_{alt}, it is put into a winning state and therefore *expects* alternators.

Now the concept of taking depends on that of a winner, and also on the thesis that all input strings in immediate experience are in part vague or fuzzy except in context. For instance, if you are the slightest bit myopic all visual input is fuzzy for you. But even if you enjoy good sight, the chances are you ordinarily take a second look at things to make sure in cases that matter for action.

There is a small circle of thought in support of the thesis that all input is vague. For an illustrious trio – Peirce, Quine and Wittgenstein – all hold that predication is vague, which seems to entail the fuzziness of objects. However, there is a running debate in the literature which pits vagueness of objects against vagueness of words but which leaves proximal stimuli out of account. But as we have seen in introducing '*Re*', vagueness (as a matter of empirical fact) attaches to patterns, not to distal objects – which are what they are in themselves – and the referring words as physical items are precise enough. On the line I am taking, if there were no vagueness in proximal objects as experienced there would be no intentionality.

A part of a pattern is vague or fuzzy if the acceptor cannot certainly tell what it is. For instance, the alternator pattern token 010lo1 might occur as would-be instance of 010101, where o is not one of the defined inputs 0, 1 but (we imagine) is a smudged or slightly defaced 0. The sequence is *nearly* an alternator, and might be taken as such to fulfill expectations. It might be that the writer of the sequence indeed intended it to be the clear string 010101.

Letting all such vague characters be represented by '*B*', let us write the example 0101*B*1. To say *B* is vague or fuzzy is formally just to say it is not a member of the input set of the relevant acceptor A_{alt}. If this string is input to A_{alt}, the acceptor goes into successive states, by the production rules, as it encounters each input. By the time it gets to *B*, A_{alt} is in a winning state, for, mathematically speaking, there is a string continuing 0101 that would lead to a yes. Such a string is 010 (which might not actually occur). By (3), the acceptor therefore expects an alternator, but in fact it next sees B, which it cannot identify.

This brings us to the notion of taking. If an acceptor is in a winning state and has input *B*, it selects an input – in our example from the specified set {0,1} – that would lead to another winning state. In more colorful language, it tacitly 'imagines' a favorable input. It determines itself to win, so to say, by taking 0101B to be 01010 – it *replaces B* by 0. Then continuing the input, it would get 010101, which is accepted as an alternator. This is an example of case (a).

Suppose, however, the original vague string is 0101*B*0. Then when the machine sees *B* it is in a winning state, for the same string 01 (as before) would lead to acceptance (the acceptor has a disposition to accept 01). So it expects an alternator. As before it now *replaces B* by 0, and continuing on, the total input is 010100. But this string is *not accepted* since the part 00 does not alternate. This is an instance of case (b) wherein an expectation is not satisfied even by judicious taking.

Finally, if an acceptor is in a nonwinning state when it has input *B*, it does not accept the string. For instance, rejection would occur if the original string were 0100*B*0; for the head of the string up to *B* is not the beginning of an alternator; hence when scanning *B* it is not in a winning state as no possible continuation could make the string an alternator. 0100*B*0 is an example case of (c).

The crucial notion in analyzing 'taking' within a strictly extensional idiom is self-description. The acceptor has to 'know' that it expects an individual of a certain type to occur – to know, that is, it is in a winning state; and the acceptor must know which replacing symbols might be successfully taken to put itself in another winning state. It must know what satisfies.

Acceptors are endowed with these self-fulfilling attributes by virtue of 'knowing' their own production rules. If *A* is hung-up on a blank, *B*, it can, if so endowed, look up its rules and tacitly 'see' what input supplied for the errant *B* might result in a string that would fulfill what it expects. 'Knowing' what to replace is a matter of self-description.

A *self-description* of an acceptor *A* is an encodement of its own production rules *in itself*. One may draw a parallel here with the role of the genome in genetics, for the acceptor coded description determines its structure just as the genetic code determines the characteristic biological traits of an organism.

Again, for readers familiar with programming, the idea is a bit like the notion of recursive subroutine, which is to say of a subroutine that calls itself out to a main program. In both the acceptor and the computer program, an algorithm (in one case embodied and in the other free) uses knowledge of itself to carry out a computation.[11]

In later parts of this discussion if there is need to talk about taking I shall refer to the above process of scanning, replacing and judging by use of a coded self-description as the 'routine'. It is formulated precisely as a free algorithm in the appendix section on taking and self-description. For the reader who dislikes that sort of detail, a rereading of the above description now and then should help in getting at the rest of our business about intentions.

Having this rough idea of vague string replacement in mind we can explicate taking as follows.

(4) An acceptor A_α in state *q* *takes z* to be *y* (or takes *z* for *y*) at *t* if and only if *q* is a winner and A_α follows the routine for obaining *z* from *y*, at *t*.

Throughout the sequel I will abbreviate 'A_α takes *y* to be *z*' by '$K_\alpha(y, z)$'. If pattern *y* has no degraded input elements, the acceptor simply takes *y* for itself, and I write '$K(y, y)$'. When the identity of the acceptor is understood from the context of discussion I shall write simply '$K_a(y, z)$'. Also, (4) makes taking relative to winning state. We suppose the routine includes making a decision whether the current state of an accepter is a winner. (See appendix on taking and self-description.)

An expectation, we said, is either fulfilled or disrupted. In our technical terms,

(5) *x fulfills* A_α at *t* if and only if A_α is in a winning state at *t*,

there is a y such that $Re(x, y)$ at t and, for some z, $K_\alpha(y, z)$ at t and A_α accepts z.

Note that the distal pattern x fulfills, albeit not directly, but through a path in which the proximal pattern y is caused by x and is, in turn, taken to be z.

Relation (5) may be read as explicating 'fulfills' for either individual objects or properties. For the first, read 'α' as a distal object a (eventually as a name bearer); for the second read it as a property F.

(6) *x disrupts A_α* at t if and only if A is in a winning state at t, there is a y such that $Re(x, y)$ at t and, for every z, if $K_\alpha(y, z)$, A does not accept z.

Relations (5) and (6) together with the explication of 'expects' in (2) and (3), implies Chisholm's condition (1) above and is therefore an adequate extensionalization of the intensional terms involved, as all of the expressions in the analysis (with the exception of 'Re', which is a physical relation) are computational. To aid in checking this out, note that his two cases 'fulfilling and 'taking to fulfill' in (1) are covered in (5) by '$K(y, y,)$ and '$K(y, z,)$' plus 'accepts'. Likewise disrupting and taking to disrupt are covered in (6) by the K-predicate and 'not accept'.

Although our target topic is reference, we must briefly mention that many acceptors for named individuals and attributes work in parallel (as described earlier) and as a consequence there is overlap and ambiguity of response. Many expectations could be fulfilled and disrupted at once. Suppose there are n acceptors for properties $F_1, \ldots, F_n$ operative at the same time. There is a single transduction of x to y under relation Re; but then all n work in parallel, each running the routine with respect to its own self-description and each deciding for or against F_1 or $\ldots$ or F_n. More than one computation might decide yes, since taking is incorporated in the process and a system could switch from tracking F_i to F_j ; and for the organism to act, ties would have to be broken, presenting an extraordinarily complex task. But this is a topic for empirical study of a deeper sort than this. Some possible uses of context and other ways of resolution of conflicts and ties of output are discussed in my *The Logic of Mind* (1989a: Ch. VI, especially p. 194) and elsewhere throughout the literature.

Any time after a baptism, reference to the newly named on direct occasions depends on perception. An individual p-refers on the spot only if he or she perceives the referent. Perception is sometimes distinguished from psychological attitudes proper as being a direct grasp of an individual or quality, not a grasp of a proposition or Russellian atomic fact. Thus it might be maintained that an individual perceives **red box**, say, not that x is a red box, or perceives the individual Jones, not that x is Jones. However, from a mechanist point of view the distinction simply turns on a confusion of reception with perception. Reception fetches the pattern into the system, while perception decides set membership computationally. The 'content' of machine decision is that x is such and such. Hence, following the lead of the model itself, we understand perception of a property to be fulfillment of an expectation thereof.

It is time to return from exclusive treatment of abstract Turing machines to full-blooded persons. Persons perceive things, and the analysis therefore attributes realization of the appropriate acceptors to them. For an individual i,

(7) *i perceives $x = a$ at t* if and only if i realizes an acceptor $A_{=a}$ that x fulfills at t.

Similarly for a property F,

(8) *i perceives x is F at t* if and only if i realizes an acceptor A_F that x fulfills at t.

Perception is thus satisfied expectation stimulated by received input, and the steps leading to (7) and (8) explain away the intentional quality computationally.

The epistemological tradition (Chisholm 1957: Part I) draws a distinction between appearance and perception, perception being veridical. If we were to follow that tradition, (7) and (8) would need amending to include expressions '$x = a$' and 'x is F' respectively. However, we must face the fact of vagueness, and of taking false to be true and true to be false. So (7) includes a case such as Schmid perceiving Bush in the parade whereas the distal object is really the advance man. And so for (8).

On the other hand, the normative concept is picked up, in §6, in our treatment of truth for core English, wherein i is replaced by an exemplar who accepts directly – without expectations or takings.

We have now almost caught p-reference as well as we are going to and are simply called on to replace 'fulfill' in our aboriginal (0) above with 'perceive'.

(9) '*a*' *p-refers* to x for i at t if and only if i perceives $x = a$ at t and '*a*' is associated to the yes state of A_a.

and,

(10) '*F* ' applies to x for i at t if and only if i perceives x is F at t and '*F* ' is associated to the yes state of A_F.

Relation (9) unpacks to an analysis using the *Re* relation, *K*-predicate and Turing acceptance. To emphasize the sense of (9) with all concepts made explicit, let us see what Schmid's referring to Russell (assuming Russell were around) breaks down to.

'Russell' p-refers to x for Schmid at t if and only if Schmid realizes an acceptor A_{Russell} that is in a winning state at time t, there are y and z such that $Re(x, y)$, $K_{\text{Russell}}(y\ z)$, the acceptor accepts z at t and 'Russell' is associated to the yes state of A_{Russell}.

Substituting 'Russell' for x, (9) provides a theoretical explanation of disquotation and of the intentionality of p-reference, and it satisfies condition (*R*).[12]

Relation (9) holds name-by-name for each proper name of English for each individual i and similarly (10) for each predicate.

Inasmuch as we mean to turn received cognitivist theory upside down, we have an obligation to look up to belief in order to see where the cognitivist's concerns with attitudes and representations fit with respect to core. Full-fledged perceptual belief that a is F rests on our earlier study of the simplified concept belief^, which resembles Field's (2) of Chapter 8, §4, and which the reader might want to review. But now taking is written into that account.

(11) i (perceptually) *believes* that a is F at t if and only if there is an x such that '*a*' p-refers to x for i at t and '*F* ' applies to x for i at t, and i knows the sentence 'a is F '.

Cognitivist theory considers belief to be a relation to a mental object. Relation (11) of course does not express any such relation as it has been deliberately omitted. But making some assumptions about the semantics of occasion sentences I will show in §5 that believing a is F entails perceiving a is F, which in turn is quite close to Russellian acquaintance. Perceiving a is F is apprehension of a *singular proposition* (see Kaplan (1979) and Chapter 11, §1) which is an amalgam of subatoms.

Before considering singular propositions and the related subject of indexicals I want to comment on desire and other attitudes, which cognitivism, lacking any apparent means of individuating, replaces with the nonconcept of boxes (Chapter 8, note 12). For reasons already discussed in many places here it seems a bottom-up approach is required. The problem is how to get adequate analyses of 'desire', 'act' and other terms using just the computational ideas we already have, which we know are certifiably extensional.

The question is far from our main concern with reference, and presents a whole new set of complexities that boggle the mind. We might creep away from it with a plea that if it cannot be answered bottom-up it cannot be answered, and that skeptical irreductionism could be right after all. However, I have made an issue of it; and I do propose a next step in my *The Logic of Mind* (1989a, Ch. VIII), which I note here as another part-argument against the doctrine that the intentional and noncircular semantics is beyond the pale of natural science.

The issue here directly concerns the attitudes, not semantics, but again I restrict it (I know no better) to desire, act etc. in directly experienced situations such as are reported in core language. In that domain we already have Turing-based explanations of taking, expectation, fulfillment, disruption and perceptual belief as well as of reference, application and intensions of sensible predicates.

We can go on to explain 'desire', and 'act' and the folkish paradigm belief–desire–action laid down in (a), Chapter 8, §2, by way of satisfying a certain adequacy condition that runs essentially the same as (a). This condition says, where 'p' and 'q' are atomic sentences,

(12) i desires p implies that if i believes q, then if i acts in a way depending on q, then i expects p.

An example is 'Schmid desires to stay dry implies that if he believes getting under the tree will enable him to stay dry, then if he acts to stay dry by getting under the tree, then he expects to stay dry'. The idea, as in all attempts at adequate explanation, is to define 'desire' and 'act' so that condition (12) follows.

Using certain technical ideas borrowed from the algebraic theory of acceptors and other more complex Turing automata, it appears to be possible to explicate 'act' and 'desire' in terms of taking so as to deduce (12). Both concepts depend on previously analyzed notions of expectation and fulfillment; and in particular, intentional act is distinguished from mere bodily movement in its being based on prior belief and expectation of outcome (ibid.: 225ff). If this works as I think it does, it is a step toward getting intentional wholes from parts, all on the level of intentions as they arise in direct experience, and on the plausibility of assuming machine models (Turing's thesis), of course.

5. Indexes and subatoms

For the students of the matter (ourselves) discussing i's beliefs, (11) ties reference to application by way of existential quantification. 'There is an x' *binds* the two: if x_0 is the x we want, 'a' refers to x_0 and 'F' applies to x_0. Consequently we have from (11), 'a is F' for i.[13]

However, for i, including Schmid-like i, in live first-person experience, binding is effected by *indexicals*, and that binding is essentially *social*.

Tracing back through the steps (9) and (10) leading up to (11), we see that 'i believes that a is F at t' entails 'there is an x such that i perceives $x = a$ at t and i perceives x is F at t'. Now for the moment assume the following scope property (let $x = x_0$):

(1) i perceives $x_0 = a$ at t and i perceives x_0 is F at t if and only if i perceives $x_0 = a$ and x_0 is F at t;

and also the substitutivity property:

(2) for i (tacitly), if $x_0 = a$ and x_0 is F, then a is F.

From (1), (2) and (11) and its antecedents, we conclude

(3) i believes that a is F if and only if i perceives that a is F and knows 'a is F'.

In explaining these two inferential steps we shall have at hand a small theory of how i comes to know 'a is F' from 'a' and 'F'. We shall also find a suggestion of a holistic way of distinguishing singular from general, and of distinguishing the identity from the copula of predication in core – all in terms of indexicals.

Relation (1) is subject to doubt as it stands unless x is specified *for i*. For if Schmid were to perceive $x =$ Rover at t and to perceive x

is mangy at t, there would be little guarantee, given Schmid's past performance, that he would perceive at t that Rover is mangy. Relation (1) needs support, which we see comes from a certain account of the reference of 'that' or other indexical as follows.

If the object x were demonstrated by an observer or friend of Schmid or by Schmid himself, (1) would seem to hold. For suppose 'that' refers to x for Schmid when he points at x, looks at it from several angles, nods toward it etc.; and that his friend does the same. They individuate x by physical means plus uttering 'that' plus assent. Then certainly that is x – or better, that that is what we are talking about – holds for Schmid and friend.

Now assuming he is at worst only marginally human, Schmid concludes to the propositions that is Rover and that is a dog, since he already perceives (x =) Rover and perceives (x is) a dog and he grasps 'that is x'. For although there is likely to be a short lapse of time from one demonstration to the next, Schmid *uses** 'that' as a *bond* to tie his perception of the particular Rover to the general dog.

Furthermore we suggest he is tacitly equipped to make an identity substitution (2) wherefore he perceives that Rover is a dog, and knows the sentences 'that is Rover' and 'that is a dog' and 'Rover is a dog'. In some such sense, i moves to belief that a is F and to knowing the full sentence 'a is F'. He comes to believe a proposition during the generation of the semantics of a sentence from the semantics of the lexical terms.

Whether this rough hypothesis is on the right track is surely an empirical issue, and not one of hunting through anyone's intuitions of persons' powers of inference. If it is right to think belief depends on p-reference, we seem to be led to the question of hooking-up reference and application, in some such way as is just described.

For those doing theory, the existential quantifier, (11) of §4, does the binding. We could have written, 'there is an x such that x is Rover and x is a dog'. However, for Schmid and his ilk we have to attribute knowledge of a specific, named thing for (2) to obtain. Quantification is not sufficient for colligation by the live speaker as he must know the thing identified and the thing described are the same before he applies a quantifier (the variable must be the same within common scope, which of course it is, trivially, for theory).[14]

Demonstratives and personal pronouns (those used on occasions of direct observation) are essentially social. Schmid alone in his neighborhood, confronted by a dog, mutters 'that is Rover', say; but he would seem to be communicating to himself – the I to the me. In the more elemental social case, the sense of 'that' is approximately as follows:

(4) 'that' (or 'this') refers* to x for i at t means x is pointed out to some listener j (who might be i) by speaker i at t when 'that' is uttered and x is acknowledged by j; and 'that' binds with respect to some events, realized by i and j, of accepting $x = a$ or x is F or both.

Personal pronouns are likewise nondisquotable, situational and seem to have a binding virtue in the singularly sense that they can generate 'you is (are) F' from perception that x is F. On this account, 'you' is logically more primitive than 'I' as is suggested by the following:

(5) 'you' refers* to x for i at t means i is a speaker, there is a listener j, such that $j = x$, present at t, and 'you' binds with respect to some perceived atomic facts (i.e. patterns accepted by both i and j, who know the relevant sentences).

Similarly,

(6) 'I' refers* to x for i at t means i is a speaker, $i = x$, there is a listener j (not necessarily other than i) present at t such that 'you' refers* to x for j, and 'I' binds in the relevant respect.

'He' seems to me to be far more complex than 'you' or 'I', and my convictions, such as they are, weaken in the face of it. However, whatever the direction of an appropriately social analysis might be, 'he' might have the very same reference as 'I' or 'you' or 'that' while the expressions differ in indicative meaning.

'You are happy' uttered by me has the same extension as 'I am happy' uttered by you, showing that these pronouns have the same reference but different meaning, as the intuitions of many causalists attest. The meaning here is not, of course, Fregean sense, but is the flexible social practice of use in a binding role (more in §6; also compare Wettstein 1986).

In illustration of acquaintance-type atomic beliefs, integrating some of these points, we have

(7) i believes that that is a at t if and only if 'that' refers* to some

x and i realizes $A_{=a}$ such that it accepts x at t and i knows 'that is a'.

Also,

(8) i believes that I am F at t if and only if 'I' refers* to some x (= i) and realizes A_F etc. and i knows 'I am F'.

Indexicals are the fundamental agents of joining subjects and predicates in natural, occasion-sentence language. And as such they play a role in our explanation of 'singular', 'general' and predication – as will be made explicit in Chapter 11, §1. But first we shall take an idealized look at truth.

6. *Warrant and truth*

The core language is not rich enough for ordinary expressive use or for the semantics of a corpus of very complex phrases. But it is a vehicle for coming to terms in a careful way with reference and meaning. The course is Russellian, for we are studying immediate acquaintance and observational language. And as for Russell (Chapter 4, §5, in response to Strawson), truth applies to sentence tokens.

The next step, then, is a theory of truth for observational language. In Chapter 5, §3 we noted the lack of any hint of linkage in reference. Now that we have got it truth reenters the picture. The focus, as in Tarski's theory, is reference and application (read 'satisfaction'); but now we have enough linkage to the world to promote a version of a correspondence theory.

Correspondence, in my book, of sentence to fact must involve mind. Truth is related to belief^ (shades of Plato's *Theatetus!*) essentially; but for the core this involves belief in objective states of affairs 'out there', and not of mental representations. According to naturalism the language of science and mathematics, including the semantics of it, is a refinement of daily language. As we well know this view, following American pragmatism, turns Frege and Tarski around: we move from natural to exact language, they the other way. However, the regimentation we have here is not a question of moving to austere, Quinean syntax, for core is itself basically predicate logic interpreted over a domain of sensible individuals and attributes. What makes natural core unrefined and inexact is the intentional. Our refined, exact version of core for studying truth is one with the intentionality of underlying attitudes bracketed out.

So let us now specify that core syntactically speaking is just language L of Chapter 5, §2, interpreted as in earlier paragraphs, and truth is defined recursively as in Tarski, except for clauses pertaining to atomic sentences. As in language L, there are names 'a_1', 'a_2', . . . ; variables 'x_1', 'x_2', . . . ; one-place predicates[15]: 'F', 'G', . . . ; the connectives '-' and '&', the existential quantifier '∃' and parentheses. Individual variables, names and indexicals are *terms*. An *atomic sentence* is defined as before, and *sentence* is defined as before, with possible exceptions as mentioned in the note above.

Imitating the Tarskian format of Chapter 5, to obtain a truth definition we need semantical interpretations of terms, which we have. However, for truth of sentences of exact core we want reference, not p-reference, and we want the relation $Re(x, y)$ to be a one-to-one function; in other words we want the stimulus pattern to be a veridical transduction of the distal object.[16] The best way to comply with this choice is to drop the distal–proximal distinction altogether, returning to the model of §2.

We shall therefore suppose an ideal situation, wherein all objects are precise, not vague, and wherein expectation – being in a winning state – is satisfied in nature's course of events unless the object is the wrong type: the object is taken as it is – $K(x, x)$ – and decided one way or the other absolutely, not relative to expectation. In consequence we shall return to belief^ as explicated in (5), §2. These limitations on the distal–proximal relation and taking are our *idealizations* transforming a cognitive cum semantical theory into primitive epistemology. Together they are our approximations of regimentation.

Now since meaning and truth in our theory are relative to computation, and since we have so far only dealt with atomic sentences, we must explain what it means for an individual to have beliefs cum computations associated with compound truth functions and quantification.

If i believes^ a is not F then he realizes a not-F acceptor[17] and knows '-$F(a)$' is the right sentence.

If i believes^ a is F and b is G, then he realizes acceptors for identifying objects a and b and for applying 'F' to a and 'G' to b and knows '$F(a)$ & $G(b)$'.

For us to explain what it means for an individual to believe^ a quantified atomic open sentence we need a hypothesis about the indefinite reference of a quantifier. The variable of quantification 'x' in '$F(x)$' does not refer to any definite object under immediate surveillance or demonstration, as in our recent observations on indexicals, even though the belief^ is in the specious present. The reference, or 'denotation' as Russell would have it, is indefinite, since attention is not fixed on a specific object. But for acceptance there must be a trace of a previous reception in short-term memory for the acceptor to compute. We shall suppose this is explained by use of a simple on–off device or flip-flop cell which is set or reset in the specious present (Nelson 1989a: 280). Therefore, for i to believe a quantified sentence of core *within his or her attention span in the specious present* there has to be in his or her memory cell a mark of a named or demonstrated thing.[18] We express the idea as follows:

(0) If i believes^ that something x is F at t then i realizes an acceptor A_F that accepts at an earlier time t some y that is a memory mark of x and knows '$\exists x(F(x))$'.

Next, we drop relativization of reference etc. to specific individuals i, as all are disposed to refer in the same way. They all enjoy the same accepting competence, which is hereby declared incarnate in an exemplar 'X', the name connoting his role and his nonidentity. Since we are assuming X's complete competence we are also taking phrases such as 'X syntactically knows the sentence S' for granted and do not give space to them.

A sentence is true (it will turn out) just if it is believed^ by X. However, I am going to replace 'belief^' by 'warrant' for the Exemplar, as we are about to deal with truth, not intentionality, and want to rearrange the explication of 'truth' so as to coincide as closely as possible with the format of Chapter 5, §2, Tarski's theory. Therefore to start with we replace 'believes^' with 'warrant'[19] in (5) of §2, and relativize warrant to our champion X, obtaining

(1) X *warrants a* is F at t if and only if there is an x such that 'a' refers to x for i at t and 'F' applies to x for i at t.

We are not quite finished doctoring, as we wish to copy the style of Tarski by setting out a comprehensive reference scheme as header for the definition of satisfaction. The way is simply to strip all references to 'refer' from the characterization of 'warrant', writing

X warrants a is F if and only if 'F' applies to a for X.

Then we specify disquotation, 'a' refers to a, 'b' to b etc. (suppressing our analysis, which can now be taken for granted) as a header. Next, as before, in Chapter 5, §2, we let $\sigma = \sigma_1, \sigma_2, \ldots$. designate sequences of objects of the domain, and use the function σ' to set up an interpretation scheme. The scheme is much the same as before.

if a term t is a variable 'x_i', then $\sigma'(t) = o_i$
if a term t is a proper name 'a_i' then $\sigma'(t) = a_i$ (disquotation)

With these assumptions at hand, the first thing is to define a new recursive definition of 'satisfaction'. Following that I shall give an *explicit*, not a recursive, explication of 'satisfaction'. And finally truth.

Following Tarski, we define 'satisfaction':

   (a) A sequence σ *satisfies* '$F(t)$' if and only if X warrants that $\sigma'(t)$ is F;

   (b) σ *satisfies* a sentence $-S$ if and only if it does not satisfy S;

   (c) σ *satisfies* S & T if and only if σ satisfies S and σ satisfies T.

   (d) σ *satisfies* $(\exists x_i)S$ if and only if some sequence differing from σ in at most the ith place satisfies S.

Clauses (b)–(d) contain little new; but the involvement of a theory of reference beyond Tarski's bare disquotation schema calls for comment on (a).

As often remarked, (a) is really a scheme for a large, finite number of clauses depending on the number of names and predicates in core. Clause (a) unpacks for each predicate in two ways according as the term 't' is a variable or a name. If it is a variable, 'x_i', '$F(t)$' is an open sentence and satisfaction is reduced to acceptance of an arbitrary object o_i by an acceptor A_F realized by X. If t is a name, 'a_i', '$F(t)$' is a closed sentence and satisfaction is reduced to a condition that holds if and only if there is an x which 'a_i' refers to, for X, and 'F' applies to x for X; and the latter reduces further to acceptance of x by $A_{=a}$ and of x by A_F, both realized by X. (For a review, see (3), (4) and (5) of §2 reading 'warrants' for 'believes^'.)

Clauses (b)–(d) involve some subtle questions about the scope of 'warrant' which emerge in seeking a more explicit version of 'satisfaction'.

Let S be a sentence of core which is satisfied by a sequence σ and let $S(\sigma')$ be its translation into the metalanguage, where σ' is the function determined by σ, as before, that inserts terms named in S into the translation in accordance with the interpretation scheme. We want to show the proposition

> (2) A sequence σ satisfies a sentence S of core if and only if X warrants that $S(\sigma')$.

To do this we are going to need the following scope principles for warrant. In effect the principles express variant but extentionally equivalent interpretations of what it means to believe negations, conjunctions and quantifications as described following the definition of 'sentence' a few pages back: these are empirical, doxastic principles which seem to be true of believers of observational sentences. At any rate, they have to be assumed; and whatever justification they are going to get here appears after the listing (cf. Nelson 1989a: 232ff).

> (A) X warrants that not-S if and only if X does not warrant S.
> (B) X warrants that S and T if and only if X warrants that S and X warrants that T.
> (C) X warrants that there is an x such that S if and only if there is an x such that X warrants S.

I claim all three of (A)–(C) are justified for X and the core, given the concepts of attention and specious present.

Relation (B) is not problematic for the Exemplar (even for Schmid), so far as I can see. He believes the left proposition when he believes the right and vice versa.

As to (A), the left side of the equivalence certainly implies the right, for X. And if X's attention is up, the relevant algorithms are on, and if X does not accept, it rejects, i.e. accepts the negation 'not-S' (see note 17). So not warranting S implies warranting not -S.

Relation (C) is the same as saying that warrant of occasion sentences is a species of *de re* belief, which is widely acknowledged (see, for example, Kent Bach 1986; William Lycan 1986; Igal Kvart 1989). Quantifiers in effect draw on memory reports of experienced objects as explained before our definition of 'warrant' in (1) above.

In basic logic terminology, the existential quantifier is *exportable* (cf. Quine 1981: §§9 and 13).[20]

Proposition (2) now follows by induction from the recursive definition of satisfaction (a)–(d) on page 230 and the foregoing scope principles. The induction is on the number of connective symbols '-', '&' and '∃' in S.

If the number is 0, (2) is just the first clause (a).

For the induction step, suppose (2) holds for up to m connectives and S contains m. Consider -S. If σ satisfies -S, then σ does not satisfy S, by (b). By the induction hypothesis, σ satisfies S if and only if X warrants that $S(\sigma')$. Hence if σ does not satisfy S then X does not warrant that $S(\sigma')$. By principle (A), it follows that X warrants that not-$S(\sigma)$. So if σ s satisfies -S then X warrants that not-$S(\sigma')$.

The step for 'and' is similar and depends on (c) and (B).

Finally, σ satisfies '$(\exists x_i)S$' if and only if some sequence τ differing from σ at most in the ith place satisfies S, by (d). By hypothesis, τ satisfies S if and only if X warrants $S(\tau)$ if and only if, for some x_i, X warrants S if and only if X warrants that some x_i is S, by (C).

Again in the wake of Tarski, Chapter 5, §2, assuming S has no free variables, a sentence S is true in L if and only if every sequence σ satisfies it. And from (2),

(3) A sentence S of L is true if and only if, for every sequence σ, X warrants $S(\sigma')$.

By considerations Tarski alludes to (1931: 195–7), one can show in principle the sentence S is true if and only if X warrants it. We might call this condition (W). An example, which should be compared with Tarski's companion (T), is

(4) 'Snow is white' is true if and only if X warrants that snow is white.

We shall discuss this notion of truth more in Chapter 11, §1, especially as a version of correspondence and as a theory that agrees on some points with Dummett's criticisms of Tarski (Chapter 5, §3).

CHAPTER 11

Mind and Semantics

1. Reflections on reference and truth

The distinguishing mark of the direct theory is its explanation of the causality and intentionality of reference in computational terms, and its locating of the semantics of spoken language in the world of material things. The idea is close to certain fundamental issues in philosophy of logic that have been scarcely touched on here, and should be reviewed. I do so in this section. I also want to say more about mental representation and the closely related topic of cause in the sense of acquisition of semantical dispositions as promised in Chapter 9. Finally, I will discuss the philosophical status of sundry models and questions of the proper method for semantics and mind.

Real-time reference of a name 'a' is computation of a characteristic function associated to an individual a. In logic and conventional semantics the individual is a fixed particular. However, in perceptual experience an individual has many faces. Rover, as we have said, might be standing at one moment, sitting the next, soaking wet the next, fatter later, mangy etc. Each Rover-event is a token of a Rover type, the latter being the referent of 'Rover'.

In logic and pure semantics there is no distinction between individual token x and individual type a. And of course our notation '$x = a$' (we might have written '$x \in a$') is idiosyncratic. In the tradition, every individual is a type, in my sense. The difference is clearly highlighted in contrasting a stock theory of belief with our core theory. In Field's version, if i believes 'a is F', then 'a' refers to a and 'F' to a property F. In mine 'a' refers to a thing x, which is a token of type a and 'F' applies to x.

Quine observes the same distinction, although he avoids anything like my use of 'token' and 'type'. An individual can appear in many guises at different times. When we quantify over individuals x, as we do throughout our study of reference, application, taking and the rest, what are the values of the variables? 'Simply the sums of physical objects of various worlds [stimulus patterns] combining denizens of different worlds indiscriminately. One of these values would consist of Napoleon together with all his counterparts . . . ; another would consist of Napoleon together with sundry dissimilar denizens of other worlds' (Quine 1981: 126). The counterparts and dissimilar denizens are tokens of my type Napoleon. For Quine they are parts of scattered physical wholes, Napoleon here, Napoleon there etc.

Stated in another way, according to my view, in referring to Rover what happens is the same as what happens in application – assignment of a universal to a particular, here an individual type to an individual token. What distinguishes singular from general is not the number of things linguistic expressions are true of, but the role played in formation, via indexicals, of 'a (singular) is F (general)' from '$x = a$' and 'x is F' as described in Chapter 10, §5.

Now the question of rigidity is just an aside to this story. 'a' refers to a no matter how imagined by i, with some restrictions; or, if we are observers, no matter how described verbally. If you want to think of a as a denizen of a possible world according as he wears one face, or another, or another, . . . then the 'name' refers rigidly to the same individual in every I-world (Chapter 8, §1): 'a' to a where and whenever.[1]

Having said this much I hasten to add that I have but few comments about the characteristic function computed by a reference acceptor. The algorithm embodied in the acceptor is not a description (although of course it could be described), as it is a neural network of some kind and pre-verbal. However, if Russell is essentially Russell as begotten by the Amberlys, and similarly all other individual things have individual essences which determine the set of individual tokens (in my sense) they are members of, perhaps algorithms are rigged to essences. The output is yes if the essence is present, and no if not.

I do not know this, and am content to fall back on Turing's thesis and let it go at that: naming is a causal process, therefore effective, and therefore Turing computable; hence there exists a Turing acceptor $A_{=a}$ that grounds the naming 'a'. Description of the embodied algorithm is a question ultimately of brain anatomy. From Marr's stance (Chapter 10, note 6), such a description would, I think, presuppose physiological knowledge of the characteristic function being computed – which is of course the very step I do not know how to take.[2]

Many friends of direct reference theories of one sort or another are anxious to maintain reference is causal and at the same time to accept Frege's compelling arguments that sentences might have the same truth value and different cognitive value.[3] '$a = a$' and '$a = b$' might both be true while having differing cognitive value; 'Cicero' and 'Tully', for instance. For the true Millean causalist, however, this is simply wrong; the names rigidly refer the same, there is one objective essence (for Kripke) and there is no subjective meaning, although this judgment runs against the intuitions of many people.

On the other hand, Wettstein (1986) thinks skepticism is a result of accepting a Fregean notion of cognitive value, i.e. of the idea that value is sense, and then denying proper names have sense (Millian version of Kripke). However, he argues that explaining difference of cognitive value by difference in sense is a semantical mistake – basically Frege's. So why not look elsewhere for an accounting of cognitive value, skirting the objection while at the same time accepting the new causal theory? Why not?

In Chapter 8, §1, we mentioned a proposal of Devitt's (1981) that the distinction might be epistemic: 'a' fixes the shared referent in a different manner than 'b'. However, it could be argued that cognitive significance is not the same as epistemic significance, and the point here concerns the former. For instance, 'God = Allah' might have cognitive significance for an agnostic who consistently suspends judgment on the existence of God but who is cognitively bored by 'God = God'.

Possible world semantics (Chapter 6, §3) cannot easily manage this puzzle without drawing on *ad hoc* devices. The sense of a name is a map from possible worlds to individuals. If this is the way, 'Ali' and 'Cassius' have the same sense since the associated maps are the same. But this puts us back where we started, as the problem was to explain differences in cognitive value. The notion of intension one can pull out of possible worlds semantics is not refined enough for making the Fregean discriminations we intuit.

However, the direct theory of reference, I suggest, explains both rigidity and significance of names.

Let us think of sense as mode of presentation of the object in terms of algorithms (as we have been threatening to do for a long time).[4] Terms '*a*' and '*b*' have the same sense if and only if the acceptors $A_{=a}$ and $A_{=b}$ embody algorithms for computing the same base partial functions. See the appendix section on partial functions. Terms differ in meaning, we argued in Chapter 10, §2, provided the base functions associated to the acceptors are unequal but defined over the same partial domain. To understand this idea in the present context it is well enough to think of the two acceptors as incorporating different programs for the same task. 'Ali' and 'Casius' name the same boxer, while the underlying computational processes are diverse.

In our theory, however, the characteristic functions associated to Ali and Cassius are extensionally the same (so on our construal of possible worlds as sets of patterns, they are logically equivalent in Carnap's sense). But they are accepted by different programs or, formally, computed by acceptors derived from different base-function Turing machines. Possible world maps and our maps are both intended to account for sense; both have possible world domains (although ours are I-maps, not the O-maps of model theory); however, our maps are computed by algorithms distinguishable according to the functions they compute.

A similar observation pertains to application. Recall that, for Carnap, 'human' and 'rational animal' are logically equivalent, but that in order to explain their supposed synonymy he has to fall back on an understanding that they mean the same in ordinary English use (Chapter 5, §4). However, from the mechanistic standpoint they are synonymous if and only if the relevant characteristic functions deriving from the same base partial functions use the same programs. Again, the meaning of 'red', or 'dog', is not the Fregean sense of a mental representation; the meaning is a mode of presentation, an algorithm operating on stimulus data.

There is a radical empiricist complaint in the wings about this notion of meaning; no direct criterion outside of that given by intuition, which is to be explained, is evident for telling one meaning from the next in either the Fregean or algorithmic theories. Explaining meaning as a cognitive algorithm is no more individuative, Quine might say, than explaining it by maps from worlds to individuals, sets or truth values. What hard, empirical criterion is there for telling one algorithm in Schmid's head from another?

In response to the question, two points are worth repeating. Pure semantics needs pure worlds – which according to Quine lack criteria of identity – while the pattern domains of computable functions are Quine's very own worlds. They are sets of distributions of bodies in space.

Further, meaning qua algorithm is not open to test-criteria in science today, but in principle could be checked via brain experiments. There is nothing in the theory that calls on anything but extensional entities plus the idea of embodied algorithm, which is an empirical, biological phenomenon. Diversity of meaning, if the theory is right, is reflected in diversity of anatomical structure, and the complexity of it does not imply there is 'no fact of the matter'. And from the mechanical point of view that ends the matter.

We now return to indexicals.

Indexical terms are causal, and a certain effort has been exercised in the literature in making clear what their senses are. 'He' and 'I' in a direct situation can refer the same while having obviously different senses, as we have amply illustrated. Indexicals play a key role in predication of property to object. That role is binding, and indexical reference is cousin to quantification in making a sentence ('saturating') of a predicate.

Indexicals are nondisquotable. By contrast, a proper name is disquotable, and its reference is perforce dispositional. Disquotability implies a *fixed* referent; and we now understand the real connection of world to thing to be a causal law, a law writ in embodied algorithm. But reference* of 'that' is no causal disposition of the mind in the sense of an embodied algorithmic structure. There is no word-to-thing causal *law* although, God knows, there must be enormously complex dispositions of some order actualized in social situations such as those described in Chapter 10, §5, where 'that' binds perceived objects. It refers in use*. Its object is picked out thereby, although there is no disposition to refer to some fixed that. Each token of the word has its object, but all have a common yet distinctive semantical role. What we have here is a concession to user* theories, for employment of demonstratives on concrete occasions is referential use* in Donnellan's sense, if anything is.[5]

In Chapter 10, §5 I suggested that indexicals derive their sense from binding perception of an object *a* and a property *F* to the generation of the sentence '*a* is *F* ' and its semantics, holistically. Adverting to an apt Fregean idiom, the unsaturated predicates '*x* = *a*' and '*x* is *F* ' bind through that agency. The more elemental step to the proposition that that = Rover is also a kind of degenerate binding, as the predicate is saturated by the index. Binding in this sense, singular as well as binary, in core observation language is at the very heart of predication (cf. Davidson 1990: 325).

A close look at the principles (1) and (2) of Chapter 10, §5, reveals that we attribute a tacit enthymemic inference to the individual in which the occurrence of the copula in the first premise 'that is *a*' is identity and in the second 'that is *F* ' is predication. In an atomic sentence containing an indexical subject, the term in the predicate position is singular if the 'is' is identity, and general if it is the copula of predication. This view is holistic in the sense that the identity is, the predicative is, and general and singular terms are individuated by roles in an inferential whole including speakers and listeners, not in the surface sentence syntax or semantics.[6] The sense of indexicals is explained by their role in practice (cf. Wettstein 1986).

In the realm of observational language the question of intentionality of reference, i.e. purported reference, and Fregean quandries about empty names boil down to either mistaken identification or hallucination. The first is not new as we motivated the introduction of taking in terms of expectations that might not fit actual things; and we introduced the distinction between distal and proximal object in order to account for disruption of expectations by objects which, to an independent observer, count as veridical and fulfilling. These are both kinds of *mistake*. Schmid might purportedly refer to a vague dog as a goat because he expects a goat; or turn away without comment from an actual dog he expects because he takes it to be a goat.

In both cases there is a p-referent. In hallucination, however, there is p-reference combined with vacuous perception. Schmid is dreaming, let us say – his attention is on no actual thing around him – or is in a paranoid state, or has recently been thoroughly rapped on the head; yet he audibly whispers 'Ronald Reagan', p-referring to that personage.

Our explanation is that Schmid has a Reagan-acceptor in him, and some internal prompting has set it off from an initial state and is taken so as to compute to an accepting yes. Fulfillment of expectation, no matter whence it springs, does not imply a distal object is there, as we have seen. Moreover the 'inner prompting' might be interpreted as vague stuff, not in the defined set of proximal inputs, but still a subject B (a vague, 'undefined' input in a string, see Chapter 10, §3) of a taking computation.

Philosophers of logic tend to group the puzzle of giving sense to names with the puzzle of nonbearing names. However, the first is a question of exact languages and full reference while the second arises, as we have just suggested, in contexts of p-reference and taking. Puzzles similar to the second attach to intentional attitudes. These are the Brentano puzzles.

The first of them, that names in belief sentences need not refer while the beliefs yet have clear truth values yes or no, is adequately explained by the above. For consider

Schmid believes Titania is in the Rose Garden.

Our analysis (assuming 'is in the Rose Garden' is a monadic, sensible predicate) yields

There is a y such that 'Titania' p-refers to y at t for Schmid and 'in the Rose Garden' applies to y for Schmid at t and Schmid knows the sentence 'Titania is in the Rose Garden'.

But y is proximal or even is, or might contain as lately observed, nothing but an undefined B subject to Schmid's taking. So the analysis does not imply there is or is not an object.

Second, we can do for the problem of substitution what we did for sameness of sense of proper names. Intuition demands notice that substitution of co-referring names in belief sentences can produce false sentences from true. Our explanation is that co-referring names do not p-refer the same; and so Schmid might believe George is in the Rose Garden but deny President Bush is. Nor does an input have to be taken to be George for a predicate equivalent to 'is in the Rose Garden' to apply to whatever it is that prompts him. Our preventive therapy is: a condition of substitution of singular or general terms is sameness of p-reference, which goes back to sameness of taking and acceptance, which in turn reduces to sameness of partial base functions.

Finally, that Schmid's belief is truth-functionally independent of

'George is in the Rose Garden' is shown by the fact that the belief holds even if 'George is in the Rose Garden' does not, owing to Schmid taking things the wrong way.

In all, what the theory does, as projected back in Chapter 2, §5, is extensionalize the belief sentence and yet display all the nonreferential, nonsubstitutional and nontruthfunctional properties of the unanalyzed intensional sentence.

Scattered throughout the remarks of this and earlier sections are many ontological asides – to objects and meanings. All proper names arise causally in namings and their intensions are algorithmic structures realized in neural patterns. There is a parallel for sensible predicates; all of them (primitive lexical items) in the direct theory are learned and the underlying acceptors and intensions are physical structures. All objects (except mathematical objects, which are not referred to in core) are individuals embedded in stimulus patterns; they are not the name bearers of abstractly thought-of 'domains of interpretation' of pure semantics. And at the observation sentence level there are no native, primitive lexical mental representations as objects to be believed or asserted of.

The objects of atomic sentences or of the atomic sentences believed are the states of affairs in which the sentence is true. 'States of affairs' is conventional, but could mean any number of things. There is no such thing in this book as a sentential semantics independent of a speaker of the language, a Peircean interpreter. A sentence of core always has meaning for, or truth for, some person – in Michael Dummett's terms, no meaning without understanding and no truth without understanding and warrant. There are two classes of speaker: the individual as incorporating intentional attitudes; and the exemplar E. I will discuss the latter only here although the same points, altered for the distal–proximal relation and taking, hold for Schmid and his ilk.

A state of affairs in which 'a is F' is true is the set of all patterns, including object x, in which 'a' refers to x and 'F' applies to x (note 1). The set of all such patterns is the set of Quinean possible worlds, and the set in which a sentence holds is the stimulus meaning of it. This is a 'propositional object', as Quine terms it (1969: Ch. 6), far removed from the Fregean True or False, but near to Russell's idea of singular proposition. They are both, Russell's object and ours, in the world or sets of worlds grasped by mind, but are not otherwise abstract objects or engendered subjectively.[7]

I agree with Field that Tarski's theory of truth needs development of the notion of reference, and have tried to provide it for simple cases. I also agree with Dummett that truth and falsity can be assigned only 'in virtue of something of which it is either true or false' (1958: 66). This something is not an abstract condition, but a state of affairs, a fact of the world that justifies assertion. And to be justified in making a statement we must have a method that warrants assertability of it. I take this to mean that truth of a tokened sentence, unlike truth of a type in logic and mathematics or of Quine's eternal sentences (Chapter 7, §3) depends on assertability, and the latter involves conditions that justify. No truth without justification; and this is precisely what X's warrant provides. This is no abstract condition. To assert, a speaker must understand the workings of the language and understand meanings; and this is what a theory of meaning must 'open to view' (Dummett 1977: 101).

The direct theory, so far as truth of core is concerned, differs from Tarski in the basis clause of its definition of 'satisfaction', but in the logic of the metalanguage it agrees in the recursions. For Dummett, however, Tarski's clause (c), Chapter 5, §2, does not hold. 'a is F or b is G' could be asserted without asserting either the first or the second clause. This claim is entailed by the more radical one that truth (or satisfaction) in natural language is assertability.[8]

However, for the sentences of core he appears to be wrong if an individual's attention is directed on the objects being talked about. This is the main notion underlying principles (A)–(C) in Chapter 10, §6, and note 20. For core the principles of classical logic, in particular the law of the excluded middle, hold. Outside of core, Dummett's notion of assertability seems right unless (possibly – I shall not attempt to defend the point here) all sentence tokens are converted to eternal sentences in Quine's way (Chapter 7, §3).

Field's requirements for a theory of reference and Dummett's (except for the stance on disjunctions) for a theory of justification settle, it seems to me, the question of what a correspondence theory of truth must entail. There exists a large literature on the subject which addresses the pros and cons of correspondence, yet disdains talk of the necessary engagement of referring and understanding minds. Discussion of truth as a mind-independent quality of sentences, whether correspondence, coherence or disquotation, is simply elliptical talk for truth as warranted or assertable or guaranteed by reason. For a semantic theory of observational language we get warrant.[9]

Before leaving truth let us return to the problem of empty names and descriptions. How do we cope with 'there is no such thing as Titania'? The name occurs in a non-opaque, purely referential spot. The sentence is plainly extensional and, except for Fregeans, is true. The canonical causal theory, so far as I am aware, is not noted for its response to this problem. But in the present theory we actually find a use for the notion of truth, as follows.

From (3) of Chapter 10, §6, we have that 'there is no such thing as Titania' is true in core if and only if X warrants that there is no such thing as Titania. There are two paths one can take from here, both leading to the same end. From scope principles (A) and (D), we get

There is no x such that X warrants x is Titania

if and only if

There is no x such that X realizes A_T and x is accepted by A_T.

The reasoning of course presupposes X fixes his attention during a short present, and that the Re relation and taking are irrelevant. These are the very assumptions underlying the scope principles and the equation of truth with warrant.

The other path uses our convention about memory, (0) of Chapter 10, §6. From (3) we have 'there is no such thing as "Titania"' if and only if X warrants that there is no such thing as Titania, if and only if X's memory cell is empty of any x such that X realizes A_T and A_T accepts x'.

In each explication, X has no experience of an x although he has somehow acquired a Titania acceptor. This is a problem of acquisition which does not differ in principle from the problem of learning the scientist's referent of 'water'. I will discuss this more in §3.

I incline toward a view advanced by Kaminsky (1982) opposed to the orthodox causal stance that fictional and speculative names, unlike proper names of real individuals, *do* abbreviate definite descriptions. 'Titania' is fixed in *A Midsummer Night's Dream* by a small number of descriptions; and any outside of that set would not only fail of Titania, but would alter Shakespeare's play, perhaps seriously. If so, 'Titania' submits to Russell–Quine analysis in terms of descriptions as well as to mine in terms of the analysis of 'true'.

242

Descriptions such as 'the present King of France . . . ' or 'the fourth moon of the innermost planet . . . ' are still replaceable in exact or regimented language as we have it today, but not in core as we doubt the availability of abbreviating names. Intuitively, the truth conditions are formulable in first-order logic, as for Russell's theory of descriptions; the first is false, and the second to this date speculative – one or the other value holds, while we do not know which.

2. Boundaries of psychosemantics

There are compelling reasons for a bottom-up theory of structural semantics rather than one top down from a dogma that beliefs and their contents are innate. A difficulty to overcome, however, is that the idealized core language we have to start with bears only slight resemblance to the full realities of natural language. Even if meaning and reference do arise causally, what is the connection of elementary semantics to contentful thought and 'higher' cognition, and especially to the semantics of full-blown English? How do we go from the bottom up, which is our wont? How and where in the bottom-up scheme do meaning-bearing mental representations come into theory, if at all?

As an introduction to this extraordinarily complex topic let me locate our destination. I am going to suggest that *tacit tokens* of English words acquired in learning names, predicates and sentences are *primitive* mental representations, are the basis of all phrasal MRs, and arise in the evolution of speech in the child and society. They are the vehicles of thought and cognition as in cognitivist theories, but are tokens of English as in Field's philosophy (Chapter 8, §4).They are *not* ingredients of a native and neutral language of thought, but are language-specific. There is no Mentalese, but only English, Russian, Bantu etc.; and semantics has to be explained in some way other than by the notion of translation of the vernacular into Mentalese or by virtue of knowledge of Mentalese.

In defense of this stance, let me first attempt to characterize the semantical enterprise. Typically, a top-down approach takes off from a recursive definition of the language and then defines 'truth' for it. From then on there are various routes. Typical ones are Donald Davidson's, Fodor's and Noam Chomsky's. Also typically, the bottom-up approach starts from lexical items and works up, generating a grammar and semantics inductively in a process of selection and adaptation.

According to Davidson (1967) the smallest unit of semantical meaning is the sentence. An ingredient of the meaning of a sentence is given directly in disquotation; thus using condition (*T*), the meaning of 'the snow is white' is given by whatever sentence it is translated into in the metalanguage. For English metalanguage this is simply that snow is white. The other ingredient of meaning is found in a Tarski-like recursive definition of truth built up in the canonical way from a reference scheme and a body of clauses defining 'satisfaction'. Davidson maintains the reference scheme at the basis cannot be determined from direct speech and listening – for much the same reasons as found in Quine's inscrutability arguments – but is the linguist's hypothesis about fundamental lexical meanings; the method runs parallel to hypothesis formation about fundamental particles in physics. You pick a reference scheme that makes the sentences of the language as a whole have an intelligible fit with each other and with science in a Quinean-type coordinate scheme. The Davidsonian approach here is about as top down as a semantical theory can get.[10] For Fodor you get a pattern similar to Davidson's in outline but more elaborate, since meaning for him is to be understood side by side with a theory of language-learning by a subject. Learning a first language, according to Fodor, is a matter of hypothesis formation, the theory of grammar being a hypothesis in the learner's head explaining the body of sentences in their syntactical and semantical unity. Getting meaning involves learning the semantic properties of predicates which, in turn, presupposes learning generalizations which 'determine the extension of' the predicates (Fodor 1975: 59).

The latter step presupposes knowledge of Mentalese, a stock of beliefs with attached representations and causal laws relating instances of natural kinds with tokens of those representations, as discussed in Chapter 8, §6. The semantics of a language is constrained by its syntax, which is in turn constrained by certain universal rules of which the individual has innate knowledge as well as by an innate system of mental representations ticked by causal events.

For the inquiring linguist, the right sort of methodology for psycholinguistics is consistent with cognitivism. Noam Chomsky is the pioneer of linguistics seen as falling under computability theory, and has championed a Cartesian psychology of language and cognitive science. Language, according to this philosophy, can be explained only in terms of certain a priori conditions known by the speaker. His position is best seen in terms of the adequacy of various rules that govern construction of grammar, semantics and phonology.

A grammatical theory must adequately describe what a fluent speaker knows. A theory of syntax is *real*, not instrumental science; a good one explains actual sentence structure, helps us understand communication, and besides tells us a good deal about the mind. A competent speaker tacitly *knows* the rules of grammar, and this means the rules inform and guide her speech production and understanding. The rules of syntax are computable, reducible to biology and, in our way of thinking about mind, are incorporable in free algorithms. The rules operate on spoken or written symbols, including 'terminal' or lexical items, and yield grammatical sentences, much as a system of axioms syntactically produces theorems in a formalized logic.[11]

Another condition on linguistic inquiry is *explanatory adequacy*. A good theory will reveal the universal principles that apply to all natural language and are tacitly known by the child when he learns the local grammar. Learning language is a form of abductive reasoning precisely in Peirce's sense. The child infers from a relatively small finite sample to the correct system of grammatical rules for his language with the help of constraining universal information which safeguards him or her from false or unreal guesses.

The speaker's knowledge of universal rules has propositional content (Fodor 1984) and we may suppose its vehicle is Fodor's Mentalese. Indeed, if rules are known (Chomsky sometimes prefers 'cognized' to avoid normative overtones), native endowment of Mentalese or something similar embodies the rule-corpus, and is a necessary attribute of all language learners and users. Moreover Mentalese presumably provides the semantics for spoken language and a bridge from one language to another in language translation. Chomsky's metaphysics of language thus appears to comport very well with Fodor's representational theory of mind.

The top-down character of the subject on this view is nicely illustrated in the relation between linguistic competence and performance. Not only does *learning* presuppose a substantial theory in the child's head which is applied top down, but *linguistic performance* is governed by that knowledge. An individual's fluency is guaranteed by knowledge of the grammatical rules. Employment of the language in daily life, which is marked by lapses, mistakes, blurs etc. in execution, is guided by knowledge of the rules, which in turn is constrained by innate knowledge of linguistic universals. Thus performance presupposes competence (Chomsky 1965: 9).

Attractive as it is, this cognitivist scheme for semantics generates trouble. To begin with, the armamentarium – consisting of native Mentalese; for each natural language *L* an internal language *I* which is a set of rules for *L* (Chomsky 1986); and principles of universal grammar – threatens several commandments, mainly that the semantical component seems to assume what it is that linguistic science is supposed to explain. Mentalese, with its full semantics of MRs and knowledge of universal grammar, comprehends what we set out to explain in the first place.

Whatever stand one might take on this point, the relation between Mentalese (or whatever informs Chomsky's universal grammar) and natural language presupposed in the learning and semantical transfer theories remains deeply problematic. What does it mean – what is the mechanism? – to talk of using Mentalese to learn the semantics of English? For Field's theory (Chapter 8, §4) the meaning of a mental object is just that of English. Without a theory of meaning for English this leaves a lot open, but it helps. However, for Chomsky, Fodor and company the semantics of the natural language is to derive from that of Mentalese in virtue of the subject's knowledge of Mentalese.

Let us suppose that tacit lexical translation is algorithmic, to give the theory a conservative accent. Now one might propose that there be one universal algorithm for learning all possible languages or a unique one for each. The first proposal, that there is one algorithm from or to Mentalese that constitutes 'knowing', is very hard to accept. Mentalese might be fixed; but the necessarily native cognitive relations to all other tongues could not possibly be the same in Mohawk, Finnish and Cantonese. I am not questioning the possibility of an algorithm representing a priori conditions for the *syntax* of natural languages, but for the *semantics*.

The alternative, that there is a different scheme (one machine or prefabricated program) for each possible language, seems equally wild, even if the brain is many orders of magnitude greater than the one we have. Myriads of complex algorithms each containing specific Mentalese to natural language lexicons would have to be inborn and ready for use, just in case. Thus even if we drop the suspect rationalist claim (that English works because we *know* Mentalese) in favor of species-specific algorithmic networks, the theory is patently absurd.

But worse, there is nothing in it for reference. In a rather sharp turn from canonical cognitivism, Fodor (1984) lately insists there are 'input systems' that feed information from the world into the central cognitive apparatuses of the mind. These systems are modules that furnish information about the world to the processing facility. On the surface, input analyzers seem to be analogous to our acceptors as they are computational and, contrary to basic cognitivist theory, process *nonsymbolic* input via embodied algorithms. 'Input systems function to get information into the central processors; specifically, they mediate between transducer outputs and central cognitive mechanisms by encoding the mental representations which provide domains for the operations of the latter' (ibid.: 42). Now from his causal theory of denotation (Chapter 8, §6) (which we shall assume combines with the idea of input system under consideration) a general term denotes a natural kind, and, as we know, instances of the kind cause tokens of the term. So we suppose the cause of the encoding of the representation via the input system is associated to or is identical to the event of causing the term. There does not seem to be any principled trouble with locating the *meaning* of the term in the Mentalese representation and the *reference* in the causing object; for the input system *infers* the character of the distal object from processing the proximal (ibid.). This is the source of the referential meaningfulness of the MR and derivatively of the associated linguistic item.

But this happy arrangement does not extend to proper names, if their semantics is truly causal. The object of a primitive observation sentence in English is often an MR with the meaning that *a* is *F* where '*a*' is a proper name. It is simply incredible that there be a *native* MR for every proper name in English, every one in Swedish, every one in Arabic etc. which is of course one of the reasons why the theory of descriptions is attractive, if only it were true. The concept of a language of thought presupposes a fixed, Aristotelian world of categories with an MR for each one. This might work for predicates, but there *cannot be* a matching MR stuffed in everone's head since the dawning of time, ready for each proper name likely to turn up in baptisms from Nome to Victoria Land.

Returning to consideration of the bottom-up approach, the entire unlikely business of a Mentalese-based linguistics is skirted if meaning is seen *to grow from causally induced lexical items on up.*

The notion of mental representation, however, is needed still to explain higher cognitions and language beyond a core, possibly by appeal to free algorithms, executive-driven systems and the like. But how do we get MRs into a direct theory?

First I will explain the need for mental symbols as it arises at a core language level, and second describe machinery that leads to a concept of MR as consisting of tacit English. There is to be a mental language for any natural language, consisting of tokens of the language itself.

We know Hesperus is the same as Phosphorus, and also consider it to be the bearer of sensible names learned in direct experience, reinforced by pointing and demonstrative reference. However, the name-pair 'Hesperus'–'Phosphorus' differs in an essential way from 'Ali'–'Cassius', say. Ali and Cassius are identified in direct exper-ience. 'Ali' refers to Cassius for some individual i at time t since Cassius is accepted by A_{Ali} (or the other way around, or both) given directed attention. Hence Ali = Cassius.

However, the same does not obtain for 'Hesperus' and 'Phos-phorus'. Although both bearers are sensible objects, the one does not occur in the same specious present or field of attention of an individual as the other. Their identity is not secured owing to A_{Hes} accepting Phosphorus (or the other way), but to scientific dis-covery, much as phenomenal water is identified as H_2O owing to scientific knowledge.

The difference is in *learning*, not in circumstance of reference or in diversity of cognitive value. The causal theory still holds in all respects, and one might still claim with Kripke that 'Hesperus = Phosphorus' is necessary if he has the applicable notion of possible worlds in mind.

The moral of the story is, 'a' and 'b' refer owing to causal connection with the object; but they might refer on site or according to stored information. In the second case, names or representations must be stored for use beyond the specious present in order to make simple identifications. Such is the primary use of MRs, which are tokens of the natural language itself and arise non-natively in experience.

In a naming ceremony, a name gets associated with a yes state of an acquired acceptor. As in Fodor's theory (for application or 'denotation' only) the name is encoded in the neutral states standing for yes, probably; but the mind in my theory is supplied with tokens of names as namings come along; each MR is new as are the phrasal MRs that incorporate it, while Fodor's subsist in an innate, natural-language neutral domain.

Continuing the bottom-up proposal, language would grow from primitive reference and application with the help of demonstration from the ground up, with the exception of innate dispositions to accept primary qualities. If brain evolution, which is the preferred choice for a theory of acquisition (next section) is right, *no* acceptor structures for lexical – in particular natural kind predicates – would be of this native sort. All mental representations playing symbolic roles in higher cognition would be tokens of terms originating in baptisms or direct experience. For English speakers, all MRs would be post-language tokens of English.

Linguistic roles, syntactical and semantical, would develop inductively under species-specific constraints built genetically in the brain and embodying an enormous number of embodied algorithms. A ground system of this sort would provide a second-order computational system having roughly the same role as a universal grammar ensconced in Mentalese. By 'second order' I mean to imply a precategorization of the world, a system of 'algorithmic principles' guiding the construction of specific grammars and a mechanism of natural selection thereby constrained. Out of the evolutionary, inductive, growth process would emerge a 'knowledge' of rules of English, say. Performance would determine competence, rather than the other way around as Chomsky believes.

I see syntax, semantics and phonology developing in individual learning and the social evolution of the system as a *whole*. The familiar disciplinary divisions – syntax, semantics etc. – are a result of the historical development of linguistics, not a reflection of separate real 'faculties' that have to be put together by mapping systems. For instance, the once-standard theory (Postal and Katz 1964) that syntactical rules are interpreted via projections of some kind from within a semantical system, goes by the board, in part because the theory depends on an idea that native, neutral representations subsisting in the head constitute a kind of Mentalese dictionary. The suggestion is now, rather, that all linguistic entities develop pretty much as reference does – holistically: reference, meaning and syntax entire within a language community.

Thus rules of a language would grow in the individual and as relatively complete would govern fluency, perhaps through free programs generating sentences pretty much as in the standard phrase-structure grammatical theory.

An analogy with programming suggests itself. In standard 'strong' artificial intelligence (AI) human cognition is regarded as adequately modeled, in principle, by free programs operating on symbols. This is of course the computer paradigm for cognitivism including speech generation. But *constructing* programs is an entirely different matter than *running* them. Construction of a clever chess player serves to show that chess, as representative of high cognitive capability, is mechanical. However, it shows nothing whatever of the process of acquisition, of designing the algorithm and the program.

I suspect, largely from considerations of the causal character of semantical input, that developing language and thought are analogous to program writing, not running – persisting in the computer 'metaphor' – and eventually are to be understood, if at all, in terms of connectionist, embodied algorithm systems in the brain. The brain probably runs programs – think of social linguistic communication or of playing a musical instrument in concert – but *acquiring* the program or learning the piece, though algorithmic, is a matter that demands a different sort of theoretical attention.[12]

In all, there is a referential input system from which representations derive; an evolution of grammatical and semantical rules and structures constrained by genetically determined species-specific pre-structures; and, intermittently, the 'running' of the rules in speech and listening in an executively driven system using free programs. None of this assumes there is anything like knowledge and antecedently categorized Mentalese symbols.

Chomsky's demand for *descriptive adequacy* of a linguistic theory seems to me to be right. The linguist has to find the system of rules (in effect the recursive definition of a language, including syntax and semantics) that account for free generation of speech and its unbounded sentences (Chomsky 1965). But the explanation of this competence or 'knowledge' cannot entirely be from a priori principles known by individual minds. The problems of semantical translation and the putative fact of *acquisition* of causal reference schemes suggest that a top-down Cartesian paradigm does not fit acquisition of semantics as it very probably occurs in life.

Evolution probably accounts for knowledge of universal grammar (or possession of species-specific algorithms) for learning syntax of natural languages as they come along (cf. Pinker and Bloom 1990). This is an interesting biological question. But I am concerned about *naming*, which seems to call for a more plastic, relatively unconstrained individual brain.

3. Evolution and acquisition

In Chapter 9, §4 we distinguished the causal event of referring and the causal law covering it, from *acquisition* of the law. A basic feature of a causal theory is that the disposition to refer arises or is brought to the fore in the original event of naming. The most plausible way of explaining acquisition of names and natural kind predicates, I shall argue here, is by evolutionary selection. I am tempted to affirm further that if a causal theory of reference is true, then it helps confirm a radically new theory (Edelman 1987) that the brain in the child develops by a natural selection process.

The slightly puzzling issues concerning acquisition of proper names and natural kind predicates do not arise in the same way for primary qualitative predicates such as 'red' and 'bell-like', which are probably innate. I do not mean to say there are native MRs for these things, but that the mechanisms of identifying things as red or salty is – unlike that for 'H_2O' or 'brook trout' – innate or, as we say better, genetic. Some dispositions, in other words, are built in and others acquired; and in the case of names and predicates for species we are faced with the question of how the disposition is formed.

English terms for fictional names and predicates such as 'Titania' and 'mermaid' and speculative terms such as 'God' or 'tachyon' are acquired along with the naming dispositions in some sort of social–environmental process on a par with acquisition of natural kind terms like 'water'.

This move is just to generalize Putnam's idea that natural kind properties are discovered by science and then delivered over to the public in some kind of social instructional process. The extensional meaning of 'water' is objective and socially constituted. Similarly fictional and speculational names and their dispositions to refer are socially acquired although there is no real-time reference, no objects or extensions, as already explained.

In all there are at least three cases (this is no doubt a gross simplification): names of actual objects, which (with dispositions) are acquired at naming occasions; qualitative predicates like 'red', which are learned and associated with native receptual dispositions; fictional names, speculative terms and natural kind terms, all of which are acquired along with their underlying dispositions to refer or apply (like the embodied algorithm A_{red}) in some experience in an English-speaking community.

The acceptors active in perception of things in naming them cannot be *native*,[13] as there would have to be one for every logical atom, just in case. In 1920 or thereabouts an eskimo would have to be pre-rigged for possible attendance at the baptism of George Bush. A lesser absurdity would come of pre-rigging natural kind terms; 'water' would correspond to a native algorithm, although its true application to H_2O originates in the practice of science.

Acquisition might mean learning or adaptation, or a higher-order process involving a disposition to acquire dispositions to refer or apply. One can imagine a spectrum of possible processes: in material place-holder terms, acquisition could mean *activating* a system – turning it on; or *learning* to use it; or *adapting* to one system rather than another; or *exchanging* the algorithm that defines a system for one more adequate to a specific *task*; exchanging the algorithm to one more adequate to *survival*; . . . or *implanting* a new piece of brain. Acquisition of an acceptor for identifying a bearer of a name would be over toward the far end, but involving reformation of neural material and probably not anything more drastic. However, there is very little in current research in cognitive or computer science, outside of an evolutionary theory, to help us understand what this might be. Here are some methods that have to be discarded as candidates for a possible theory.

Behaviorism, as we know well, makes it a professional point to keep speculation as to mind/brain structure out of science. An organism has a tendency to behave in certain ways given stimulus input, and acquires a disposition for pecking in a certain way or crying 'ouch!', when it has been trained by a trainer using a schedule of reinforcements or conditioning it to respond in the *right* way. 'Higher' processes such as learning to categorize, either precepts or concepts, is also a question of controlled reinforcing, and so can be 'explained' behavioristically.

Learning a name at a baptism, however, is what the engineer calls a 'one-shot' affair. You do not have to harp on a schedule of repetitive ritual unless your audience is hard of hearing. And it is tempting, except for the absurdity of it, to explain grasping of a distinct name by attributing native powers for each such name to the grasper.

A vast literature in cognitive science and AI has emerged in the past thirty years or so reporting a whole range of processes and models for learning, adapting, categorizing and problem solving in general. Some of these presuppose a fixed brain with a fixed repertoire of procedures that are programmable or learnable, and others a plastic brain that can be changed through experience, weighting, rule modification or selection (for a sample of recent theory see Edelman (1987); Rumelhart and McClelland (1986); Waltz and Feldman (1988); Hahlweg and Hooker (1989); Holland *et al.* (1989)).

For the most part weighting and rule-modification depend on feedback from a system goal intrinsic to a model. This means the model is rigged to learn a task or adapt to a goal, not to organize or institute a goal – not to acquire a disposition. Techniques of this kind are being used very little, if at all, to illuminate reference.

Again, the principal occupation of AI is inventing free algorithms for standard sequential machines in order to simulate or analyze the properties of real cognitive systems. The dominant interest in expert systems, knowledge representation and computer semantics is completely unrelated to questions of referential input. All input to AI programs consists of clinically clean, transferable symbols in Newell's sense (Chapter 9, §3) which are purely syntactical in office and semantically dead except to a human interpreter. For instance even Holland *et al.*'s excellent study (1989) of inductive processes presupposes full symbolic representations and a free algorithm bias (ibid.: 25f) although the models used are parallel.

It has been observed from time to time that a robot with refined sensing organs might be able to get in touch perceptually with its environment. However, a robot has trouble enough detecting a hole that does not quite fit the specifications without requiring of it knowledge that a name '*a*' refer to *a* in its humble symbology. Nevertheless, naming and application are not entirely out of the question for robots for if they were we ourselves, being mechanists, might just as well close up shop.

The point of the foregoing brief survey, other than to suggest the apparent powerlessness of cognitive science at present to explain acquisition of semantical disposition, is to invite attention to Edelman's (1987) notion of *brain evolution*, which appears to fit the acquisition bill exactly and which, in return, gets strong support from the demands of a causal theory of reference.

For our summary purposes (Nelson 1989c) Edelman's theory has four main parts: (a) a critical argument against a certain residual Aristotelianism in mind/brain inquiry;[14] (b) an inventory of facts of brain biology which challenges the Aristotelian paradigm; (c) a proposal for an evolutionary approach to brain biology that squares with the facts adduced in (b); and (d) an argument against the adequacy of computational (free algorithm, Chapter 9, §3) models of mind/brain for explaining visual perception.

(a) Much current inquiry assumes that what is up for study is an evolving, but at the moment relatively stable, natural world faced by a developmentally complete mind/brain consisting of fixed neural structures; the perceiving organism is endowed with the native ability to grasp pre-existing visual categories – a 'pre-labeled world' – owing to its adaptation to that categorization. Simply, the world comes in categories and the human brain matches, although the matching might be achieved only by learning, adapting, computing or whatever. Much of the research alluded to above, certainly that of cognitivists, rests on such an assumption, although my aim is not to expose closet Aristotelians.

(b) Residual Aristotelianism is inadequate to the known facts about the brain. '[T]he [natural] environment . . . is inherently ambiguous: even to animals eventually capable of speech such as ourselves, the world is initially an unlabeled place. The number of partitions of potential "objects" or "events" in an econiche is enormous, if not infinite . . . ' (Elderman 1987: 3); individual animal response to it is relative to the way the organism sorts things out; and one animal's response system is not always the same as that of another.

The brain is very complex – current estimates are up to 10^{11} neurons, and it has enormous redundancy and repetitive structure.

Brain anatomy is underdetermined by information in the genome, which means its determination is not solely genetic, but is in part epigenetic and possibly postnatal.

In vision there are over a dozen neuronal groups (bundles of interacting nerve cells, thousands to the bundle) working in parallel and overlapping. In a certain sense the brain is plastic, not 'hard-wired' (i.e. not hooked up the same in every individual of a species); perceptual categorization varies slightly among individuals and more greatly from culture to culture.

(c) Highly organized and relatively completed neural anatomy and the physiology of visual perception can be explained by a hypothesis of a process of natural selection working on the primary groups.

To fix the main ideas: standard Darwin selection theory explains evolution of a species in terms of selection from a population of individuals of a species who differ from one another in some salient biological respects – this is individual variation *within a species.* Edelman's neural Darwinism explains evolution of the visual system of the brain in terms of selection from a primary population of neuronal groups each having roughly the same function (they all fuzzily detect about the same visual features of things) but differing in functional detail and being anatomically diverse. This is variation *within an individual brain.* An example of the first is selection of large-eared dogs from an initial dog population marked by individual variations in ears (straight Darwin); of the second is selection of edge-detectors from a population of neuronal groups in a single brain marked by individual variation in refinement of edge-detecting (Edelman's Darwin).

It is extremely important to stress that the 'success' of selection is survival. This is what distinguishes an *evolutionary* from a *goal-adaptive* process. For instance, an adaptive system of rules for achieving a categorical goal – winning chess or correctly classifying red squares – is not a selection system, even if the rules can be altered for better adaptation (Holland *et al.* 1989). Changing a rule in midstream is not the same as selecting a surviving rule from an initial set. In the one case the change is governed by a fixed goal; in the other the 'goal' is a product of the process. Roughly, the first is Lamarckian and the second is Darwinian. The Lamarkian is residual Aristotelian.[15]

(d) The proper conceptual scheme for brain selection theory is connection machines – parallel, distributed memory processing systems (Edelman 1987). Edelman is *against* the use of standard AI practices, for they all assume categorization. In our terminology, what he opposes is free algorithm, semantically interpretable symbol, von Neuman architecture of exactly the description given in Chapter 9, §3. By default, the standard AI model of an executive or 'instructionist' system operating on symbolic data or, in the brain, on mental representations violates the crucial principles (a)–(c) of the selectionist theory.

In my view, embodied Turing automata are exactly right as they too are not driven by free executive programs, are nonsymbolic, highly parallel, systems with distributed memory.[16]

Continuing with some details on the selectionist theory, as Edelman puts it, the major constraints on *physical* brain theory are phylogenetic and quantum mechanical, assuming an in-principle reduction of cytology, molecular biology etc. to physics, while *development* is a question of selection. A selection theory is conceptually 'impoverished', meaning that it abstracts from the particulars of transduced stimuli, neurotransmitters, synapses, thresholds and spike frequencies, and deals simply with inputs and outputs, much as we do in our embodied algorithm models.[17] In our terminology, the logic of evolutionary development is functional, indeed computational.

The selection portion of vision theory proper posits a family of neuronal groups for perception. These groups are diverse in function although some of them might be approximately equivalent (see (b) above). Any group recognizes at least one, possibly many, input(s) that drives it above threshold; for other inputs it is quiescent. The initial family is large enough so that every possible input (presumably as characterized by the inquirer) is recognized by some group or other.

Neurons are 'ignorant' (ibid.: 43) at the outset of the selection process. The inputs they respond to do not fall into categories (of course from the logician's point of view they extensionally comprise categories), and thus have only 'syntactical, not semantical significance'. There is no such thing as cognitive representation or 'mapping' in the visual cortex, initially.

The selection process, which Edelman and associates model by a computer simulation (Darwin I, II and III), preserves some groups and lets others die or go inactive; and among the survivors establishes re-entrant connections both within and between groups, leading to a structure providing for growth of neuronal representations of objects.

A second-level process leads to refinement of the emerging categorization by weighting or amplifying re-entrant connections among neurons – by strengthening synaptic (roughly, neuronal input from other neurons) effect. Weighting makes the connection between A and B, say, stronger than that between A and C depending on performance. The overall process in due course eventuates in a visual processing system that is capable of generalization, discrimination and representation of features of the world sufficient for survival and continued somatic and cultural growth.

Inasmuch as reference and application in core imply an underlying perceptual system realized in the brain (Chapter 10, §3), there is plenty of interest in seeing how our question of acquisition rings in this selectionist scheme. I have already said most of what I intend to say about a nativist and Aristotelian notion of acceptance categories. Reference is not native and application of natural kind predication is environmental and social. Existing models of the 'pre-categorization' cast do not fit a causal theory in our third sense of the word. Thus we agree with (a).

As to (b) let us speculate that there are neuronal groups dedicated to hearing, touch and perhaps other sense modalities that are involved in reference. Our model assumes that an acceptor explaining reference of '*a*' or '*F* ' incorporates parallel operation realized in hearing as well as sight etc. (Chapter 10, §2). Edelman's input recognition is my acceptance; and neuronal groups might realize Turing acceptors within an extremely wide range of anatomical variation. They do not have to be binary, or Boolean or whatever the current, popular understanding of Turing machines might be. But they must be such as to realize Turing-embodied algorithms of specific sorts.

How these groups are organized is of course far from the reach of present day brain anatomy. We only assume, with the selectionist, that such groups (for '*a*' or '*F* ', for example) are roughly equivalent in the initial layout, and form an initial population repertoire determined as far as it goes by phylogenetic and other factors.

Let me dispose of point (d) before (c). Our embodied algorithm stance already agrees with Edelman's exclusion of free algorithm models: of instruction-driven, symbolic, semantically laden systems. We do have to assume in addition, however, that acceptors, now realized in neuronal groups, have the attributes qua abstract model required by the selectionist's parallel distributed systems. But I do not think the point is disputable given Turing's thesis (Chapter 9, §3) and arguments cited in note 16 immediately above.

But (c) is the rub. Selectionism presupposes a certain rough equivalence among groups all of which are 'ignorant', which is to say, they do not fall into precise categories in the sense of satisfying fixed descriptions or defining properties (see note 13). Our acceptors, except for vague input which is undefined for a system to which the taking routine does not apply, are precisely firm *categorizers* – contrary to the whole show we are trying to run. The list of acceptors for sensible individual and property types is precisely a fixed categorization.

There are several ways of altering the model so as to accommodate it to a selection theory. One way is to require that all acceptors be *probabilistic*, meaning that each acceptor A is said to emit output with a certain probability (Rabin 1964; Nelson 1984a; 1989b). If the probability is higher than a certain fiducial level π, then the output is said to be a yes, and no otherwise (if its probability is $1 - \pi$).

Then a probabilistic theory goes on to specify that the initial family of neuronal groups (realizing probabilistic acceptors) consists mainly of those responding at levels lower than π, meaning (since the systems are working in parallel) that there is no categorization. However, under selection some outputs will be driven higher (there are any number of known weighting mechanisms for this process); and under repeated stimulus-input from the environment the system will evolve so that some groups will have some inputs with high probability and will partition input with probability higher than π (deciding yes) from those with low probability. The aggregate of such groups constitutes an after-the-fact categorization, which is exactly what is needed for an acquisition theory.

There might be deterministic models more adequate than the probabilistic one to the one-shot character of acquisition of a name at a baptism. However, none of them is likely to have any more credibility as an image of the actual anatomy of perception in identifying and naming than an AI program has of the human cognitive apparatuses underlying good chess. However, it is relatively straightforward sequential circuit design to show that such a system is possible, i.e. to provide what is in effect an existence proof that one-shot acceptor-learning acquisition is not an empty or inconsistent hypothesis. That is all we need.[18]

After having delivered myself of the foregoing remarks on acquisition I find myself in the unenviable position of having little more to write that is constructive. There are limits to naturalistic speculations in philosophy, and we seem to have hit them. Most of the remarks, except for those on neural selection, are negative, against nativism, representations and even sophisticated computer models. Inquiry that does not clearly distinguish learning and adaptation to antecedently existing categories from radical neuronal selection may not be worth continued pursuit – if *reference is causal.*

Appendix

The topics included in this appendix appear in the same order as they do in the text.

Production rules

A *production rule* is a conditional imperative which expresses that if a condition C occurs in a situation, generate an operation of type O in that situation.

Processor

A *processor* is a structure that takes (digital) input x and generates a unique (digital) output y.

An *algorithm* is a finite set of production rules: a step-by-step procedure for generating output y from input x.

An *effective* processor is one that generates y from x by an algorithm.

A *computable function f* is the set of pairs (x, y) such that there is a processor that generates exactly one output y from each input x, i.e. $f(x) = y$.

An *effectively computable function* is a computable function such that there is an effective processor that produces output from input.

Turing machines

A *Turing machine* is a processor governed by a finite set of production rules which are instances of the following schema:

> If the processor is in state q with input s, then go to state q' and output s' or move L or R.

The set of all states q appearing in the rules is the *state set Q*; the set of all inputs and outputs s is the *vocabulary S*; S and Q are disjoint.

Items L and R, meaning left and right, are moves relative to a tape, as shown in the following illustration.

Appendix

SWAP is a Turing machine that moves right swapping inputs a and b as they appear on an input tape, and then moves left relative to the tape until it sees a stop sign #, in which case it halts. The vocabulary is $\{a, b, B\text{ (blank space)}\}$ and the states are $\{0, 1, 2\}$. The production rules are the following eight:

(i) $0, a \rightarrow b, 1$ (ii) $0, b \rightarrow a, 1$ (iii) $0, B \rightarrow L, 2$ (iv) $1, a \rightarrow R, 0$
(v) $1, b \rightarrow R, 0$ (vi) $2, a \rightarrow L, 2$ (vii) $2, b \rightarrow L, 2$ (viii) $2, \# \rightarrow$ stop

((i) should be read: if SWAP is in state 0 scanning input a, it prints b over the a and changes to state 1; similarly for (ii); (iii) says: if it is in state 0 reading a blank B, it moves left and changes to state 2; similarly for the other four.)

Given initial input #*abaaaba*, SWAP starts to operate when in state 0 scanning the leftmost a. Then production rule (i) applies and the result is #*bbaaaba* with the machine in state 1. Rule (v) now applies, and the machine moves to the right and returns to state 0. Next (since it has moved right) it is scanning the second b, so by (ii) it overprints a, and by (iv) moves right. And so on. The ultimate output is #*babbbab*.

Let S^* be the set of all finite-length strings of inputs of S. The sequence of strings on tape beginning with #*abaaaba* and resulting in #*babbbab* by use of the production rules is an example of a *computation*.

In general, the set of pairs drawn from S^* for some input–output set S of some machine M that are computations (produced by a set of rules for M) is a *machine function*.

Strings of input–output of S^* are called *symbols* and the input elements drawn from S are called *sub-symbols*.

Turing productions are uninterpreted expressions of a formal system, like the expressions of a formal logic. Here are four examples of interpretations: sub-symbols s are binary 0s and 1s (or ternary 0s, 1s and 2s, or other) and symbols composed of the subs are (encoded) natural numbers; sub-symbols are parts of stimulus patterns patterns on the surface of the body (presumably just-noticeable irritations), and the symbols are stimulus patterns; sub-symbols are electrochemical inputs to neurons or groups of neurons (synaptic and/or somatic) and arrays of them are symbols; sub-symbols are bytes of a standard computer, and the entities introduced by declarations in an assembly or other language or in accordance with ASCII or other are symbols.

Sub-symbols are syntactical and never semantically interpreted; only symbols are interpretable – an analogy is in the letters of a lexical item in English like 'd' which has no independent meaning; the word (symbol) 'dog' does.

Turing computable function

A *Turing computable function* is one that is identical to the machine function of some Turing machine.

261

Church–Turing thesis

Every effectively computable function is Turing computable. All of the functions (data processes) possible on commercial computers (PCs, minis, main frames etc.) are effectively computable as they follow algorithms; hence they are Turing computable, by the thesis.

Universal Turing machines; free and embodied algorithms

A *universal Turing machine* is a Turing machine U which can compute *any* Turing computable function. If a standard computer had infinite memory (access to an unlimited store of discs or tapes) it would be universal. U can imitate any other Turing machine M given an appropriate translation of sub-symbols of S as follows.

Supplied with tape as just described, the input to a U computation consists of two parts: a string of symbols on U's symbol set S^* encoding the production rules of a machine M to be imitated; and another string on U's vocabulary that represents, by a syntactical mapping, an input string to a computation on M. The left string is a *program* and the right is a *data* string.

U computes the output M itself would produce from the data string, by moving back and forth on tape, reading the instructions in the encoded production rules which tell it how to imitate M, and executing those rules by producing output as specified.

In any computation on U there are two sets of production rules to be distinguished; the encoded rules of M imitated and the rules of U itself.

The set of rules encoded on tape is an example of a *free algorithm*, while the set of rules for U itself is an *embodied algorithm*.

Both sets are just instances of the production rule schema. A free algorithm can be executed on any copy of a universal machine, while an embodied algorithm is fixed in the structure of each independent Turing machine, including the universal machine U.

Characteristic functions

A characteristic function for a subset C of S^* for some S is a function f_C on domain S^* such that, for any symbol x of S^*, $f_C(x)$ = YES if x is in C and $f_C(x)$ = NO if x is not in C.

A characteristic function for prime numbers, for instance, has a value YES if a prime number is entered as argument, and a value NO otherwise. In the interpretations here, a characteristic function for horse, for instance, has the value YES if a stimulus pattern caused by a **horse** is imposed on one's sensory equipment, and NO otherwise.

All characteristic functions of interest here are computable.

Appendix

Acceptor

The following is an idealization and simplification of the notion of a *Turing acceptor*.

An *R*-machine is a Turing machine that moves *right* only. Tape is processed as a machine moves over it to the right.

An *acceptor* is an *R*-machine for computing a characteristic function. In terms of productions, we may write that an acceptor is just a set of production rules of the form:

> If the processor is in state q with input symbol s, then go to state q' and move *R*.

As before, S and Q are sets of sub-symbols and states occurring in the set of production rules.

There is a subset Q' of the set of states Q called *final* states. There is a distinguished *initial* state q_0 of Q. The final states Q' are YES states; states of Q not in Q' are NO states.

There is a map $M: Q \times S \to Q$, and we write $M(q, s) = q'$ for the value of the mapping with arguments q, s. The expression '$M(q, s) = q'$' is just a mathematical way of writing an acceptor production rule.

The action of an acceptor over input is represented by computation of M. To facilitate this, M is extended from domain $Q \times S$ to $Q \times S^*$ by the following:

$$M(q, xs) = M(M(q, x), s)$$

Here x is a symbol of $S^{*'}$ and s of S. Example: take input *aba*. Then $M(q, aba) = M(M(q, ab), a)$; then apply the recursion to the innermost M getting $M(M(M(q, a), b), a)$. Then compute this out beginning at the interior and applying the production rules. The move R is implicit in the computation of the recursion, and we do not explicitly write $M(q, a) = q'$, R.

Acceptors are decision machines for computing characteristic functions of symbol sets.

For illustration, consider a *pattern type* of sub-symbols a and b consisting of symbols containing clusters of three contiguous bs scattered among the os, but no other occurrences of ls; or otherwise all as. A characteristic function f_3 of this pattern has the value YES if argument x is an instance of the pattern, and NO otherwise. For instance $f_3 (aba) = $ NO, $f_3(bbbaaabbb) = $ YES and $f_3(aaaaaaa \ldots) = $ YES.

Here are eight production rules for an acceptor A_3 for such strings, written in M-notation. The states are 0, 1, 2, 3 and 4; the initial state is 0, and there are two accepting states (indicating recognition) 0, 3 – with YES pasted on; the vocabulary is $\{a, b\}$.

(i) $M(0, a) = 0$ (ii) $M(0, b) = 1$ (iii) $M(1, a) = 4$ (iv) $M(1, b) = 2$
(v) $M(2, a) = 4$ (vi) $M(2, b) = 3$ (vii) $M(3, a) = 0$ (viii) $M(3, b) = 4$

Let us compute the string *aba*. Starting from the initial state 0, we have $M(0, aba)$. By the recursion scheme this is $M(M(M(0, a), b), a)$. Using rule

263

Naming and Reference

(i) on the inside we get $M(M(0, b), a)$; and using (ii) we get $M(1, a)$; finally by (iii) this is just 4. Since 4 is not a final state we obtain NO. Thus we have compared the value of the characteristic function f_3 using A_3 for the argument *aba*, and obtained NO, as we should.

The production rules could be programmed on a universal Turing machine or on an ordinary digital computer for processing the characteristic function. In such a case the algorithm is free.

Alternatively, an engineer could design an electronic switching circuit which embodies A_3, or according to mechanism, a brain might embody it in a nerve system, in which case the sub-symbols *a* and *b* would be stimulus patterns and a full symbol would be accepted by the mind/brain according as it is or is not a triple type.

Acceptance and acceptability

If $M(q_0, x)$ is computed at time t and is equal to an element q'-YES of the set of final states Q', then we say the acceptor *accepts* x at t.

If it computes to q'-NO, a state not in Q', it *rejects* x at t.

Let $x(A)$ be the set of all strings x such that $M(q_0, x)$ is YES. Then we say a string x is *acceptable* or YES-decidable to A if and only if x is a member of the set $x(A)$.

Accepting x at t is an *event*.

Acceptability of x by A (membership of x in $x(A)$) is a *disposition* of A (a mathematical property of A).

Equivalence and identity

Let A and A' be two acceptors which process exactly the same symbols S^*. A and A' are *equivalent* if and only if $M_A(q_0, x) = M_B(q_0, x)$ for every x. So for any x in S^* they both decide – accept or reject – the same. In other words, A and A' are two acceptors for one and the same pattern-type if and only if they are equivalent.

Two equivalent acceptors need not have state sets Q of the same cardinality, and hence need not have the same M – defined by different sets of production rules. They need not be embodied in the same physical configurations.

Partial functions

A Turing computable function is *partial* if its domain of definition is a subset of some domain D under study. An example is subtraction, if the domain D is pairs of positive integers. It is defined only for arguments x greater than y.

There is an infinite number of partial functions on one partial domain.

Appendix

The *completion* of a partial function f is the function g that has the value 0 wherever f is undefined and elsewhere the same values as f.

Every characteristic function g of a set is the completion of one or more parital functions f, and is obtained as follows: replace all function values for which f is defined by YES, and complete f by NO elsewhere. For instance, starting with subtraction, introduce g:

$g(x, y)$ = YES if $f(x, y) = z$ for some integer z;
$g(x, y)$ = NO if $f(x, y)$ is undefined.

g is in fact a 'greater than' characteristic function for pairs. Any function from which a characteristic function is derived is a *base function*. Example: there is an infinite number of base functions for greater than.

Equivalence of algorithms

Every characteristic function is derived from some base function. Suppose M_f is a Turing machine for computing a partial function f, and let A_g be an acceptor for the characteristic function g derived from f. Equivalently, let A_g be constructed from the productions of M_f in the obvious way.

Two acceptors on a common domain *compute the same way* if and only if their base functions are equal (in extension).

Note that computing a *different way* means different base functions. So (embodied) algorithms differ, on this account, only if they compute *different* full functions, even though they compute the *same* characteristic function.

Taking and self-description: the routine

Assume the production rules in the form of the M-function of an acceptor A are represented on a tape of a super Turing machine T (it could be a universal machine) best thought of as a conventional computer for expository purposes. This representation of A is a *description*, and in particular is a *self-description*, as A is a part of T.

T has, among usual computational powers, ability to tell whether a state q of A is a *winner*, i.e. whether there is a string of sub-symbols x such that $M_A(q, x)$ is a final YES state. In general, identifying winners is possible only if A is equivalent to a rather restricted type of Turing machine (a 'push-down' machine); and it is a part of a mechanism that the algorithms (free or embodied) we attribute to the mind/brain are limited to this class if there is to be taking and expectation accounted for.

We are to compute $M_A(q_0, s_0, s_1, s_2, \ldots, s_{n-1})$. The productions of A are coded in some appropriate way in T. In the following program (which is meant to simulate the operation of a hypothetical phenomenon) 'i' is a location in T's tape standing for indexes on sub-symbols, and 'q' for a location allocated to states of A. The sub-symbols might be in either A's

265

vocabulary S or in B, the latter of which is the set of *vague, degraded symbols*.

Given this restriction on A and ability of T, the following is a *taking routine* written as a free program in an impromptu high level language.

	Remarks
1 $i \leftarrow 0$	[Initialize productions]
2 $q \leftarrow q_0$	[Initialize productions]
3 If s_i is in S, go to 4, else 8	[If current sub-symbol is in S
4 Do $M_A(q, s_i) = q'$	compute; if in B, take]
5 $q \leftarrow q'$	[Update next state and input]
6 $i \leftarrow i+1$	
7 If $i = n$, go to 14, else 3	[Exit, if end of input]
8 If q is a winner, go to 9, else 15	[Begin *take* subroutine]
9 Search productions for all rules $M_A(q, s) = q^1$, for all s	[q is current winning state]
10 Determine which q^1 found in step 9 are winners	
11 Pick a q^1	
12 $q \leftarrow q^1$	[End take subroutine]
13 Go to 6	
14 If q is final, YES, else NO	
15 Halt NO	

Notes

1 Introduction

1 'Name' and 'predicate' should be understood in the sense of formal logic, not grammar. Pronouns and proper names are logical names; common nouns, verbs, adjectives and many adverbs are predicates. In modern linguistics 'noun phrase' and 'verb phrase' are roughly the same as 'name' and 'predicate'.

2 To fix usage: Charles Morris (1938) proposed in his *General Theory of Signs* the terminology 'syntax' for the study of the relation of signs to signs, 'semantics' for the study of the relation of signs to things and 'pragmatics' for the study of the relation of signs to users. I shall use 'semantics' as short for the study of reference and application.

2 Natural Signs

1 Anaphora is use of a pronoun (or other) to refer to the referent of another word in a sentence. For instance 'John wanted to read it, so Schmid gave the book to him'. In this sentence, 'it' refers to whatever 'the book' refers to; and 'him' refers to John. Substantial research is going into anaphora (e.g. Chomsky 1981). However, this is a technical problem in linguistics. The direct reference of terms like 'John' and 'the book', but not the indirect reference of anaphors like 'it' and 'him', is of course the main topic of this book. A theory of direct reference plus one of anaphora would make a major step toward understanding the referential semantics of language.

2 'Semiotic' means quite different things to different people. For Morris (Chapter 1, note 2) it means the theory of signs. For Peirce (Chapter 2, §4) it also means theory of signs, but his theory of signs comprehends an entire philosophy including logic, metaphysics and epistemology. Today 'semiotic' is often used in Augustine's sense, borrowed by Locke in one of his two theories of names.

3 I use the standard convention for citations of *An Essay Concerning Human Understanding*: for example, IV, i, 2 is the second numbered section in Chapter I of Book IV.

4 In some editions of *An Essay Concerning Human Understanding* the editors included parts of Locke's correspondence with one Bishop of Worcester who suspected Locke's doctrines, especially of knowledge as perception of relations amongst ideas, of having 'dangerous consequences' for articles of faith. See, for example, Locke (1760: vol. II).

5 From Augustine's *De Doctrina Christiana* (Deely 1982: 57). This way of understanding 'sign' appears up through Occam and beyond. In Occam the idea sometimes includes a (physically) causal ingredient, since 'any effect is a sign of a cause' (William of Occam 1954: I, c. ii). This is almost word-for-word Fodor's causal view of the application of mental representations. See Chapter 8, §6.

The doctrine of natural sign is not dead in professional philosophy. See Addis (1989), who proposes a doctrine of 'intrinsic' reference which is as semiotical as can be.

6 Brentano gave up on the ontological thesis, since evidently its incredibility grew on him: an object that is not actual must be immanent, an object of inner awareness; but then it is just the thought or emotional pang itself. So he retreated to an ontology of concrete individuals: no objective unactuals, not even mental ones.

However, in order to frame the problem, in this section I imagine, and so invite the reader to imagine, that Brentano held fast to the notion of objective inexistence.

7 References to Peirce's *Collective Papers* are conventionally made to volume and paragraph (paragraph numbers are independent of chapters). Thus (5.312) means paragraph 312 of volume 5.

8 For some detail: Peirce classifies signs according as they are themselves more *qualities* (for instance the quale **red** you experience in looking at a label on a can of paint), as *concrete* thing (the physical red label), or as *law* (the type red label); and cross-classified according as they represent *iconically* (the quale red is a veridical picture of an object red-paint-in-the-can), *indexically* (the red label is causally connected to the paint – it points to it) or *symbolically* (the type red expressed by 'red paint') represents in virtue of 'an association of ideas' (or as we shall later say, 'computationally'); and again cross-classified according as the interpreter (signs in a mind) takes the sign as a sign of *abstract* quality, as a sign of an *actual object* or of a *law*.

9 The relation between intentionality as a feature of mind and intensionality as a feature of words and sentences is more fully explored in Chapter 10, §§3 and 4.

3 Sense and Reference

1 The text for this summary is Frege's landmark essays 'Function and object' and 'On concept and object' (Frege 1891, 1892a).

2 This is just the right place to explain substitutional quantification, which might be a not unreasonable way of interpreting Frege at times, and which figures prominently in our first attempt at 'references', in (0), Chapter 1, §1. In substitutional quantification one supposes there is

given a list of singular terms $a_1, a_2, \ldots$. Then 'for every x $F(x)$' is true just in case substitution of any term a_i, $i = 1, 2, \ldots$, for x yields a true sentence '$F(a_i)$'. Here the mapping of the concept is from named objects, not from arbitrary objects as in objectual quantification. Still more about (0) and substitutional quantification in Chapter 5.

3 In other respects, e.g. that of function, Frege's exact language is not extensional as a function is not just a set of ordered pairs but a map or a rule. His functions are *intensional*.

4 I think Haack is wrong on this point (1978: 62). Frege (1892b: 58n) is as close as he gets to a description theory.

5 This is not easy to square with an equally explicit statement in 'On concept and object' (1892a: 43n): a concept 'is, in fact, the reference of a grammatical predicate' (ibid.: 43).

6 This is Dummett's (1981: 298) interpretation of Frege, and does not quite square with some passages. Judgments are advances from a thought to a truth value (Frege 1892b: 65), not assertions.

4 Naming and Describing

1 Russell habitually confuses 'sentence' with 'proposition' and 'belief'; however, most of the fuzziness can be ironed out by heeding context. Here read 'sentence' for 'belief'.

2 There is an evolution from idealism and Meinongian realism (possible as well as actual beings) through critical realism, neutral monism and phenomenalism, to naturalism in Russell's philosophy. Quine (1981) believes that there is a steady move toward naturalism – epistemology just part of science itself – in Russell. All these views can be used more or less convincingly to secure a theory that truth is objective, and Russell tried them all.

3 Russell and Wittgenstein diverge here, but not widely. For although both think of true sentences about particulars as picturing reality, only Russell strove for a theory of truth. Wittgenstein holds the mirroring to be ineffable, which I suppose everyone knows about Wittgenstein even if he or she knows nothing else; while Russell holds acquaintance to be the ground of correspondence.

4 The proper way of viewing Russell's analysis is that there are two ways of reading the unanalyzed sentence. For either reading, the law of the excluded middle holds true. His analysis should not be understood as delivering an analysis that is true, or otherwise false, in two ways. The readings of the true sentence may be indicated by scope operators. Thus if '0' is the operator, '0[the present King of France is bald] indicates the description is secondary, and in 'the present King of France is 0(bald)' it is primary in occurrence.

5 In Frege's more precise way: an existential quantifier combines with a predicate to form a new predicate or a sentence. Ontologically, existence operates on concepts (propositional functions) to form more concepts or thoughts.

6 By the mid-nineteenth century Russell himself had come to doubt the equivalence of names and descriptions (1948: 77–9).

7 Since Russell's time philosophers of language have made much of a *de re–de dicto* distinction in belief sentences. A belief sentence is *de re* if it is a report of the attitude of a believer toward an object. A sentence is *de dicto* if read to report the attitude toward a proposition (or possibly a sentence or state of affairs). A good enough example is the report of George VI 'wanting to know . . .'. Read the description or name as having a primary occurrence and the sentence is *de re*, as having a secondary occurrence it is *de dicto*. A perennial problem is whether there are objective marks of a sentence enabling you to tell which reading is correct. For a definitive, skeptical, discussion see Quine (1966: 183–94, 1981: 113–23) and references there.

8 In response to this possibility John Searle (1958) proposes to treat proper names as abbreviations of *clusters* of descriptions. Thus 'Russell' would be an abbreviation of 'the junior author . . .' clustered with 'the 3rd Earl of . . .', 'the son of Lord and Lady Amberly', 'the oldest friend of Lady Ottoline . . .' etc. This theory as well as Russell's comes under criticism later in Chapter 6, §2, and Chapter 8, §1.

5 Truth Without Reference

1 'One of themselves, even a prophet of their own, said, "The Cretans are always liars . . ." ' (Epistle of Paul to Titus 1: 12). If 'liar' means 'never tells the truth' and thus the Cretan prophet never tells the truth, we have a contradiction. In simpler form, the story says ' "This sentence is false"; but if that very sentence is true, then it is false, and if false, true.'

The liar is an example of a *semantical* contradiction, to be kept apart in thought from Russell's paradox of sets and other *syntactical* paradoxes (see Chapter 4, §1). For a good review discussion see Haack (1978: Ch. 8).

2 The division is due to the mathematician David Hilbert, while the sanctions on the use of semantical terms is Tarski's.

3 Thus a symbol is a variable, constant, predicate etc. if it occurs on the list of variables etc. The only requirement (in the present exposition) is that the variables etc. be recursive sets. This is technical talk for saying a computer program must be able to tell whether a symbol is a variable, a constant etc. just by its physical properties. The category of every expression 'is unambiguously determined by its [syntactical] form' (Tarski 1931: 166). This is unlike our semantical requirement of Chapter 1 that lists of disquotations express only those names intuitively identified as such by competent speakers of English.

4 In another paper (1935: 406) commenting on his own theory Tarski claims that unless semantics can be brought into harmony with the principles of the unity of science and physicalism it will not enjoy accord with the rest of the science. Tarski's 'The semantic conception of truth' (1944) contains more on the theme of the connection between his

theory and mid-century philosophy of science. Also see Davidson (1990) for an exhaustive discussion of the question whether the truth theory is purely formal and stipulative or explicative of 'truth' in scientific languages.

5 Tarski's explication (1931: 194) literally says that N refers to an object o if and only if o satisfies the predicate consisting of 'three parts in the following order: a variable, the word "is" and the given name "N" '. If Tarski means by 'consisting of parts' *concatenation* in this scrap of an explication, then you supposedly get the treatment in the text, which is due to Hartry Field.

6 The equivalence, given disquotation, of the conditions depends on the existence of the object. If disquotation is just p-reference without the full condition (R) of Chapter 1, §4, this enlightenment fades. Observe, too, that if 'N refers to o' were analytic, which Tarski denies, the theory would hardly be a correspondence theory. Putnam thinks disquotation is analytic and for this reason, partly, thinks Tarski's theory is a 'failure' (see also Davidson 1990: 283).

7 The condition of holding for a quantified statement in effect supplies the missing clause – the one for quantified sentences – in the definition of 'true'. Call the state description in which all elements are true 'the true state description' (see below). Then '$(x)P(x)$' is true if and only if it holds in the *true* state description. This is tantamount to substitutional quantification when extended to arbitrary P, where at most 'x' is free. Compare with Chapter 3, note 3.

8 Unfortunately he frequently uses 'designation' for both, as well as for application. In the following I shall always use 'designate' for his meaning in rule (1) and 'reference' for our meaning, which seems the same as his in the rule of truth and the rule of identity.

9 In 1941 Carnap in conversation already referred to ' "a" designates a' as L-true.

6 Reference and Speech Act

1 Compare with Strawson (1950: 120 nl) who sees a similar difference between 'use' as 'rules for using' or 'meaning' and 'use' for 'way of using' in acts.

2 We have to put up with both the jargon and the inconstancy of its employment. Morris's three-way division of the theory of signs (Chapter 1, note 2) into syntax, semantics and pragmatics was meant heuristically to mark three sections of overlapping inquiry, just vague enough to cover everyone's interest in language, from Wittgenstein to Korzybski. But times change. Today 'semantics', 'pragmatics' etc. cover what one's pet theory presupposes; there is no common coin. Semantics in ordinary language philosophy has a nearly null connection with Tarski's semantics. As we shall see here and in the next few chapters, Chomsky–Fodor semantics has nothing in common with either California semantics or Oxford semantics. Computer semantics is not relevant to reference at all. And Presidential semantics – 'I am not

talking semantics' – is not relevant to anything.

3 Of course I do not mean there are three kinds of language-knowers. I do mean a language-knowing individual qua intender, grasper of meaning etc. is *user*; the individual qua asserter, questioner, promiser etc. is a *user**; and the individual qua abstract mathematical element *à la* Montague is a *user*ᵃ.

4 Compare with Gilbert Ryle's 'Ghost in the Machine'. The *locus classicus* is his *The Concept of Mind* (1949: 15ff). Also see Chapter 8, note 2.

5 Elsewhere Searle (1980) plumps for a materialist theory of mind; the mind is the brain. This is not Rylean, behaviorist theory.

6 In recursive definitions of languages (think of Tarski's definition of 'satisfaction' in Chapter 5, §2), the reference schemes and clauses that apply to open atomic predicates correspond to (b); while the clauses that apply to compound sentences and quantifiers correspond to (a).

7 This is the place to mention that purported reference and intended reference are not the same. Reference is purported when there is not, or may not be, an object, and applies to name types like 'Pegasus', 'God' or 'the fourth moon . . .'. Intended reference is Gricean 'reference meant to influence'. See §2 of this chapter.

7 Steps Toward Naturalism

1 I am going to feel free to use 'semantics', avoiding Quine's longer 'theory of reference and meaning', now that we have divorced the term from dyadic semantics of the older tradition.

2 'Disposition to respond' is a favored expression in the behaviorist repertoire. The term is less clear than persistent use by Quine and others might suggest. What Quine means is something like this: an individual has a disposition to respond to a stimulus if and only if he would respond to it in a certain way if a stimulus were imposed. I argued in Chapter 6, §2, that user* theorists also follow Gilbert Ryle in taking intended reference, belief in truth conditions etc. as dispositional. For the ordinary language philosopher that ends the matter; they get on without a mediating mind or brain by using subjunctive conditionals that relate input and act, as just mentioned. For Quine, however, dispositions are 'place-holders' for future physical brain theories of mind. I adopt this notion in Chapter 10.

3 I mean for 'cognitive process' to include perception, memory, thought, linguistic mechanisms etc. as currently studied in cognitive science. Behavioral and cognitive psychology both eschew feelings, subjective impressions, qualia etc. But Quine additionally has no truck with either cognitive process (except conditioning, habit formation and discriminations in a quality space – if those things count as cognitive) or conscious mental phenomena in his prescription for austere science.

4 Strictly to sets of stimulus patterns. Contrast this with Russell's idea that the meaning of an expression in acquaintance is the atomic fact. In

Quine's writings, however, there is nothing like atomic sentence to fact correspondence for true sentences.

5 I have been taking it for granted that 'individuation' and 'identity' are clearly understood expressions in these contexts. 'Individuation' applies to individuals that fall under a term like 'rabbit': what to count as one rabbit and what as another. It applies as well to properties – what to count as a rabbit, but not a cat. Identity or similarity is the instrument that individuates. An early occurrence of Brer and a later occurrence are of the same rabbit, and the similarity plays the role of individuating Brer (Quine 1973: 55–9).

6 Belief sentences could be part of a recursively defined language in modern pure semantics (Montague 1974). Quine's view, however, is that of the text above. Nevertheless, he has led the way in exploring substitutivity and quantification in intensional sentences, pretty much in the spirit of Russell (Quine 1966, 1981).

7 If L contains no proper names, however, proxy functions operating on the domain over which the variables range do not disturb condition (T). It is easy to see that schemes of assignment of objects to variables as in Chapter 5, §3, can be varied by permutation of objects with no effect whatever on the truth values of sentences. So if all names disappear in descriptions, *truth conditions* and not only truth values stay the same under permuting schemes. See John Wallace (1979).

8 Even Skinner (1984: 542) in response to a criticism of mine (1984b: 529f) admits to use of inner state terms, which implies tolerance of 'recursive habits'. Also see Suppes (1975) and Zuriff (1985).

9 There is a similar argument in Field (1972) to the effect that Quine's arguments are given as products of philosophical reflection – thought experiments in a behaviorist vein – 'prior to scientific information' (ibid.: 373). The procedure is external to ongoing science and a priori, whereas a naturalistic approach should, on Quine's own grounds, be from within science as a developing concern.

10 Inasmuch as there is no reference relation for Quine it does not matter what the coverage of the term is – language by language, individual speaker by speaker, or whatever. Since I maintain there is a relation to be explained I must accept at the very least that the list of disquotational pairs in Chapter 1, §1, is in the extension of a single relation. Of course this is already done in (1) of Chapter 1, §2, and in Field's Tarski. However, at the moment I leave the question open whether there is a single relation for English but not one for all languages, or a single relation for each speaker of English but not one for all of English-speaking society (cf. Davidson 1990).

11 Of course I am skimming over some nonburning issues in philosophy of science. I am saying that simple, inductive generalization is not a necessary condition for firming-up a concept in science and using it in theories. Of course I do not mean to say definitions are a priori, just that fastening on them is not a matter of accumulating prior successful criteriological tests.

12 This is Peirce's use of the distinction between *logica utens* and *logica*

docens (II. 188). If we follow Peirce on signs (I do), reference itself is an inferential relation. See Chapter 2, §4.

13 Again, as I mentioned at the end of the previous section, I am not assuming there is a single formalization of the mathematician's logic; there are many. But set theory being underdetermined by the theorems of mathematics does not mean inference is inscrutable.

8 Cause and Function

1 I-worlds as capturing the idea of imagined counterfactual affairs seem to be ontologically safer than O-worlds by Quinean standards (cf. Quine (1981: 171) and Chapter 7, §3). However, counterfactual conditionals are not extensional sentences, as is well known; so their use is a departure from strictly regimented scientific language. Putnam (1986: 67) tries to get by (sometimes) with Carnapian state descriptions. Obviously this will not work if we try to apply it to Kripke's programme, as then necessity is just analyticity (*L*-truth) – smudging a distinction Kripke is at great pains to promote, as we shall see soon.

2 This distinction and its implications for philosophy of science is extremely interesting; it occupies a large part of Kripke's 'Naming and necessity' (1972). For instance 'heat is kinetic energy', which is a popular example of a contingent, a posteriori identity, is really necessary, as both terms of the identity are rigid. However, this doctrine of Kripke's is remote from concerns of rigidity and causality based on the notion of I-worlds.

3 Kripke includes Quine as a description theorist. But Quine uses descriptions therapeutically, i.e. as replacements for names, certainly not as synonyms for them (or vice versa), and certainly not as reference-fixers; one of Quine's purposes is to replace natural language puzzles about nonreferring names by canonical language in which the puzzle vanishes, not to explain how minds manage reference.

4 'Natural kind' can be understood here, nearly enough, as meaning what Aristotle in the *Categories* calls secondary substance.

5 Recall that an explicit definition of a term *x* does not include any occurrences of *x*, or any occurrences of any *y* such that *y*'s definition depends on *x* in the definiens. For more on implicit definition in psychology see Hill (1988).

6 Quine's holism arises from indeterminacy, and science and its sentential meanings is constructed within a 'coordinate system' fixed by ongoing scientific inquiry. Intentional holism on the other hand is holism of the fabric of folk thought a priori.

7 For a sample of the functionalist literature, see Lewis (1970, 1972b), Field (1978) and Stich (1983). Functionalism is not exclusively material-istic, as I have made it; one could have functionalism under an idealistic interpretation of belief etc. The mental would still be role etc. But more on this observation is not part of our game.

8 For both Lewis (1972a) and Stalnaker (1976) semantics of belief, or

semantics in general, is one thing, and mind and intentionality another. So neglect of belief as semantical relation to object does not seem to be accidental.

9 This criticism is leveled at fusion functionalism, not at folkism. Hill's laws (a) and (c) in §2 involve the truth of attitudes. Also, his 'reference' (b) is not intentional, hence not fused to anything.

10 Turing machine language can be formalized in either first- or second-order predicate calculus, thus strengthening the analogy with Russell and Quine.

11 For a survey of views in Fodor's neighborhood see Dennett (1986).

12 Believe it or not it has been proposed by someone (I forget who) that, just as MRs can be thought of as inscriptions on a chalkboard, beliefs are housed in belief-boxes, cubes most likely; desires in other boxes, perhaps prisms; expectations in tesseracts etc. Sometimes there is just one 'intention box' that 'churns' when there is an intention to act provided the right occasions are believed to obtain (Fodor 1987: 136). No one, so far as I know, has suggested the causal interaction of attitudes is 'boxing'.

13 For Fodor as functionalist, beliefs are token identical to brain complexes and are individuated according to their causal roles with other attitudes. If two individuals have the same or similar brains, including tokens of MRs with the same semantics, they have the same mental 'states',

14 It is hard for me to see how i and i' could be identical molecule for molecule if they are made of water in part and water is chemically different in the two Earths.

15 'Denotation' is Fodor's word, and I am not translating it 'reference' as it turns out his theory is limited to application.

16 A property is not an abstract object instanced differently in different worlds (as Field presupposes but does not attempt to explicate in (2), §4); the property red here is instanced in the actual world. So the meaning of 'x is red' is not a propositional object as usually thought of in belief semantics, but is a law. '[W]e get the meaning by quantifying over the routes from a symbol to the denotation' (ibid.: 126).

9 Mechanism

1 Various nondescriptional theories of names are often called 'direct'. For a survey see Devitt (1989).

2 Here is a short argument, assuming belief and the rest are computational, interacting states. Examining the format of Turing productions (see the appendix section on Turing machines) we see that a state–input pair (belief–MR pair) is mapped to another 'next' state (a belief or desire, or the like). Mathematically, there is a set of states S, a set of inputs I, the Cartesian product $S \times I$, and a map from the product back to S. Now throughout science, including classical mechanics, a set having a certain topology (trivially satisfied by a finite set) and having the property that

there is another set and a map from the product of the two back to the first is called a 'state space'. So our S is a state space. If a state-to-state sequence under perturbations from elements of I is intentional in the Turing world, owing solely to the abstract relation described, then it is also intentional in the domain of physics. This is absurd. If there is more to the holist's role-playing than what I just described (that the states are instantiated in a living brain, for example) it is never explained.

3 Turing machines and generally all programming rules are varieties of formal rules of inference, introduced by the logician Emil Post (1940). Hence from this formal point of view a computation is an *inference*, yet causal. The Peircean, abductive character of it will be described *passim* as we proceed.

4 It does strike me as odd that in most cognitivist thought the truth of folk psychology is taken for granted in setting up the discipline of cognitive science (e.g. Fodor 1987: Ch. 1). This is true of both functionalism and RTM. But knowledge of mind is a product of cognitive science, one hopes, not a presupposition of it.

5 The thesis (1) is equivalent to Church's thesis (Church 1936), which is referred to in the literature more frequently than (1). Church's thesis states that all effectively computable functions are recursive. The recursive functions include addition, multiplication, integer polynomials etc. and are objects of study in ordinary arithmetic. Turing computability is the same as recursiveness provided the intended domain consists of the positive integers and functions of them. In cognitive science the domain is stimulus patterns, brain or machine entities homomorphic to the integers (which means one can map certain relevant machine or brain entities into integral numerals and treat them as such). For arguments as to the empirical status of the thesis in cognitive science, see Nelson (1987). For more on the thesis and philosophy of mind see Nelson (1989a: especially Ch. 4). For more technical details see the appendix.

6 An essentially equivalent idea, with a proof that such a limited device can compute all computable functions, is discussed in Boolos and Jeffrey (1980).

7 In evolutionary neurobiology (Edelman 1987), neuronal systems are considered to be kinds of discrete processing systems which embody algorithms and hence are basically Turing automata.

8 As long as I am writing this incidental review, it is worth pointing out that in radical empiricism the only evidence for a disposition is manifest behavior; so if there is no empirical basis for identifying a referent unequivocally, there is no disposition – another way of expressing the inscrutability of reference. However, Quine also has some tolerance for the 'place-holder' view of disposition, soon to be introduced here, provided there is scientific reason to sustain it within a broad theory. If so, a built-in disposition to refer would seem to contravene the inscrutability thesis.

9 Let me disabuse the reader right now of his or her belief (if he or she has it) that a disposition to respond is a physical 'state' that causally yields a

verbal response correctly when a stimulus pattern is input. We indicated the refutation of this behaviorist rule in challenging Quine's behaviorism. In my theory a disposition is an embodied algorithmic *structure*, which is a far cry from a 'state' and, as we shall see in great detail, an individual might respond to 'chair' or 'dog' in many diverse 'incorrect' ways depending on how he or she takes things; yet the taking itself is algorithmic. This sort of treatment would be impossible using behavioral 'states' only.

10 Direct Reference

1 The theory of observational semantics, on which this section and the following four are based, goes back to my 'Are humanly recognizable patterns effective?' (1971), and is developed in my *The Logic of Mind* (1989a) via a string of intervening papers, chiefly Nelson (1976, 1978).

2 The possibility of equivalence of function of anatomically diverse neural structures is a basic theme of brain biology. For a discussion, with pictures, see Edelman (1987: especially 33ff).

3 Persons who insist that substitutional quantification is benign have a choice: either (1), or an amendment of the minimal proposal of Chapter 1, §2, as follows:

N refers to y for i if and only if there is a z (on the original list) and i realizes an acceptor $A_{=z}$ for which y is acceptable and 'z' = N and 'z' is associated to yes,

where 'N' is as usual a dummy proper name. Here the supposition would be that 'there is a z' is substitutional. So we get the economy over repeating (1) a large finite number of times. Do we also get a proof of God's existence?

4 The idea is Quine's (1969), although he uses 'historical description' rather than 'event description'. I use the latter to avoid confusion with Donnellan's notion that causal reference is historical (Chapter 6, §2). Of course reference at a time does resemble reference*; and an interesting task would be to attempt to connect up Donnellan with the present theory, a task I avoid until the last chapter.

5 For the time being we assume an Aristotelian world of firm, unchanging, types, and a one-to-one mapping of distal objects (chairs) to proximal objects (chair stimulus patterns) into object types. However, we are not also assuming that acceptors involved in reference are innate. Acquisition is still an open question at this stage.

6 David Marr's *Vision* (1982) employs a similar scheme. My use of characteristic function corresponds to his 'computational level' of inquiry, which focuses on the *function* processed in vision; his algorithmic level of description consists essentially of Turing computers; and implementation for him is a question of nerve anatomy, which he regards functionally. For a philosophically oriented discussion of his ideas see Patricia Kitcher (1988: 10). Also see Dennett (1986: 71ff).

7 I am paraphrasing Smith and McIntyre (1971: 542).

8 The user* theorist, whom I urged we drop several chapters ago, might maintain Schmid is using* 'Bush' to refer to an advance man. He is, of course; but that is not Schmid's intention. His p-reference has the accidental semantic force of reference* to the man for the crowd and perhaps for himself, but this is not our worry. We want the intention.

9 One might suspect that this consequence of using Turing, deterministic models could be escaped by use of probabilistic models. The idea would be that an input is accepted or not, but accepted with a probability. However, it turns out that a probabilistic model does not help get around the problem. See Nelson (1984a, 1989b).

10 Another detail: a receptor in neurophysiology *transduces* input from the surface of a sense organ to signals that can be processed by the nervous system. For instance the rods and cones of the retina transduce light to electrical signals. It is hopeless (and unnecessary) to get down to such detail; and I shall simply assume that reception includes transduction some place along the line.

11 The idea of self-description goes back historically to Goedel's device of self-reference in his celebrated incompleteness theorems. The circle of ideas including genetic description and self-encodement of Turing rules stem from the recursion theorem of computability theory (Rogers 1967), and were first used in machine construction by Lee (1963) and Thatcher (1963) and in biology and theory of reproduction by von Neumann (1966).

12 Stevan Harnad (1990) offers a strikingly similar view in many respects. Adopting connectionism (which I insist is a variety of embodied algorithm theory) he argues that mental representation theories require 'grounding' of semantics in natural explanation and not assumed a priori. He differs from the present direct theory in finding the engendering of meaning in the *iconic* (which I would dispute, if pressed) representation of distal by proximal object, and in the *categorical representation* of the object in the cognizing mind. The first step is similar to my reception, *Re*, and the second to Turing machine acceptance. The fact that his semantics is bottom up – finding reference in a direct relation of object to representation – is a heartening switch from old-fashioned AI (before 1980, say), which simply ignored reference.

13 Recall that in Chapter 5, §2, we noticed that '*a* is *F* ' is true if and only if *a* is *F* (Tarski condition (*T*) if and only if '*F* ' applies to the (unique) object referred to by '*a*', given disquotation.

14 Compare Quine's view that objects x and y are judged the same outright and then a predicate applied to both, rather than the other way around, as suggested by Geach (Chapter 7, §4). I am saying the same holds for quantification.

15 *N*-place predicates are excluded as they are not semantically instructive in core. Connective '*or*' can be defined in the usual way. Likewise, 'if – then' is omitted, but can be readily supplied for the reader who believes indicative conditionals are adequately reflected in the material conditional of quantification theory. So far as I am concerned the point is moot. See, however, Vann McGee (1985).

16 This is a decision, not a finding. Truth is an epistemological, not a psychological, concept; and we want a definition that characterizes true sentences. Criteria of truth – scientific confirmation – is a different question. Any causal correspondence theory – correspondence of sentence to fact by way of a knowing mind – must presuppose veridical transduction or reception.

17 If A_F is a Turing acceptor, there exists a complementary acceptor A_{-F}, since what the first rejects the second accepts (see the appendix section on acceptors). We posit that an individual who knows English realizes A_{-F}, either natively or by acquisition.

18 Technically, if '$F(x)$' is Turing computable so is '$(\exists x)F(\exists x)$' for a bounded quantifier '$(\exists x)$'. So we assume acceptors A_{EF} exist. Although the boundedness requirement for a mechanist theory of mind is neither trivial nor irrelevant, it is outside of our range.

19 'Warrant' vaguely suggests John Dewey; however, I do not mean by truth a quality of science at the end of inquiry. I mean, as all the steps leading to this note show, an ideal correspondence for the core as perceived by X. Note that for X there is no need to demonstrate x (as there was for Schmid), and hence no truck with indexicals. The quantifier 'there is an x' does the binding. See the earlier discussion in §5.

20 There is a companion scope principle for 'or'. It is less intuitively evident than (B) according to some, but can be proved from (A) and (B). This task is left to the reader.

11 Mind and Semantics

1 Kripke's I-worlds (Chapter 8, §1) are ranges of stimulus patterns according to the present theory. Take the actual world as the grand distal pattern mapped on the surface of i's body at time t. The pattern relative to i is Quine's naturalization of the notion of possible worlds (1969: 147–53). The ones we can imagine are Kripke's I-worlds.

2 My comment assumes Marr (Chapter 10, note 6) would count visual perception of an individual named object as falling into the same class of scientific questions as perception of qualities and kinds.

3 There are several nice discussions in the literature of the puzzles involved in accepting the notion of causal reference, and also of problems of giving answers to Frege's questions about sense and empty names. See especially Wettstein (1986), Salmon (1986) and Devitt (1989).

4 Frege's mode of presentation is from the mind to the object, while computation is from the object to the mind. But no matter. For one meaning it is 'subjective', or at any rate grasped by the mind from a Platonic realm, and for the other it is objective, a function of patterns.

5 It is a good idea to keep reference* at t apart from p-reference at t. The latter is an event in an attitudinal psychology of expectation, taking and Turing acceptance. Reference* is part of pragmatics, concerned with how we refer to or attribute to things in social contexts, and its

associated meaning is Gricean (Chapter 6, §2). I am promoting the idea that reference* is a salient ingredient of perceptual belief, but not of p-reference as such.

6 Similarly Quine (1960: 95f) notes that 'actually the difference between being true of many objects and being true of just one is not what matters in the distinction between general and singular. . . . It is by grammatical role that general and singular terms are to be distinguished.' He does not, however, go on to notice anything like the social role we give to indexicals in observation sentences. His sentences are whole, indeed holophrastic, to begin with, and this discourages analysis of predication.

7 Russell's singular proposition $\{a, F\}$, the object of 'a is F', can be obtained from the set of patterns by reckoning a as the individual type, in my sense, of the tokens x accepted by X in the relevant Quinean possible worlds, and F as the embodied algorithm (to get a concrete object, rather than the abstract property) for computing the characteristic function f_F, or that function itself. David Kaplan (1979) has a similar notion of singular proposition, but it is derived from pure semantics, not from a computational theory.

8 Dummett (1958: 67) means by 'assertable' decidable in the sense of intuitionistic logic, while I mean by 'warrantable' decidable in the sense of computability theory. He denies the law of the excluded middle, whence rejection of clause (c), and I do not. See Nelson (1987: 592ff).

9 See, for a survey, Haack (1978: §7). Donald Davidson's 'The structure and content of truth' (1990: especially §II) is the best discussion of truth, as it follows in the Aristotelian tradition, on record.

10 Davidson (1990) has shifted to a view which is in a certain respect bottom up.

11 In addition, there are higher-level transformational rules that operate on phrases and sentences to produce other sentences, and rules that govern intra-sentence reference (anaphora). This is no place (nor am I the one) to give anything like the coverage Chomsky's theory deserves. A good sample of his views plus some commentary on it relative to philosophy of mind can be found in Chomsky (1965), which is still basic, and Chomsky (1972, 1975, 1981). In recent writings (1986) the theory is elaborated. For commentary see Nelson (1978, 1989a).

12 The analogy with learning a piece on an instrument can be improved. A better parallel to learning rules of competence would be learning rules of common practice musical composition, by listening to Haydn. Learning a first language is quicker, but that does not imply it requires tacit propositional knowledge. This idea emerged in conversation with Hendrieka Nelson.

13 'Native' means 'by birth', not that humans were made by an Aristotelian architect with eternal perceptual and conceptual categories built in. The distinction here and hereafter is between what the individual as a product of evolution is born with – his genetic endowment – and what he acquires by adaptation, further evolution of the brain, morphological change or whatever.

14 'Mind/brain' is Edelman's locution expressing a materialist view of mind: he does not deny mind; but he also does not intend to assume anything ontologically other than matter. And the proper approach to the mind is via understanding of the brain plus attention to psychological fact.

15 'Categorization' might mean either a process of putting items in the right slots or a process of constituting the slot system. Contextual English is often not sufficient for resolving the ambiguity. Edelman should always be read as meaning 'categorization' in the second sense.

16 A stronger statement is that connectionist machines of Edelman's sort are all embodied algorithm (basically Turing) machines. This need not be settled here, one way or the other, however, as the important characteristics for selection theory are shared. For views *pro* identification see Arbib and Caplan (1979) and Nelson (1988b); for views *con*, see Smolensky (1988) and Reeke and Edelman (1988).

17 A handy source of review of some of the relevant details of brain biology is Patricia Churchland's *Neurophilosophy* (1986), written in a clear style accessible to nonspecialists. Unfortunately she identifies the 'computer metaphor' with free algorithm machines (ibid.: 458ff), and many of her criticisms do not apply to embodied algorithm Turing automata.

18 One can envision embodied algorithm networks having no fixed bond to any particular characteristic function. This is a technical counterpart to Edelman's 'ignorant' neuronal groups. The idea is as follows. Network inputs are partitioned into *biasing* (B) and *working* (W) inputs. If B consists of n binary inputs, it has 2^n states and the network has so many functional potentialities. Pick one of these states; bias it yes, and the network computes characteristic function 1 from input on W. Pick another, bias it yes, and it computes 2 from the *same* input data on W. If all biasing inputs are no, the network computes at random and is indeed ignorant. A real example is a certain parallel network in a central processing unit in a computer. Bias the appropriate input one way and the network is an *adder*; bias it in another and it is a *subtractor*.

In the abstract case, a single network can embody 2^n functions (if n is binary), each one selectable in the right sort of environment, on a one-shot basis. It might be of interest to see whether neuronal groups might be doing anything of a related kind according to Edelman's scheme.

Bibliography

Addis, L. (1989) 'Intrinsic reference and the new theory', in P. A. French, T. E. Uehling, Jr. and H. K. Wettstein (eds) *Midwest Studies in Philosophy*, vol. IV, Notre Dame, IN: University of Notre Dame Press, pp. 241–57.

Arbib, M. A. and Caplan, D. (1979) 'Neurolinguistics must be computational', *Behavioral and Brain Sciences* 2: 449–83.

Bach, K. (1986) 'Thought and object: *de re* representations and relations', in M. Brand and R. M. Harnish (eds) *The Representation of Knowledge and Belief*, Tucson, AZ: University of Arizona Press, pp. 187–218.

Boolos, G. S. and Jeffrey, R. C. (1980) *Computability and Logic*, Cambridge: Cambridge University Press.

Brand, M. and Harnish, R. M. (eds) (1986) *The Representation of Knowledge and Belief*, Tucson, AZ: University of Arizona Press.

Brentano, F. (1924) *Psychologie vom Empirische Standpunkte*, Leipzig: Dunker.

Burks, A. W. (1972) 'Logic, computers, and men', *Proceedings and Addresses of the American Philosophical Association* XLVI: 39–57.

Carnap, R. (1937) *The Logical Syntax of Language*, London: Kegan Paul, Trench & Trubner.

—— (1942) *Introduction to Semantics*, Cambridge, MA: Harvard University Press.

—— (1951) *Logical Foundations of Probability*, Chicago, IL: University of Chicago Press.

—— (1956) *Meaning and Necessity*, Chicago IL: University of Chicago Press.

—— (1963) 'The philosopher replies', in P. Schilpp (ed.) *The Philosophy of Rudolf Carnap*, Lasalle, IL: Open Court.

Chisholm, R. (1957) *Perceiving: a Philosophical Study*, Ithaca, NY: Cornell University Press.

Chomsky, N. (1959) 'A review of B. F. Skinner's, *Verbal Behavior*' reprinted in J. Fodor and J. Katz (eds) (1964) *The Structure of Language*, Englewood Cliffs, NJ: Prentice Hall.

—— (1965) *Aspects of the Theory of Syntax*, Cambridge, MA: MIT Press.

—— (1972) *Language and Mind*, New York: Harcourt, Brace, Jovanovich.

Bibliography

—— (1975) *Reflections on Language*, New York: Pantheon Books.

—— (1981) *Lectures on Government and Binding*, Dordrecht: Floris.

—— (1986) 'Changing perspectives on knowledge and use of language', in M. Brand and R. M. Harnish (eds) *The Representation of Knowledge and Belief*, Tucson, AZ: University of Arizona Press, pp. 1–58.

Church, A. (1936) 'An unsolvable problem of elementary number theory', *American Journal of Mathematics* 58: 345–63.

Churchland, P. S. (1986) *Neurophilosophy*, Cambridge, MA: MIT Press.

Davidson, D. (1967) 'Truth and meaning', in J. F. Rosenberg and C. Travis (eds) (1971) *Readings in the Philosophy of Language*, Englewood Cliffs, NJ: Prentice Hall, pp. 450–65.

—— (1977) 'Reality without reference', *Dialectica* 31: 248–58.

—— (1979) 'The method of truth in metaphysics', in P. A. French, T. Uehling, Jr. and H. K. Wettstein (eds) *Contemporary Perspectives in the Philosophy of Language*, Minneapolis, MN: University of Minnesota Press, pp. 294–304.

—— (1990) 'The structure and content of truth', *Journal of Philosophy* 87: 279–328.

Davis, M. (1958) *Computability and Unsolvability*, New York: McGraw-Hill.

Deely, J. (1982) *Introducing Semiotic*, Bloomington, IN: Indiana University Press.

Dennett, D. C. (1969) *Content and Consciousness*, London: Routledge & Kegan Paul.

—— (1978) *Brainstorms*, Montgomery, VT: Bradford Books.

—— (1986) 'The logical geography of computational approaches: a view from the east pole', in M. Brand and R. M. Harnish (eds) *The Representation of Knowledge and Belief*, Tuscon, AZ: University of Arizona Press, pp. 59–79.

Devitt, M. (1981) *Designation*, New York: Columbia University Press.

—— (1989) 'Against direct reference', in P. A. French, T. E. Uehling, Jr. and H. K. Wettstein (eds) *Midwest Studies in Philosophy*, vol. IV, Notre Dame, IN: University of Notre Dame Press, pp. 206–40.

Donnellan, K. (1966) 'Reference and definite descriptions', *Philosophical Review* 75: 281–304.

—— (1979) 'Speaker's reference, descriptions, and anaphora', in P. A. French, T. Uehling, Jr. and H. K. Wettstein (eds) *Contemporary Perspectives in the Philosophy of Language*, Minneapolis, MN: University of Minnesota Press.

Duhem, P. (1954) *The Aim and Structure of Physical Theory*, Princeton, NJ: Princeton University Press.

Dummett, M. (1958) 'Truth', *Proceedings of the Aristotelian Society* 59: 141–62.

—— (1973) *Frege: Philosophy of Language*, London: Duckworth.

—— (1977) 'What is a theory of meaning', in S. Guttenplan (ed.) *Mind and Language*, Oxford: Clarendon, pp. 97–138.

—— (1981) *The Interpretation of Frege's Philosophy*, London: Duckworth.

Edelman, G. (1987) *Neural Darwinism*, New York: Basic Books.

Evans, G. (1982) *The Varieties of Reference*, Oxford: Clarendon.

Field, H. (1972) 'Tarski's theory of truth', *Journal of Philosophy* 59: 347–74.

—— (1978) 'Mental representations', *Erkenntnis* 13: 9–61.

Fodor, J. A. (1975) *The Language of Thought*, New York: Thomas Crowell.

—— (1981) *Representations*, Cambridge, MA: MIT Press.

—— (1984) *The Modularity of Mind*, Cambridge, MA: MIT Press

—— (1987) *Psychosemantics*, Cambridge, MA: MIT Press.

Føllesdahl, D. (1969) 'Husserl's notion of noema', *Journal of Philosophy* 66: 680–7.

Frege, G. (1879) *Begriffschrift*, in P. Geach and M. Black (eds) (1966) *Translations from the Philosophical Writings of Frege*, Oxford: Basil Blackwell, pp. 1–20.

—— (1884) *Grundlagen der Arithmetik*, Breslau: Wilhelm Koebner.

—— (1891) 'On function and concept', in P. Geach and M. Black (eds) (1966) *Translations from the Philosophical Writings of Frege*, Oxford: Basil Blackwell, pp. 21–41.

—— (1892a) 'On concept and object', in P. Geach and M. Black (eds) (1966) *Translations from the Philosophical Writings of Frege*, Oxford: Basil Blackwell, pp. 42–55.

—— (1892b) 'On sense and reference', in P. Geach and M. Black (eds) (1966) *Translations from the Philosophical Writings of Frege*, Oxford: Basil Blackwell, pp. 56–78.

French, P. A., Uehling, T., Jr and Wettstein, H. K. (eds) (1979) *Contemporary Perspectives in the Philosophy of Language*, Minneapolis, MN: University of Minnesota Press.

French, P. A., Uehling, T. E., Jr and Wettstein, H. K. (eds) (1989) *Midwest Studies in Philosophy*, vol. IV, Notre Dame, IN: University of Notre Dame Press.

Geach, P. (1962) *Reference and Generality*, Ithaca, NY: Cornell University Press.

Geach, P. and Black, M. (eds) (1966) *Translations from the Philosophical Writings of Frege*, Oxford: Basil Blackwell.

Goedel, K. (1931) 'Uber formal unentscheidbare satze der *Principia Mathematica* and vervandter systeme I', *Monatsheft fur Mathematik und Physik* 38: 173–98.

Grice, H. P. (1957) 'Meaning', in J. F. Rosenberg and C. Travies (eds) (1971) *Readings in the Philosophy of Language*, Englewood Cliffs, NJ: Prentice Hall.

—— (1974) 'Method in philosophical psychology', *Proceedings and Addresses of the American Philosopical Association* 48: 23–53.

Grover, D. (1990) 'Truth and language-world connections', *Journal of Philosophy* 87: 671–87.

Haack, S. (1978) *Philosophy of Logics*, Cambridge: Cambridge University Press.

Bibliography

Hahlweg, K. and Hooker, C. A. (eds) (1989) *Issues in Evolutionary Epistemology*, Albany, NY: State University of New York Press.

Harman, G. (1973) *Thought*, Princeton, NJ: Princeton University Press.

Harnad, S. (1990) 'The symbol grounding problem', *Physica* D42: 335–46.

Hill, C. (1984) 'Animadversions on the inscrutability thesis', *Pacific Philosophical Quarterly* 65: 303–12.

—— (1987) 'Rudiments of a theory of reference', *Notre Dame Journal of Formal Logic* 28: 20–40.

—— (1988) 'Intentionality, folk psychology and reduction', in H. Otto and J. A. Tuedio (eds) *Perspectives on Mind*, Dordrecht: Reidel, pp. 169–80.

Hintikka, J. (1969) 'Semantics for propositional attitudes', in L. Linsky (ed.) *Reference and Modality*, London: Oxford University Press.

Holland, J. H., Holyoak, K. J., Nisbett, R. E. and Thagard, P. R. (1989) *Induction*, Cambridge, MA: MIT Press.

Hwang, K. and Briggs, F. A. (1984) *Computer Architecture and Parallel Processing*, New York: McGraw-Hill.

Kaminsky, J. (1982) *Essays in Linguistic Ontology*, Carbondale, IL: Southern Illinois University Press.

Kaplan, D. (1979) 'On the logic of demonstratives', in P. A. French, T. Uehling, Jr and H .K. Wettstein (eds) *Contemporary Perspectives in the Philosophy of Language*, Minneapolis, MN: University of Minnesota Press.

Kitcher, P. (1988) 'Marr's computational theory of vision', *Philosophy of Science* 55: 1–24.

Kockelmans, I. (ed.) (1967) *Phenomenology*, New York: Anchor Books.

Kripke, S. (1963) 'Semantical considerations in modal logic', *Acta Philosophical Fennica* 16: 83–94.

—— (1972) 'Naming and necessity', in D. Davidson and G. Harman (eds) *Semantics of Natural Language*, Dordrecht: Reidel, pp. 253–355.

—— (1976) 'Is there a problem about substitutional quantification?', in G. Evans and J. McDowell (eds) *Truth and Meaning*, Oxford: Clarendon, pp. 325–419.

—— (1977) 'Speaker's reference and semantic reference', in P. A. French, T. Uehling, Jr and H. K. Wettstein (eds) *Contemporary Perspectives in the Philosophy of Language*, Minneapolis, MN: University of Minnesota Press, pp. 6–27.

Kucklemans, J. J. (ed.) (1967), *Phenomenology*, Garden City, NJ: Doubleday.

Kvart, I. (1989) 'Divided reference', in P. A. French, T. E. Uehling, Jr and H. K. Wettstein (eds) *Midwest Studies of Philosophy*, vol. IV, Notre Dame: University of Notre Dame Press, pp. 140–79.

Lakeoff, G. (1987) *Women, Fire, and Dangerous Things*, Chicago, IL: University of Chicago Press.

Lee, C. Y. (1963) 'A Turing machine which prints its own code script', in J. Fox (ed.) *Proceedings of the Symposium on Mathematical Theory of Automata*, Brooklyn, NY: Brooklyn Polytechnic Press, pp. 155–64.

Levi, I. and Morgenbesser, S. (1964) 'Belief and disposition', *American Philosophical Quarterly* 1: 1–12.

Lewis, D. (1970) 'How to define theoretical terms', *Journal of Philosophy*, 61, 427–46.

— — (1972a) 'General semantics', in D. Davidson and G. Harman (eds) *Semantics of Natural Language*, Dordrecht: Reidel, pp. 169–218.

—— (1972b) 'Psychophysical and theoretical identification', *Australasion Journal of Philosophy* 50: 249–58.

Loar, B. (1981) *Mind and Meaning*, Cambridge: Cambridge University Press.

Locke, J. (1760) *An Essay Concerning Human Understanding*, 2 vols, 15th edn, London: D. Brown *et al.*

Lycan, W. G. (1986) 'Thought about things', in M. Brand and R. M. Harnish (eds) *The Representation of Knowledge and Belief*, Tucson, AZ: University of Arizona Press, pp. 160–86.

Marr, D. (1982) *Vision*, San Francisco, Freeman.

Marsh, R. C. (ed.) (1956) *Logic and Knowledge*, London: George Allen & Unwin.

McCulloch, W. S. and Pitts, W. H. (1943) 'A logical calculus of the ideas immanent in nervous activity', *Bulletin of Mathematical Biophysics* 5: 115–33.

McGee, V. (1985) 'A counterexample to modus ponens', *Journal of Philosophy* 82: 462–71.

Mill, J. S. (1843) *A System of Logic*, 8th edn, London: Longmans, Green, 1941.

Minsky, M. (1988) 'Connections models and their prospects', in D. Waltz and J. A. Feldman (eds) *Connectionist Models and Their Implications*, Northwood, NJ: Ablex, pp. vii–xvi.

Montague, R. (1974) *Formal Philosophy*, New Haven, CT: Yale University Press.

Morris, C. W. (1938) 'Foundations of the theory of signs', in O. Neurath, R. Carnap and C. Morris (eds) *International Encyclopedia of Unified Science*, Chicago, IL: University of Chicago Press, pp. 79–137.

Nagel, E. (1961) *The Structure of Science*, New York: Harcourt, Brace & World.

Nelson, R. J. (1968) *Introduction to Automata*, New York: Wiley.

—— (1969) 'Behaviorism is false', *Journal of Philosophy* 66: 417–51.

—— (1971) 'Are humanly recognizable patterns effective?', in J. Fox (ed.) *Computers and Automata*, Brooklyn, NY: Brooklyn Polytechnic Press, 327–36.

—— (1976) 'On mechanical recognition', *Philosophy of Science* 43: 24–52.

—— (1978) 'The competence–performance distinction in mental philosophy', *Synthese* 39: 337–81.

—— (1984a), 'Naturalizing intentions', *Synthese* 61: 174–203.

—— (1984b) 'Skinner's philosophy of method', *Behavioral and Brain Sciences* 7: 529–30.

—— (1987) 'Church's thesis and cognitive science', *Notre Dame Journal of Formal Logic* 28: 581–614.

—— (1988a) 'Mechanism and intentionality: the new world knot', in H.

Otto and J. A. Tuedio (eds) *Perspectives on Mind*, Dordrecht: Reidel, pp. 137–57.

—— (1988b) 'Connections among connections', *Behavioral and Brain Sciences* 11: 45–6.

—— (1989a) *The Logic of Mind*, 2nd edn, Dordrecht: Kluwer.

—— (1989b) 'Correction to "Naturalizing intentions" ', *Synthese* 80: 315–17.

—— (1989c) 'Philosophical issues in Edelmann's *Neural Darwinism*', *Journal of Experimental and Theoretical Artificial Intelligence*, vol. 1, 195–208.

Newell, A. (1980) 'Physical symbol systems', *Cognitive Science* 4: 135–83.

Partee, B. H. (1979) 'Montague grammar, mental representations, and reality', in P. A. French, T. Uehling, Jr and H. K. Wettstein (eds) *Contemporary Perspectives in the Philosophy of Language*, Minneapolis, MN: University of Minnesota Press, pp. 195–208.

Peirce, C. S. (1931–57) *Collected Papers*, vols I–VII, ed. by C. Hartshorne, P. Weiss and A. Burks, Cambridge, MA: Harvard University Press.

Pinker, S. (1991) 'Rules of language', *Science* 253: 530–5.

Pinker, S. and Bloom, P. (1990) 'Natural language and natural selection', *Behavioral and Brain Sciences* 13: 707–27.

Post, E. (1940) 'Formal reductions of the general combinatorial decision problem', *American Journal of Mathematics* 65: 85–104.

Postal, P. M. and Katz, J. J. (1964) *An Integrated Theory of Linguistic Descriptions*, Cambridge, MA: MIT Press.

Putnam, H. (1975) *Mind, Language, and Reality*, Cambridge: Cambridge University Press.

—— (1978) *Meaning and the Moral Sciences*, Boston, MA: Routledge & Kegan Paul.

—— (1981) *Reason, Truth and History*, Cambridge: Cambridge University Press.

—— (1986) *Realism and Reason*, Cambridge: Cambridge University Press.

—— (1988) *Representation and Reality*, Cambridge, MA: MIT Press.

Pylyshyn, Z. W. (1984) *Computers and Cognition*, Cambridge, MA: MIT Press.

Quine, W. V. (1953) *From a Logical Point of View*, Cambridge, MA: Harvard University Press.

—— (1960) *Word and Object*, New York: Wiley.

—— (1966) *Ways of Paradox*, New York: Random House.

—— (1969) *Ontological Relativity*, New York: Columbia University Press.

—— (1973) *Roots of Reference*, LaSalle: Open Court.

—— (1974) 'Methodological, reflections on current linguistic theory', in G. Harman (ed.) *On Noam Chomsky*, Garden City, NY: Anchor Books, pp. 104–17.

—— (1981) *Theories and Things*, Cambridge, MA: Harvard University Press.

—— (1982) *Methods of Logic*, Cambridge, MA: Harvard University Press.

—— (1987) *Quiddities*, Cambridge, MA: Harvard University Press.

—— (1990) *Pursuit of Truth*, Cambridge, MA: Harvard University Press.

Rabin, M. O. (1964) 'Probabalistic automata', in E. F. Moore (ed.) *Sequential Machines*, Reading, MA: Addison-Wesley, pp. 98–114.

Reeke, G. N., Jr and Edelman, G. M. (1988) 'Real brains and artificial intelligence', *Daedalus* 117: 143–73.

Rogers, H., Jr (1967) *The Theory of Recursive Functions and Effective Computability*, New York: McGraw-Hill.

Rosenberg, J. F. and Travis, C. (eds) (1971) *Readings in the Philosophy of Language*, Englewood Cliffs, NJ: Prentice Hall.

Rumelhart, D. E. and McClelland, J. L. (1986) *Parallel Distributed Processing*, Cambridge, MA: MIT Press.

Russell, B. (1905) 'On denoting', in R. C. Marsh (ed.) (1956) *Logic and Knowledge*, London: George Allen & Unwin, pp. 39–56.

—— (1912) *The Problems of Philosophy*, New York: Galaxy.

—— (1914) 'On the nature of acquaintance', in R. C. Marsh (ed.) (1956) *Logic and Knowledge*, London: George Allen & Unwin, pp. 125–74.

—— (1918a) *Mysticism and Logic*, New York: W. W. Norton.

—— (1918b) 'The philosophy of logical atomism', in R. C. Marsh (ed.) (1956) *Logic and Knowledge*, London: George Allen & Unwin, pp. 175–282.

—— (1940) *An Inquiry into Meaning and Truth*, New York: W. W. Norton.

—— (1948) *Human Knowledge, its Scope and its Limits*, New York: Simon & Schuster.

—— (1959) *My Philosophical Development*, New York: Simon & Schuster.

Ryle, G. (1949) *The Concept of Mind*, New York: Barnes & Noble.

Salmon, N. (1986) *Frege's Puzzle*, Cambridge, MA: MIT Press.

Schiffer, S. (1986) 'Foundationalism and belief', in M. Brand and R. M. Harnish (eds) *The Representation of Knowledge and Belief*, Tucson, AZ: University of Arizona Press, pp. 127–59.

Schwartz, S. P. (ed.) (1977) *Naming, Necessity, and Natural Kinds*, Ithaca, NY: Cornell University Press.

Searle, J. R. (1958) 'Proper names', *Mind* 67: 166–73.

—— (1969) *Speech Acts*, Cambridge: Cambridge University Press.

—— (1980) 'Minds, brains and programs', *Behavioral and Brain Sciences* 3: 417–57.

—— (1990) 'Is the brain a digital computer?', *Proceedings and Addresses of the American Philosophical Association* 64: 21–37.

Shapiro, S. (1980) 'On the notion of effectiveness', *History and Philosophy of Logic* 1: 209–30.

—— (1981) 'Understanding Church's thesis', *Journal of Philosophical Logic* 10: 353–65.

Skinner, B. F. (1953) *Science and Human Behavior*, New York: Macmillan.

—— (1957) *Verbal Behavior*, New York: Appleton-Century-Crofts.

—— (1984) 'Theoretical consequences', *Behavioral and Brain Sciences* 7: 541–6.

Bibliography

Smith, D. W. and McIntyre, R. (1971) 'Intentionality and intentions', *Journal of Philosophy* 68: 541–61.

Smolensky, P. (1988) 'On the proper treatment of connectionism', *Behavioral and Brain Sciences* 11: 1–23.

Stalnaker, R. (1976) 'Propositions', in A. Mackay and D. Merrill (eds) *Issues in the Philosophy of Language*, New Haven, CT: Yale University Press.

Stich, S. P. (1983) *From Folk Psychology to Cognitive Science*, Cambridge, MA; MIT Press.

Strawson, P. F. (1950) 'On referring', in J. F. Rosenberg and C. Travis (eds) (1971) *Readings in the Philosophy of Language*, Englewood Cliffs, NJ: Prentice Hall, pp. 175–94.

—— (1959) *Individuals*, New York: Doubleday.

Suppes, P. (1975) 'From behaviorism to neobehaviorism', *Theory and Decision* 6: 269–86.

Tarski, A. (1931–5) 'The concept of truth in formalized languages', in A. Tarski (1956) *Logic, Semantics, Metamathematics*, translated by J. H. Woodger, Oxford: Clarendon, pp. 152–278.

—— (1933) 'The establishment of scientific semantics', in A. Tarski (1956) *Logic, Semantics, Metamathematics*, translated by J. H. Woodger, Oxford: Clarendon, pp. 401–8.

—— (1944) 'The semantic conception of truth', in H. Feigl and W. Sellars (eds) *Readings in Philosophical Analysis*, New York: Appleton-Century-Crofts, pp. 52–84.

—— (1956) *Logic, Semantics, Metamathematics*, translated by J. H. Woodger, Oxford: Clarendon.

—— and Vaught, R. (1957) 'Arithmetic extension of relational system', *Compositio Mathematica* 13, 81–102.

Thatcher, J. W. (1963) 'The construction of a self-describing Turing machine', in J. Fox (ed.) *Proceedings of the Symposium on Mathematical Theory of Automata*, Brooklyn, NY: Brooklyn Polytechnic Press, pp. 165–72.

Turing, A. M. (1936) 'On computable numbers with applications to the entscheidungsproblem', *Proceedings of the London Mathematical Society* 42: 230–65.

von Neumann, J. (1961) *Collected Works*, vol. V, New York: Macmillan.

—— (1966) 'The theory of automata: construction, reproduction and homogeneity', in A. W. Burks (ed.) *Theory of Self-Reproducing Automata*, Urbana, IL: University of Illinois Press.

Wallace, J. (1979) 'Only in the context of a sentence do words have any meaning', in P. A. French, T. Uehling, Jr and H. K. Wettstein (eds) *Contemporary Perspectives in the Philosophy of Language*, Minneapolis, MN: University of Minnesota Press, pp. 305–25.

Waltz, D. and Feldman, J. A. (eds) (1988) *Connectionist Models and Their Implications*, Northwood, NJ: Ablex.

Wettstein, H. (1986) 'Has semantics rested on a mistake?', *Journal of Philosophy* 83: 185–209.

Whitehead, A. N. and Russell, B. (1925) *Principia Mathematica*, vol. 1,

Cambridge: Cambridge University Press.

Wiener, N. (1948) *Cybernetics, or Control and Communication in the Animal and Machine*, Cambridge, MA: MIT Press.

William of Occam (1954) *Summa Totius Logicae*, ed. by P. Boeher, Bonaventure, NY: Franciscan Institure.

Williams, B. A. O. (1951) 'The hypothesis of cybernetics', *British Journal for the Philosophy of Science* 2: 1–24.

Wittgenstein, L. (1925) *Tractatus Logico-philosophicus*, London: Kegan Paul, Trench & Trubner.

Zuriff, G. E. (1985) *Behaviorism: A Conceptual Reconstruction*, New York: Wiley.

Index

291